U.S.–ISRAELI RELATIONS
AT THE CROSSROADS

U.S.–ISRAELI RELATIONS
AT THE CROSSROADS

Edited by
GABRIEL SHEFFER

FRANK CASS
LONDON • PORTLAND, OR.

FRANK CASS AND COMPANY LIMITED
Newbury House, 900 Eastern Avenue, London IG2 7HH, England

and in the United States of America by
FRANK CASS
c/o ISBS, Inc.
5804 N.E. Hassalo Street, Portland, Oregon 97213-3644

British Library Cataloguing in Publication Data

A catalogue record for this book is available from the
British Library.

ISBN 0 7146 4747 0 (hbk)
ISBN 0 7146 4305 X (pbk)

Library of Congress Cataloging-in-Publication Data
U.S.–Israel relations at the crossroads / edited by Gabriel
Sheffer.
    p. cm.
Includes bibliographical references and index.
ISBN 0-7146-4747-0 (hbk). -- ISBN 0-7146-4305-X (pbk)
1. United States -- Foreign relations -- Israel. 2. Israel --
Foreign relations -- United States. I. Sheffer, Gabriel.
E183.8.I75U23 1996   96-19072
327.7305694--dc20   CIP

This group of studies first appeared in a Special Issue of *Israel Affairs*,
Vol.2, No.3&4 (Spring & Summer 1996), [U.S.–Israeli Relations at the
Crossroads].

Printed in Great Britain by
Antony Rowe Ltd., Chippenham, Wilts.

Contents

Preface

The dramatic global, regional, and domestic changes that occurred after the unpredicted collapse of the Soviet Union have created a need to reexamine a host of theoretical and practical issues in all spheres, and particularly in regard to security and foreign relations. Most of the old concepts, as well as actual political arrangements, have been put to the test by these and ensuing developments.

The "special relationship" between the United States and Israel is no exception. Although this seemed one of the solid and stable political arrangements of the Cold War period, the new international and domestic reality in the U.S. and Israel warrants a thorough re-examination.

That is the main purpose of the present collection of original essays by a group of distinguished American and Israeli scholars. The essays in this volume discuss the special relations between the "only remaining superpower" and the "only democracy in the Middle East" within American global, Middle Eastern regional, domestic American, and domestic Israeli contexts. These candid and provocative essays explore the role of the United States in world affairs; the new bases of policymaking in the United States; American regional politics with a special reference to the Middle East; several aspects of American domestic politics that have direct and indirect bearing on relations with Israel; the issue of Israel's nuclear status; problems of Israel–Diaspora relations, and other relevant issues. They deal, that is, both with strategic dimensions affecting U.S.–Israeli relations and with the less tangible aspects such as the attitudes of American religious communities toward these relations, the situation of the American Jewish community, the influence of public opinion and the media in general on U.S. policy toward Israel, and Israeli attitudes toward America and American Jews.

By design, most of the essays are not only descriptive and analytical, but deal with major theoretical issues such as the bases of policymaking and the validity of the main approaches to foreign policy and strategy, including the neorealist and domestic-politics approaches. Though since the completion of the articles in this volume, in 1995, a few dramatic events occured in Israel – Rabin's assassination and the 1996 elections in which the Likud and its leader, Binyamin Netanyahu, returned to power – we believe that the volume will be of interest to the general public; to those with a special interest in Middle Eastern and Israeli politics; and to scholars and students of American foreign policy, American–Israeli relations, and international relations in general, including international relations theory.

Introduction: The United States and the "Normalization" of the Middle East and Israel

GABRIEL SHEFFER

There is hardly a need to repeat here that the sweeping global changes that occurred after the abrupt and unpredicted collapse of the Soviet Union and its empire, which entailed the end of the loose bipolar regime of the Cold War era, have affected the United States and its standing in the international system, its position in various regions in the world, and its relations with particular states in each of these regions. Moreover, as the main themes, as well as the results, of the 1994 congressional elections in the United States have shown, these global changes have also had ripple effects on American domestic politics. These elections have demonstrated that, though not entirely disinterested in international affairs, greater segments of the American public regard domestic politics as having greater priority than external affairs and commitments.

By the same token, it need hardly be repeated that most regions and states, including the Middle East and its various countries, were also profoundly affected by these sweeping changes.

In regard to the United States' relations with the Middle East as a whole and with particular states of the region, these recent global developments have caused major alterations, both in the political and economic structures in which all actors that are involved in this volatile region operate, and in these actors' patterns of bilateral and multilateral behavior. The global transformation, of course, eliminated the Soviet Union as a major force in Middle Eastern politics. Hence, the relatively well-defined American and Soviet spheres of interest and influence in that part of the world were eradicated as well. Overall, these structural and behavioral changes have markedly enhanced the United States' prestige and influence in

Gabriel Sheffer is Professor of Political Science and former Director of the Leonard Davis Institute for International Relations, the Hebrew University of Jerusalem.

Thanks should go to the Leonard Davis Institute for International Relations, and especially to Mr David Hornik, for their support and help in initiating this volume, and in its publication.

the Middle East. Indeed, the United States has improved its position in the region to the extent that this "only superpower" could initiate and implement something that had previously been almost unthinkable: it could form a coalition consisting of a wide range of states, most notably including many Arab states (even Syria, not entirely surprisingly, decided to join this coalition), then launch the 1991 Gulf War, defeat Iraq, and impose severe sanctions on it.

These developments led to the formation of a large group of Middle Eastern states that either are blatantly pro-American (such as Egypt and more recently, Jordan) or are seeking American support (such as Syria). In turn, this new environment has created the backdrop for the Jordanian-Israeli peace agreement as well as for the peace process between Israel on the one hand and Syria and the Palestinians on the other. The United States has been actively involved in both processes, but particularly in the Israeli–Syrian track. Moreover, the formation of this pro-Western and pro-American group of states and the ongoing multilateral negotiations about peace arrangements in the Middle East have increased the chances of economic cooperation in the region, in which the United States takes an interest as it may well stand to benefit.

In short, these profound structural and behavioral changes are paving the way toward the "normalization" of the Middle East. In terms of the main concerns of this volume, these developments are also conducing toward the "normalization" of Israel's position as an accepted member of the international community. Basically, this involves a greater readiness by most Arab states to accept Israel's existence in the international and regional arenas. Unquestionably this growing legitimation of Israel, as well as its acceptance by most countries all over the world, has been enhanced by the global alterations. Thus, like a number of other countries that during the Cold War period had a pariah status (such as Taiwan, South Africa, and Chile), Israel no longer belongs to the category of rejected states.

Signs of such a gradual "normalization" of Israel's international position are already evident in a number of spheres. East European, African, and Asian countries that after the 1967 or 1973 Arab-Israeli wars severed their diplomatic relations with Israel have resumed these relations. Most notable among these states are Russia itself, many of the former Soviet republics, and India. A number of other states that had never formally recognized Israel have done so, most notably China, Morocco, Tunisia, and some smaller states in the Persian Gulf. Furthermore, the political boycott and the secondary and tertiary economic boycotts that had been imposed on Israel by and at the behest of Arab states and their allies have largely been revoked; Israel's relations with the European Union have improved; Israel has found new markets for its products, especially in Asia; immigration from the former Soviet Union and Soviet empire has brought about 600,000 Jews to Israel, contributing to a tremendous boost in its economy; and Israel has become a respected member in various international political and economic forums.

One of the basic underlying assumptions of this volume is that these profound processes must also have discernible implications for Israeli internal politics. Despite Netanyahu's victory, probably the most striking change has occurred in the attitudes of the majority of Israelis toward the peace process with the Palestinians and in their readiness to accept a withdrawal from the Israeli-occupied territories. This significant shift in Israeli public opinion may partly be attributed to the new and more relaxed international environment, which has enhanced Israelis' sense of security. Undoubtedly, most Israelis welcomed the collapse of the Soviet Union and its disappearance from Middle Eastern politics; like many Americans, most Israelis viewed the Soviet Union as an "evil empire" that posed major direct and indirect threats to Jews and to their state.

This shift should also be attributed in part to a growing sense among Israelis of the futility of war and conflict with Israel's Arab neighbors, especially against the backdrop of the new and more relaxed international environment. Such sentiments have led large segments in Israeli society to prefer a state of imperfect peace over the continuation of tension and strife with these countries, even if this involves what some of them regard as "sacrifices" or concessions to the Arabs.

No less noticeable and significant internal changes which resulted from these global trends and which have affected Israel's position including its relations with the United States, have occurred in the economic sphere. As a result of new patterns of allocation of national resources (connected to the peace process, and mainly involving reduced funds for the administration of the occupied territories and for the Jewish settlements there, coupled with certain cuts in military expenditure), the Israeli Labor government has invested more in transportational, educational, and industrial infrastructures. Such patterns of resource allocation, new and greater investments from abroad, reduced and controlled inflation, and the economic activity involved in the absorption of the huge Russian Jewish immigration have contributed to an impressive economic growth and prosperity (Israeli GDP per capita is about $15,000 a year). In this respect, Israel resembles some other smaller states that on the whole are performing better than the larger ones in the economic sphere.

Without delving too deeply into the cultural and social changes that have been underway in Israel since the late 1980s, on the whole Israeli society is becoming more secular, pluralistic, multicultural, and invidualistic. Consequently, personal, social, and political rights are more fully observed, and by and large Israelis enjoy a greater freedom of movement and action. In short, like most small countries, Israel has been affected by various aspects of globalization.

From all these perspectives, then, Israel is becoming more "normal," losing its previous special features of a garrison state, and is becoming more similar to other small democratic states that have not been locked in a protracted international conflict or belonged to the pariah category. Indeed, normalization was an important secular-Zionist tenet. Hence, about a century after the establishment of the Zionist political movement, a combination of global and domestic developments are contributing to the realization of a part of the "Zionist dream."

THE IMPACT OF "NORMALIZATION" ON U.S.-ISRAELI "SPECIAL RELATIONS"

Before the beginning of these gradual processes of "normalization", not only politicians and rank-and-file but analysts, too, regarded Israel as a unique case. Indeed, this view has been reiterated in numerous speeches, books, and articles about the Jewish State. Israel's uniqueness was mainly attributed to its ongoing involvement in the Arab–Israeli conflict and the purported existential dangers it had faced since its establishment in 1948; to the resulting predominance of the military and defense sectors in its social, economic, and political development; to its being an immigrant society; and to a number of aspects involved in its foreign relations, particularly its isolation and pariah status. Another perceived unique feature has been its "special relations with the United States", including what are sometimes regarded as part of these special relations and sometimes as a separate phenomenon, namely, Israel's "special relations" with the American Jewish community.

The central question posed by this volume is whether these "special relations" between Israel on the one hand, and the United States and the American Jewish community on the other, can withstand the dramatic changes that have occurred in the global, American, Middle Eastern, and Israeli arenas – including what we have called the normalization of the Middle East and Israel, and, not least, the changes in the United States itself and in its foreign policy. Indeed, in this volume the focus is mainly – though by no means exclusively – on the American side of the U.S.–Israeli equation, as we have sought to shed some additional light not only on questions of the United States' relations with Israel, but also on its foreign policy and international relations in general.

THREE THEORETICAL APPROACHES TO THE ISSUE OF THE "SPECIAL RELATIONSHIP"

The "special relationship" between the giant superpower and its small ally has been noted since the mid-1950s, and has been the subject of numerous empirical as well as theoretical studies. Yet since there has not been agreement on what are the relevant empirical data that should be analyzed to explain these relations, it is not surprising that not one but a number of theoretical approaches have emerged to explaining the origins and nature of this relationship.

Not surprisingly, most of the explanations that were suggested during the Cold War period were influenced by the neorealist-structural or power-politics approach to international relations. The many books and articles that were published up to the early 1990s as part of, or under the influence of, this approach emphasized the significance of structural global conditions and arrangements, and of American and Western-bloc strategic calculations, which purportedly were based on rational or bounded-rational considerations, in shaping the relations between the two allies. Most of the general and specific arguments of this school are familiar; what follows is only an overview.

Realists and neorealists maintained that the main source of affinity between these two states was their mutual strategic outlooks and interests. Uppermost in American considerations, these writers suggested, was the fact that the basically pro-Western Israel, small but militarily strong, was an essential outpost of the Western bloc in a highly volatile but extremely significant part of the world, serving as an important element in the American and Western-bloc sphere of interest and influence in the region, and capable of securing American and Western interests against the malevolent Soviet Union, which had encroached on the region and established its own sphere of influence there. Above and beyond these factors, Israel was supposed to serve as an American proxy vis-à-vis the pro-Soviet Arab states. To these considerations, some analysts added that Israel was a good market for American weapon systems, that in the recurrent Arab-Israeli wars the Israeli army had tested these weapons and passed information about their performance to the United States, and that Israel had captured Soviet weapons and supplied information about their performance to the Americans. Often, Israeli intelligence and covert operations (such as support for the Kurds) were also cited by proponents of this *realpolitik* interpretation; such analysts stressed the contributions of the Israeli Mossad, Security Services, and military intelligence to the security of the West in general and of America in particular.

According to this school of thought, such factors not only explained but also justified the special relations between these two unequal partners, and especially the enormous military, economic, and political aid extended by the United States to Israel.

The second approach, in a sense antithetical to the realists' and neorealists' position, is known as the domestic-politics approach. Its proponents have instead stressed the complex interplay of political, bureaucratic, and social forces in the United States in determining its attitudes and policies toward the Jewish State. The forces cited in this context have been the "Jewish vote"; the "unbeatable Jewish lobby"; the "Jewish money" donated to American politicians' campaigns; pro-Israel interest groups such as fundamentalist Protestants; certain segments of the Democratic Party; powerful members, both Jewish and non-Jewish, of different White House staffs; the Jewish advisers of various presidents; the American intelligence community, parts of which highly valued the cooperation with Israel; certain research institutions, and so on. The basic argument of this school has been that the particular and cumulative power and leverage of all these forces, constantly interacting within America's pluralist political system, was predominantly responsible for the ongoing special relations.

In this context, it should be noted here that most of the contributors to this volume would agree that the results of the 1994 congressional elections have not substantially changed the main configuration of the pro-Israeli forces in American internal politics, and that Israel's position on both Capitol Hill and the White House is still strong. This has been demonstrated by the continued, unaltered economic and military aid to Israel and by the support for aid to both the Jordanians and Palestinians which was approved by the House and Senate in 1995.

There has emerged a third distinctive interpretation of the "special relationship". It might be termed an "idealist" or "ideationist" approach, and its proponents have emphasized the "soft" rather than the "hard" factors cited by the previous two schools. This approach focuses on the intangible bases of the affinity and co-operation between the United States and Israel, such as "guilt feelings about the United States' inaction during the Holocaust", the need to help "the little David in its gallant fight for survival against the Arab Goliath", the "natural affinity between the largest democracy in the world and the only democracy between India and Italy", the "mutual Judeo-Christian cultural origins of the two societies", the "basic mistrust shown by Americans and the American government toward the Arabs", and the purported affinity between two democracies that were both facing evil forces (that is, the Soviet Union and the Arab dictatorships). This approach, then, stresses American idealist and humanitarian tendencies.

Directly and indirectly, the essays in this volume explore and reassess these three theoretical approaches in view of the more recent, major global changes.

THE VOLUME'S ORGANIZATION

The two parts of this volume correspond to two levels of analysis.

This reflects the view that there are close links between the developments on each of these levels, and that changes on one level influence what occurs on the other.

The first level is that of the United States' position and interests in global affairs, and in the broader context of U.S.–Israeli relations. Beginning the volume on this level enables reexamination of the perennial question of whether and to what extent there are connections between America's global interests and policies and its "special relations" with the small Jewish State, especially since the end of the Cold War.

The second part focuses more directly on the level of U.S.–Israeli relations, and includes contributors on the political, strategic, religious, and public opinion aspects of these relations.

The First Cut: American Global and Regional Interests

In the opening essay of this volume, "America's Response to the New World (Dis)order', George Quester considers some of the expectations generated among Americans by the end of the Cold War and of the often disappointing realities that have ensued. These have included Iraq's aggression against Kuwait and the resultant Gulf War, as well as ongoing conflicts in other parts of the world; continuing proliferation, despite the demise of the Soviet Union, of both conventional and nonconventional weaponry; and increased belligerent ethnic nationalism as well as Islamic and other religious fanaticism. In discussing the issue of U.S. foreign policy toward this difficult new world, Quester highlights the paradox that just at the time when the United States should be, according to some outlooks, exploiting the new "unipolar" situation of being the only superpower, it has become more chary of international involvements and more preoccupied with its domestic problems.

In "The Strategic Implications of Emerging International Security Conditions", John Steinbruner suggests that the revolution in communication technology, which has stimulated an increasingly integrated global economy, together with unprecedented global population growth will undermine the coherence of existing political systems. The strategic implications of this situation, in his view, are that: large-scale ground offensives have become increasingly unlikely, as they are too expensive and too easy to detect and disrupt; instead, capacities to attack precise targets and to inflict mass destruction have grown, so that there is a greater threat of long-term destruction; and the main political source of threat is now internal disintegration rather than foreign invasion. What is needed, he maintains, is a process of establishing generally inclusive, cooperative security arrangements in which the United States, Russia, and China must all play a part, since none can cope alone with the kinds of security threat that now exist. In Steinbruner's view the Middle East, too, which faces threats of technical diffusion as well as political disintegration, will eventually have to form co-operative security arrangements that include Israel in order to cope with the dangers.

Richard Ned Lebow, in "Psychological Dimensions of Post-Cold War Foreign Policy", discusses the effects on U.S. foreign policy of the loss of the powerful, clearly defined enemy that the Soviet Union constituted. The United States now faces a world with enemies – Iraq, Libya, Iran – that are far less powerful than itself, and with conflicts like those in Somalia, Haiti, or Bosnia to which the commitment of U.S. forces is questionable and meets determined opposition at home. Lebow argues, however, that since Americans have always regarded themselves as a chosen people with an international mission, a trend of greater pragmatism and pursuit of limited self-interest in foreign policy, rather than of trying to effect grand transformations in the name of ideals, may be a salutary development signaling the "normalization" of America.

In his contribution on "The Clinton Administration and Regional Security: The First Two Years", Samuel F. Wells, Jr., analyzes the new situation confronting U.S. policy from the standpoint of regional security. During the Cold War, and especially during the 1980s under the Reagan administration, the superpower conflict provided a basic framework in which to pursue regional security. But the Clinton administration, in Wells's view, has not developed a coherent approach to the new world reality and instead has pursued regional security in a haphazard, often ineffective way. Thus, although in the Middle Eastern region the United States has both given consistent support to the Arab-Israeli peace process and conducted an effective dual containment policy against Iran and Iraq, the Clinton administration has encountered many frustrations and failures on other fronts such as Bosnia, China, and North Korea. Overall, Wells is critical of the administration for enunciating regional security policy in terms of abstract ideals while conducting the policy through bargaining processes that are more appropriate to domestic policy.

In "Israel, the United States, and the New World Order Crisis: Fuzzy Logic and Conflicting Principles", Robert L. Rothstein focuses on the tension between, on the one hand, growing trends of globalization in the post-Cold War world, caused by the spread of the democratic/free-market paradigm and the diffusion of economic power, and, on the other, the intensification, especially in the Third World, of localism of ethnic, national, or religious hues. In the Middle East, he notes, the localizing trend is still strong and poses dangers of violent and especially nuclear conflict, although Rothstein suggests that success in the Arab–Israeli peace process can counteract these trends. In considering how the developed world, on the whole, can make the world more stable, Rothstein suggests that the answer lies in subsidiarity – the development of appropriate mechanisms for dealing with problems at the international, regional, or local level; and in equity – that is, in making aid available to the Third World, both for its own sake and for the sake of overall global stability.

The contribution by Steven R. David, "The Continuing Importance of American Interests in the Middle East After the Cold War", serves as a direct analytical link between the first and second parts of this volume. This essay is also concerned with the question of how the demise of Soviet power affects U.S. foreign policy – in this case, in the Middle East. During the Cold War Israel came to be seen as a U.S. strategic asset against Soviet expansion, and many have suggested that Israel will now be much less important to America. David, however, argues that because of the Middle East's ongoing instability and proneness to warfare, which threatens U.S. access to oil, as well as the dangers posed by nuclear proliferation in the region, U.S.–Israel ties will be maintained. Israel, in his analysis, remains a key U.S. ally vis-à-vis radical Middle Eastern states; moreover, the United States has an interest in helping Israel achieve peace so as to promote the region's stability.

The Second Cut: The United States and Israel

Shibley Telhami and Jon Krosnick, in "U.S. Public Attitudes Toward Israel: A Study of the Attentive and Issue Publics", note that although much of the recent discussion of U.S. foreign policy has focused on the international ramifications of the post-Cold War era, the domestic arena, which has always been central, may have become even more so with the diminishing interest of the U.S. public in foreign affairs. The conduct of U.S. policy toward Israel, the authors assert, is no exception. This analysis seeks to assess the importance in this context of the "issue-public" (or those Americans who assign high priority to a given issue) in comparison with the general and "attentive" (that is, better-informed) publics. Telhami and Krosnick found that U.S. policy toward Israel seemed most in line with the views of the relevant issue-public – presumably, in this case, American Jews and evangelical Protestants - though they did not find evidence as to whether there is a causal link. The authors also note the possibility that Israel's importance to this issue-public could be affected by success in the Arab–Israeli peace process.

Taking a different view, Charles Lipson, in "American Support for Israel: History, Sources, Limits", argues that U.S. support for Israel is primarily grounded in such strategic factors as Israel's military power, its opposition to radical Arab states, and its political stability, as opposed to the strength of lobbying groups or the role of shared values. Thus, U.S. support for Israel grew in the late 1960s and early 1970s as Israel demonstrated military prowess and a potential to help contain Soviet expansion in the region. Lipson maintains that because, after the Cold War, the U.S. still has major stakes in the region, the U.S.–Israel relationship will continue – though probably at a lower level with reduced aid.

In their contribution "Reclaiming Zion: How American Religious Groups View the Middle East", Kenneth D. Wald *et al.* pose the question – largely overlooked except with respect to American Jews – of whether, and how, religion affects the views on the Middle East of ordinary Americans. Wald and his coauthors suggest that in the United States, the relative lack of interest in world affairs in their own right, together with the strong public role of religion, gives religion a potential impact on opinion formation. The authors classify Christian Americans into evangelical Protestant, mainline Protestant, and Catholic, then examine survey results on how these groups view U.S. Middle East policy. The most pro-Israel are consistently the evangelicals, with both mainline Protestants and Catholics considerably less so. Wald and his colleagues suggest that the main factor at work here is theology about the return of the Jews to the Promised Land, linked to the strong nationalism found among evangelicals. The authors caution, however, against relying too heavily on evangelical pro-Israelism, because, among other reasons, evangelicals tend to oppose foreign aid, may become less pro-Israel with the decline of the Soviet role in Middle East, and may ultimately be more concerned with U.S. social issues.

Arthur Hertzberg, in "Israel and the Diaspora: A Relationship Re-examined", argues that Israel and the Diaspora have failed each other's expectations, and are destined to drift farther apart though without totally relinquishing each other. Israelis have tended to think of their country as the authoritative center of Jewish life, and diaspora Jews have tended to think that through pro-Israel involvement their own Jewishness can be maintained. Both assumptions, Hertzberg suggests, have proved wrong; Israel no longer commands unquestioning allegiance and agreement from the diaspora, and the diaspora is experiencing serious assimilation and demographic diminution despite pro-Israel involvement. In his view, the two communities face separate tasks: Israel must learn to integrate into the Middle East, and American Jews must find effective ways to preserve their Jewishness in an increasingly multiethnic America. Nevertheless, he believes that some measure of Israel-diaspora interaction will continue.

Exploring the topic of "U.S. Nuclear Non-Proliferation Policy: Implications for U.S.–Israeli Relations", Shai Feldman notes that despite America's overall efforts to stem nuclear proliferation, Israel, because of the security threats it faces, has been regarded by the United States as a special case and has been exempted from these efforts. Thus Washington has refrained from pressuring Israel to sign the Non-Proliferation Treaty, and did not support Egypt's attempt to make Israeli denuclearization an international priority. Feldman maintains that for the foreseeable future as well, the nuclear issue will not become a source of tension between Israel and the U.S. – all the more so because of the increased security risks that Israel will be asked to take in the context of the peace process. Since Washington attaches high value to this process, it will not likely take measures that would weaken Israel's existential deterrence.

In Edward N. Luttwak's consideration of "Strategic Aspects of American–Israeli Relations", he asserts that, despite negative assessments of Israeli's strategic value by the U.S. military, intelligence, and diplomatic bureaucracies, Israel in fact had great strategic value for the United States during the Cold War. By defeating Arab armies equipped and trained by the Soviets, Israel caused the Arab world to turn away from the Soviet Union and toward the United States, which had been (or was perceived to be) the patron of the winning side. Luttwak then questions whether in the post-Cold War era this alliance still has strategic value to the United States, and takes a view different from that of David and Lipson. He argues that although a new common threat of Islamic fundamentalism has arisen, there can be no consensus between the United States and Israel on how to deal with it, since, for various reasons including Israel's unpopularity in its own region, Israel cannot contribute much toward U.S. efforts to counteract this threat. Yet the alliance, Luttwak observes, seems to be continuing, which he attributes to bureaucratic momentum as well as sympathy between U.S. and Israeli elites.

In her essay "Israel and the United States: Images of Flawed Paradise", Judith Elizur points out that in our age, national images – nations' images of themselves as well as of other nations – are largely shaped by television and other media, and by government policies as reflected in media. Thus, the American image of Israel has been shaped, especially since the 1967 War, by televised images of violence. Israel has sometimes, as in the 1967 and 1973 wars and the 1991 Scud missile attacks, been regarded as a laudable David, and sometimes, as when dealing with the Palestinians especially during the intifada, as a reprehensible Goliath. The overall image, however, has become that of a country involved with Middle Eastern violence. The Israeli image of the United States is far less one-dimensional; Israelis tend to admire the United States as an exemplary and powerful democracy on whose friendship and largesse Israel is dependent. However, increasingly negative depictions of the United States in Hollywood movies and cable TV, highlighting crime, drugs, violence, urban blight, and AIDS, have tarnished this image. Nevertheless, the United States remains highly appealing to Israelis as a successful country with a high standard of living.

WHITHER AMERICAN–ISRAELI RELATIONS?

Probably in part because of the selection of the contributors to this volume, and because of the continued predominance of the neorealist-structural approach in American and Israeli political science, most of the essays in this volume suggest that despite the major strategic changes that have occurred in the world and in the United States itself, in the final analysis, global-structural, power-politics, and bounded-rational factors still determine American, and for that matter also Israeli, foreign and defense policies. An implicit assumption in most of the essays that deal with these issues is that this tendency will be even stronger while both the White House and Congress are controlled by the Republicans.

Hence, despite the current confusion in the United States concerning its global posture, regional politics, and role in various difficult, mostly ethnic conflicts such as those in the former Yugoslavia, in various parts of the former Soviet Union, and in Africa; despite the debate over resource allocation now raging in America, especially after the Republican victory in the 1994 elections (with the military budget having been increased without a request by the administration); despite Americans' reduced interest in international affairs and a clear emphasis on the need to deal with serious domestic problems; and despite growing questions about the neorealist (as well as about the neoliberal) approach – most of the contributing authors to this volume still believe that world politics in general, and the United States' policies in particular, will unfold in accordance with this model. Hence, the basic assumption of these analysts is that the United States will continue to be involved in world affairs – specifically, in various regions and states that are deemed strategically significant for American well-being.

Thus, these authors argue that America's bounded-rational security calculations will determine the degree of its involvement in the various regions. Some of the authors suggest that the United States will show either continued, or even greater, pragmatism and selectivity in choosing the regions and conflicts in which to become involved; others emphasize the trend toward cooperative security arrangements, in which the United States will try to persuade its allies to participate; others still suggest that the United States' policy should be determined by such principles as subsidiarity and equity; none, however, predicts total American isolation or detachment from international affairs. Underlying these views is the rather pessimistic position that despite the collapse of the "evil empire" and the ongoing processes of liberalization of other dictatorial regimes, the world is not becoming a better and safer place but probably a more dangerous one.

The continued theoretical and empirical support for the neorealist interpretation also colors the main conclusions concerning the trends in American attitudes and policies toward Israel. Here, too, there is discernable agreement among most of the contributors. While some express doubts about Israel's strategic significance for the United States in the foreseeable future, especially in connection with the "normalization" of the situation in the Middle East on the one hand, and with Israel's somewhat tarnished image on the other (relating to its treatment of the Palestinians during the intifada), yet, because of what the authors regard as the largely unaltered strategic and economic significance of the Middle East for the United States, and because of the volatility of regional politics and possible nuclear proliferation in the area (though, notably, relatively little significance is attributed to Islamic fundamentalism), there seems to be agreement that Israel will continue to be perceived as an irreplaceable strategic asset and enjoy the benefits of close relations with its traditional superpower ally.

This "business as usual" view of American attitudes toward Israel, which is mostly influenced by neorealist strategic calculations, is somewhat balanced by those who suggest that certain shifts are occurring in American public opinion in general, particularly among the two segments of American society – namely, the American Jewish community and the evangelical Protestants – who have strongly supported Israel and the "special relationship". The argument here is that questions about Israel's centrality in the Jewish nation, new trends among various Protestant groups, the perception of the normalization of the situation in the Middle East and Israel, and Israel's tarnished image may, eventually, adversely affect the relationship between the "only remaining superpower" and the "only Jewish State".

In applying the analyses to current events of the mid-1990s, most of the authors, as I have already noted, would agree that the 1994 congressional elections have not altered much in U.S. attitudes and policies toward Israel; hence there are no substantial new trends that would warrant a fundamental review of the analyses presented here. Thus, support for Israel in the White House, the administration, and Congress will remain massive; and Israel, so long as it coordinates and synchronizes its policies with the United States, should not be apprehensive about any major pressure or diminution in American support. This is borne out by the agreement between the Clinton administration and the Rabin–Peres government (which apparently is also endorsed by a vast majority in the U.S. Congress, including most of the Republicans) about the essential steps to be taken in the bilateral and multilateral peace negotiations. It seems that for the time being these attitudes have not changed after the establishment of the Netanyahu government in 1996. Consequently, the levels of American aid in the peace process and to its main actors (Israel, Egypt, Jordan, and the Palestinians) have, as noted, remained solid and substantial.

In sum, although as expected there are occasional disagreements between these two traditional allies, and such disagreements may be greater during the tenure of Netanyahu's government, one does not detect clouds on the horizon that might lead to dangerous storms in American–Israeli relations. Based on the analyses in this volume, and learning from the history of the Anglo-American "special relations", it may be concluded that even full "normalization" of the situation in the Middle East and in Israel not only would not impair the close relationship between the United States and Israel, but would even further strengthen it.

PART I

The Strategic Implications of Emerging International Security Conditions

JOHN STEINBRUNER

When people use the word "strategic," the context they usually have in mind is that of a military confrontation among nation states, and the topic they are addressing usually has to do with the possible use of military power on behalf of some national interest. Perhaps the first thing to be said in any contemporary strategic discussion, however, is that the traditional context and intuitive meaning of the term is undergoing radical alteration. The entire pattern of international relationships is being transformed, and any valid strategic assessment must now extend well beyond the traditional issues of military capability.

That, of course, is easier said than done. The ongoing transformation of international relationships is clearly not the result of a deliberate initiative or any trend of opinion. In fact the conceptions of strategy that evolved during the Cold War still dominate prevailing thinking, and they are bolstered by emotional and political commitments that have accrued over four decades. Nonetheless there is good reason to believe that relentless events will eventually change even the most entrenched habits of mind. The transformation we are in the early stages of experiencing is a spontaneous phenomenon driven by at least two fundamental developments whose implications are powerful enough to impose themselves.

NEW CONDITIONS

The first of these transforming forces is the revolution in information technology, an event whose immediate manifestations are quite familiar even if its full implications are still obscure. Over the past two decades the inherent costs of performing the basic functions of storing, processing and long-range transmission of information have undergone precipitous declines. Though agreed measures of these

John Steinbruner has been Director of Foreign Policy Studies at the Brookings Institution since 1978. He is a member of the American Academy of Arts and Sciences, the Council on Foreign Relations, the International Institute of Strategic Studies, and the Committee on International Security and Arms Control at the National Academy of Sciences.

cost declines have not been fully established, they clearly amount to several orders of magnitude – factors of a thousand to a million or more. That appears to be the largest efficiency gain of any commodity in economic history, and the unfolding consequences are commensurately strong. Highly facilitated information flows are stimulating a globalization of economic activity and in fact the spontaneous formation of an integrated international economy. This process is also diffusing technology and is changing the basic circumstances of making military investments.

At the same time we are encountering an unprecedented surge of the world population – the rapid rise associated with an exponential growth sequence before it reaches some natural or induced limit. The world population is projected to double by the middle of the next century, adding roughly a billion people per decade over the next five decades. Ninety-five percent of the increase will come in what are currently the poorest communities. Both the scale and the composition of this surge will have consequences powerful enough to affect, potentially even to dominate strategic assessments.

Since the revolution in information technology and the population surge are well outside the bounds of any historical experience, it is prudent to assume that many important implications are yet to be discovered and that some major surprises are likely to be encountered. Nonetheless some central features of this new strategic environment are already apparent. Economic performance will clearly be an objective of overriding priority. Unless the globalizing economy successfully extends its reach to those people in the lower economic strata, where the population surge is occurring, then the coherence of many if not all political systems is likely to be in question and some would almost certainly be torn apart. The expansion of economic participation required to assure a favorable trend in standards of living implies that the global economic product will have to increase by a factor of five or more, including a probable tripling of energy and agricultural production. That in turn implies that massive investment programs will have to be undertaken bringing about large structural and technical shifts within virtually all national economies. It also implies an increasing sensitivity to the balances of material flows and to their environmental effects, a development likely to be of decisive importance in the more burdened regions and potentially so on a global scale as well.

The national governments subjected to these implications can expect to experience a diffusion of their own power; that is, the ability to determine the outcome of matters they care about. Information technology is enabling, probably in fact compelling the decentralization of many decision processes, thereby eroding the degree of control they can expect to exercise within their societies. It is simultaneously enabling/compelling the global extension of basic economic activities thereby dispersing effective control into the international economy as a whole. In responding to new problems under new circumstances, national governments will clearly have to devise new methods, and the content of what they consider to be strategy will be drastically altered.

STRATEGIC IMPLICATIONS

If it is too early to attempt to draw conclusive strategic implications from these broad trends, it is not too early to advance some strong presumptions.

First, it appears likely that large scale ground offensives designed to seize and hold territory – historically the primary focus of strategic calculation and of military investment – are no longer the central security problem for the simple reason that in most important instances classic aggression of this sort is infeasibly expensive. With modern technology large offensive operations can be detected and disrupted in their initial stages, and even an initial success could not be sustained. Basically in the new era political jurisdiction cannot be maintained by coercive means since that method is ruinously inefficient in economic terms.

Second, the traditional problem of massive aggression intended to acquire territory is apparently being superseded as a security concern by capacity for long-range destruction. That presents itself in two forms – the ability to attack precisely defined targets and the ability to cause mass casualties in human populations. The potential to develop both of these capabilities is being proliferated by the inexorable diffusion of technology. Information technology is itself inherently internationalized, and its use is internationalizing access to most other technologies as well. Many of the technologies that are relevant to advanced weapons applications are being developed in commercial markets for commercial application and general access to them cannot be denied as a practical matter. That means that advanced delivery system technology and most of the materials required to make weapons of mass destruction will be accessible to small states and substate organizations. That will not confer the ability to seize territory but it will propagate the potential for producing severe social and economic damage. Weapons of mass destruction and weapons of precision delivery share the characteristics that they are strategically meaningful in small numbers regardless of what the overall balance of military capability might be.

Third, it appears that the primary political source of threat is no longer the impulse for imperial or irredentist expansion but rather the danger of internal disintegration. The globalizing economy is producing rapid structural shifts in patterns of production and is stripping away the protective devices used by national governments to buffer their populations from the effects of these shifts. This process has imposed endemic austerity on some regions serious enough to undermine not only the authority of particular political regime but also the entire legal structure on which it is based. In extreme instances of this process basic civil order can break down, and in those instances armed intimidation becomes the residual form of social organization. Disintegration of this sort has recently occurred in a sufficient number of places to suggest that a general pattern may be emerging. Against the background of the impending population surge that constitutes a sharp warning, a suggestion that legal order generally might be threatened.

As Inflicted on the United States

The problem of assessing these presumptions and of adjusting to the results of the assessment confronts all governments, but it falls particularly heavily on the United States. Without explicitly intending the result, the United States has emerged from the Cold War period with the predominant military establishment. Its annual defense budget is five times larger than that of any other military establishment and is more than twice the size of the combined budgets of all the major ones with which it is not formally allied and might conceivably come into confrontation. The annual defense expenditures of Russia, China, Iran, Iraq, Syria, Libya, India and North Korea, for example, are altogether less than half of those of the United States. As a consequence of this disparity, the United States has the only establishment in position to project military power on a global basis and the only one able to undertake some of the most advanced military operations. It sets the standard against which all the others compare themselves. It is unavoidably the primary element of any international security arrangement.

The United States military establishment, or more broadly speaking its security establishment, also has the substantial internal inertia that naturally accompanies its relative preponderance. It was created over the course of the Cold War to conduct large scale operations – those associated with the objectives of deterrence and containment. In the aftermath of the Cold War it is in the process of reducing its force structure by nearly 30 percent and no longer explicitly focuses its plans and deployment patterns on a specific enemy or a specific theater of engagement. It nonetheless continues the basic operations developed for the Cold War – preparation for both nuclear and conventional war on short notice. Deterring and resisting large-scale, deliberately calculated aggression continues to be the fundamental strategic commitment of the United States.

The international security order, such as it is, undoubtedly depends on that commitment to an appreciable extent. It is reasonable to assume that the potential to defeat any major exercise of aggression has a general settling effect whether or not it is formalized in an explicit alliance arrangement. The most urgent emerging security requirements are not addressed by that residual background effect, however, and are not necessarily compatible with it. The putative villains cannot justify the magnitude of investment the United States is making and cannot carry the burdens that investment indirectly imposes upon them. The predominant strategic problem under the new international security conditions is not that of propagating a decisive deterrent effect in order to restrain aggression but rather that of providing systematic reassurance that legitimate security interests can be met with acceptable risk and tolerable cost. Failures of reassurance would drive some states toward limited but dangerous adaptations of advanced technology and others toward internal disintegration.

As Emanating from Russia

As during the Cold War so in the new situation, the leading instances of the emerging security problems occur in the successor states of the former Soviet Union and in China. The Russian military establishment in particular is in very great difficulty and will undoubtedly need formalized arrangements for reassurance if it is to master those difficulties.

The Russian military planning system, which inherited the prime elements of Soviet forces including provisionally all of the nuclear weapons, is aspiring to preserve a 1.5 million person establishment out of that inheritance. In traditional terms that is a reasonable aspiration. The Russian state must defend new borders with turbulent neighbors very few of which are inclined to be allies. Using standard military planning logic, they must imagine a series of moderate contingencies along their southern periphery, some of which are immediately active. They must also contemplate the possibility of major ones both in Europe and in Asia. In assessing their ground force capabilities in Asia against the potential of China and their general air defense capabilities against sophisticated Western operations, they have solid reason for concern.

If it is easy for the Russians to justify a 1.5 million person establishment, however, it is virtually impossible to finance it while simultaneously pursuing economic regeneration. The current defense budget, approximately the equivalent of $30 billion, is perhaps a third of the minimum that would be required to sustain a establishment of that size. To make it competitive at the standard that the United States sets would require a yet greater level of financing.

For the foreseeable future it will not be feasible for Russia to sustain a military establishment that would be independently competitive in performing traditional military missions, but no alternative arrangement has been prepared.· Nor is Russia in a position to create such an arrangement solely or even primarily at its own initiative. Meaningful reassurance would require a general understanding about the size, configuration, deployment concentrations and operational practices of military forces all along its periphery, an area extensive enough to require what would in effect be global standards. The reassurance of Russia necessarily entails the reassurance of neighboring states as well, and that is an exercise in which all of the major establishments would have to be integral participants.

POLICY PRINCIPLES

The process of establishing arrangements for systematic reassurance would necessarily be different from the adversarial bargaining characteristic of the Cold War. The basic purpose is not to maneuver for relative advantage but rather to establish general conditions of security that ease what otherwise promise to be intractable burdens for most states. It is the strongest who must initiate such a process, and it is very much in their interest to do so. The diffusion of technology is neutralizing the advantages of large-scale military operations and a widespread process of political disintegration would overwhelm them.

As the strongest of the strong, the Unites States cannot avoid special responsibility for initiating this process and in fact appears to be in the early, inchoate stages of doing so. Without yet articulating a strategic conception to replace the Cold War formulation, the United States military establishment is beginning to engage with its Russian counterpart in a series of collaborative ventures on issues of immediate practical concern. These have featured the most immediate and most obvious matters of mutual interest, in particular the deactivation of nuclear warheads and the decommissioning of military officers, but some form of dialogue has also been established on a very broad agenda. What they have accomplished so far does not constitute the partnership that both sides have cautiously espoused as an aspiration, but given the press of circumstances it is reasonable to project a serious trend in that direction.

And fortunately there is relevant tradition to evoke. In the course of the Cold War the United States did acquire considerable experience in the practice of systematic reassurance since that was the character of the relationship established with its previous enemies, Germany and Japan. This was done, to be sure, in the motivating context of a joint confrontation with the Soviet Union, but the strikingly successful results are certainly valid outside of that context. In fact the principles and operational practices developed in those relationships provide the natural basis for a generalized international security arrangement that is responsive to the new conditions. One should not be surprised to discover that the new order, when it emerges, has been incubated in the old one.

In order to see the outlines of a new arrangement embedded in the past, it is necessary to view the past with a somewhat different focus. It has been customary to understand the Cold War period as a confrontation between opposing alliances in which the two major establishments extended a particular type of security guarantee to their respective allies – that is, a commitment to fight in their defense if they were attacked by the opposing alliance. That guarantee was articulated in article V of the NATO treaty and has been considered to be the essence of the organization. Embedded in that arrangement, however, was a very different type of guarantee and a different security relationship. While confronting the Soviet Union, the members of NATO were reassuring each other that they would not fight among themselves as they had long been in the habit of doing. In that respect they were preventing the circumstances of an attack from arising in the first place, essentially by intermingling their military operations to a degree that effectively precluded their turning on each other. The United States arrangement with Japan was similar in character.

Because they have been embedded in a more prominent confrontation, the principles involved in these internal alliance relationships have been more practiced than preached. It is not too difficult to extract them, however, once one thinks of doing so.

The central element is transparency. The participating members of these relationships share a great deal of information about the current and projected size, technical configuration and operational disposition of their national forces. They do not by any means reveal everything to each other, but they do share enough to instill confidence in their respective intentions, which are rarely perfectly harmonious but certainly are not directly threatening. The Belgians, for example do not worry that the Germans might attack them despite their historical experience and despite very substantial German military capabilities. They know enough about the details of German military operations that the question simply does not arise.

An important supplement is operational integration which contributes substantially to transparency. The allied military establishments exercise together and perform common functions to an extent that the exchange of reassuring information is continuous and automatic. The respective governments continuously host foreign military forces under operational rules that protect the basics of national sovereignty while clearly qualifying national autonomy on everyone's part. The practice of collaboration is deeply and routinely embedded among them.

Abstracting from the traditional rationale of responding to a common external threat, the integrating theme of these cooperative arrangements has been the restriction of military preparation to a single legitimate objective – the defense of national territory. The implicit rule is that forces are to be configured for that purpose rather than for the more dangerous purpose of power projection. This is the standard embodied most significantly in the German and the Japanese military establishments. Both have highly capable military forces and technically advanced economies but both have strictly focused their efforts on territorial defense and have systematically integrated their operations into international arrangements. If all military establishments were in that configuration, the basic conditions of international security would be far more stable and far less expensive than they have been over the course of the Cold War.

There are obvious problems with that formulation, and they are sufficiently daunting in fact to be grounds of summary rejection by anyone operating within the traditional logic of strategic assessment. The Russian and Chinese military establishments are isolated from the collaborative arrangements that were explicitly developed to contain them. The United States, which is at the core of the arrangements, violates the standard. The United States military establishment is a power projection machine, and there is no direct reason for it to be defensively configured in terms of military operations. The United States is isolated from any contiguous threat. The exceptions, it might be said, overwhelm the rule.

But that certainly will not be the end of the story and probably will not be its ultimate character either. In order to fit the resources it plausibly will have available, the Russian military establishment will have to be reduced to less than half of its current planning goal, and that monumental exercise cannot be reasonably accomplished unless it is enveloped in comprehensive collaborative arrangements. Nor can it be readily accomplished unless China is also included. Because China's economic performance is currently much better than Russia's, China is usually attributed with both the capacity and intention for completely independent and implicitly confrontational military development. That, however, is a highly impractical conclusion. China is decades behind the leading edge of military capability and its annual rate of investment is at least five time less than that of the United States alone. Under the emerging conditions the incentives for China to enter collaborative arrangements are at least as powerful as they are for everyone else. For its part, the United States cannot legitimately sustain its configuration and relative advantage outside of collaborative arrangements, nor can it hope to regulate the very dangerous process of technical diffusion and weapons proliferation unless Russian and China are included. For all the major military establishments, the attempt to evolve a generally inclusive cooperative security arrangement is an unavoidable strategic imperative, no matter how implausible and uncomfortable it might currently seem.

REGIONAL IMPLICATIONS

The Middle East has historically been and undoubtedly will remain one of the last redoubts of skepticism, if not to say cynicism about the feasibility of any meaningful security cooperation. Obviously the politics and the military postures of the region are highly confrontational. The region will surely be affected, however, by the new strategic environment. If one thinks in terms of years and decades rather than weeks and months, some plausible effects of the general transformation can be imagined.

First, the region is not an exception to the general suppression of large ground force operations. The prospect of territorial conquest – the changing of political jurisdiction by force – may well continue to flourish in myth and rhetoric but it has become very improbable in practical terms. The trend toward engagement among the major military establishments and the predominant power projection capabilities of the United States create conditions that would almost certainly produce decisive resistance to any aggressive mobilization. The Persian Gulf war set both the norm and the precedent of international enforcement. The United States has focussed its military preparations on exactly that eventuality. The two regional contingencies that are currently advanced as the justification for United States conventional forces are well understood political code for the Middle East and North Korea. For the foreseeable future the acknowledged possibility of defiant political calculations that might challenge the norm will sustain the preparations to defend it.

Second, the region is a prime instance of the problem of technical diffusion, and that fact is a special problem for Israel. The technical advantages that the Israeli military establishment currently enjoys in comparison with the others in the region cannot be sustained indefinitely if the pattern of confrontation is itself sustained. No other regional military establishment is likely to match Israel's overall capability, but many of them will very predictably develop an offsetting capability for long-range destruction unless agreed arrangements for restraint are established. Relative advantage is a wasting asset for Israel in the region just as it is for the United States globally. The basic security requirement in both instances is to translate current advantage into co-operative arrangements to regulate the application of dangerous technology.

Third, the incentive for cooperative regulation is powerfully reinforced in the region, just as it is globally, by the underlying issues of economic equity and the associated problem of political disintegration. The first and most fundamental requirement of security is the existence of coherent government, and increasingly that is not something that can be taken for granted. None of the governments in the region can afford to sustain stark military confrontation, and all of them are directly or indirectly threatened by the possibility of internal disintegration. None of the military establishments can reasonably expect to cope with the social violence that emerges when radical disintegration occurs. For all their celebrated historical disputes, the governments in the region have a powerful common interest in their own viability and a commensurately powerful incentive to redirect assets from military preparation to economic investment. That drives them toward a process of systematic reassurance and toward the principles of cooperative security necessary to implement it, despite their ingrained political antagonism.

In general for the Middle East and for the world as a whole neither past experience nor current political sentiment provides a very good guide to the emerging strategic environment and the problems of security it poses. That is, of course, a major burden for anyone who attempts to think about strategy, since history and opinion are the things we most readily know. Perhaps the best conclusion to be drawn therefore is simply this: better start exercising the imagination; the emerging world promises to be very different than it has been.

America's Response to the New World (Dis)order

GEORGE H. QUESTER

We have encountered at least three major themes of uncertainty or surprise about international affairs since 1989, all of which will be entangled with our discussion here.

First, no one predicted that the Cold War would end so suddenly.[1] Second, if anyone had been able to forecast this collapse of the communist side in the Cold War, most westerners would initially have then predicted very beneficial political, economic, social and military consequences. What we have seen instead, in the "post-Cold War" years, is at least very confusing and mixed, and seemingly unpredictable, on all these counts. Third, again, if anyone had predicted the communist collapse, there would have been great uncertainty about the nature of America's role in the world thereafter.[2]

This essay will not dwell very much on the initial collapse of communism, or on why it came as such a surprise. Rather, the intention is to focus on the second and third ranges of uncertainty. We will first survey the series of confusions and disappointments about what the world would be like now; and then, in light of this, will discuss the implications for America's role in the world.

George Bush spoke of a "new world order" as the USSR was breaking up; if people today see as much disorder as order, is such pessimism well taken, or could it be temporary and overstated? And what are we to predict about the willingness of the American people and their government to become engaged with either order or disorder?

EXPECTATIONS OF PEACE: THE FUNDAMENTAL PARADOX

A great many Americans drew one immediate optimistic conclusion from the end of the Cold War: that military threats and burdens would now be markedly reduced.[3] Economically, this could be

George H. Quester is Professor of Government and Politics at the University of Maryland.

expected to produce a "peace dividend," allowing for tax cuts or greater civilian spending. In general, it would allow Americans and everyone else around the world to exult in a peace based on democracy. When George Bush spoke of a "new world order," various commentators noted that this might indeed at last be the realization of the Wilsonian dreams of collective security.

Yet there has always been a paradox associated with such an exultation about peace, in that it tempts someone like Mussolini or Saddam Hussein to exploit this as the cover for aggression. One of Clausewitz's most trenchant observations was that "The aggressor is always peace-loving."[4] What the Prussian analyst was pointing to is our common intuition that war does not occur unless the victim *resists* aggression. Someone like Saddam Hussein or Mussolini could thus confront a world now eager to enjoy peace with the intuitive message of "since you value peace so very much, surely you will not want to start a war when I am simply taking over territory that is rightfully mine"; and the world would be confronted with the horrible choice of electing to initiate what anyone would remember as war.

To really prevent aggression, and to make peace meaningful, one thus has to be ready to go to war. George Bush succeeded in girding Americans and others to transcend this paradox in the Persian Gulf War, but this is a very taxing test to have to pass, amid risks that it is a test that will have to be faced over and over again.

EXPECTATIONS OF PEACE: DEFENSIVE DEFENSE

Even before the Cold War ended, one could draw hope for the confrontation between NATO and the Warsaw Pact in the analysis that new attention should be given to the distinction between offensive and defensive weapons.[5] The Soviet acquisition of some 80,000 tanks had very much exacerbated the threat inherently posed by the central geopolitical position commanded from Moscow, and (under prodding from western analysts) Soviet commentators had begun to acknowledge this.[6] Interesting discussions were underway as to how to reconfigure the armed forces on each side so that they would be robustly able to defend their own territory but much less effective when they crossed the border to enter someone else's territory. Shrugging off references to "Maginot mentality," new consideration would be given to fixed fortifications and to "platform-stopper" anti-tank weapons, and to territorially-based militia systems.[7]

Approving references were made to the models of several countries which had such a defensively-oriented system, discouraging anyone from invading their territory, but holding no meaningful capability at all to invade their neighbors: Switzerland, Sweden, Finland, and ... Yugoslavia.

But here one comes to another major paradox. If we generally welcome defense over offense, what will then happen when a society tears itself apart amid horrendous atrocities, and the outside world needs to intervene for the most humane of motives?

Yugoslavia caused the West relatively little concern about the prospect of a Warsaw Pact invasion, because (like Finland and Sweden and Switzerland), it trained all its males for military service, and because it knew all the right places in its mountains for an ambush of invading Soviet or other forces. But the same Serb, Croat and Bosnian Muslim males all thus know how to operate mortars and machine guns, and hence how to hurt each other's women and children, all the while threatening that they could also impose substantial casualties on any American or other peace-restoring force of intervention.

When asked to explain the U.S. professional military officers' reluctance to get involved in Yugoslavia, after their achievement in liberating Kuwait, some have responded off-handedly: "We do deserts, we don't do mountains."

EXPECTATIONS OF PEACE: THE LOSS OF SOVIET COMMAND AND CONTROL

To repeat, no one predicted that the Soviet Union would cease to exist. A theorist of nuclear strategy would not even have looked forward so positively to such a breakup, moreover, on the elementary logic that the outside world could never dare put the communist leadership into a position of "use "em or lose "em" with regard to the Soviet nuclear arsenal.

Yet anti-communist forces did take over the streets of Moscow, posing a host of worrisome unanswered questions about the control, and even the elementary accounting, what had been this nuclear arsenal.[8] And there are indeed depressing questions, for anyone aspiring to a world *order*, about the disposition of *conventional* weapons as the Cold War comes to an end.

Instead of a world where weapons are unimportant, it has turned out to be the case that nuclear weapons are *very* important. If they did not exist, almost no one in the United States would know where Ukraine was, or would care about the future of Kazakhstan. If nuclear weapons did not exist, the U.S. would not be so concerned about keeping President Boris Yeltsin in power and keeping democracy on track. If nuclear weapons had never been invented, the United States, and most of the outside world, would probably welcome any and all additional signs of division and chaos inside the former Soviet Union. The old adage was "divide and conquer." Since nuclear weapons do exist, however, Americans have to worry a great deal about the maintenance of unified command-and-control systems over Soviet Inter-Continental Ballistic Missiles (ICBMs) and other nuclear weapons.

There are problems even in the realm of conventional weapons. While there is no longer a unified force of some 80,000 Warsaw Pact tanks to be feared, the sale and transfer of such weapons, and the production of similar weapons for export in the former communist military-industrial complex, generate arms control concerns for many places around the globe.[9]

Much the worst, of course, would be if any *nuclear* weapons were to be transferred, as rumors sometimes have it, to Iran or Serbia, or to any other erstwhile "nth" nuclear power. The change in the communist "evil empire" is very welcome, but it has dramatically reduced the status and well-being of the Soviet military-industrial complex, leaving some of its individuals possibly desperate. Even if bombs were not to be missing under the sloppy Soviet accounting system, and then slipped to such a foreign power, the skills of nuclear weapons designers who used to work in the USSR could be of great value to a Saddam Hussein or a Mu'amar Gaddafi.[10]

Before 1989, it was also the case that Moscow held a sort of veto over the military actions of North Korea, as the USSR was instrumental in getting Pyongyang to sign and ratify the Nuclear Non-Proliferation Treaty (NPT). With the end of the USSR, and opening of trade and diplomatic relations between Russia and South Korea, most of such leverage has been lost. The new concerns Americans face about the possibility of North Korea acquiring its own nuclear weapons are thus another part of the "peace dividend."[11]

At the very beginning of the 1990s, there were hopes that relations might improve dramatically between North and South Korea, including prospects for additional guarantees of a non-nuclear status for both portions of the peninsula, for reunification of families, and for an opening of trade.

Yet the outside world very much lacks information on what is happening inside North Korea, with Chinese and Russian diplomats having little more access than anyone else. During Kim Ilsung's last year, there was an inevitable power struggle about whether his son or some other person would succeed him, and some analysts concluded that this explained the "on again, off again" nature of all North Korean cooperation with the outside world, including relations with South Korea, with the International Atomic Energy Agency (IAEA), with the United States, and even with China and Russia.

The net of the happenings in Korea has thus been to generate one more of what have been a series of disappointments for the U.S. about how the 1990s would evolve. Rather than amounting to another category of international conflict that fades with an outbreak of peace, this has indeed become one of the most serious foreign policy challenges for the Clinton administration.

The bottom line in this entire category of predictions and reality has been that the "peace dividend" has been smaller than anticipated, and that the role of "security" issues has remained larger than most Americans would have hoped. Rather than a unified colossus threatening the U.S. and its allies, there is the prospect of disorganization and proliferation, of more "fingers on triggers."

THE RETURN OF ETHNIC NATIONALISM

Liberals and Marxists agreed that it was ridiculous for people to hate each other and shoot at each other because of religion or language. In the West, this saw old Franco-German hatreds seem to fade as the Common Market became the European Community/Union, and in the East the same could be expected between, for example, Hungarians and Romanians, under the guidance of Moscow, through the Warsaw Pact and "socialist internationalism."

Looking ahead in 1989, Americans would have expected even more of a demise of petty nationalist feelings, as Western Europe committed itself at Maastricht to the elimination of border controls and to the adoption of a unified currency. Very few of such Americans would have guessed that Azeris and Armenians still knew how to hate each other, and massacre each other, after 70 years of communist rule, a rule in which both Christians and Moslems were persecuted. Very few would have predicted that Eastern Europe would so quickly see disintegration rather than integration, as the Soviet Union broke into many pieces, as Yugoslavia violently broke apart, as even Czechoslovakia could not stay unified.

To repeat, the one part of the Marxist world outlook shared by most Americans, because it is also so central to the liberal world outlook, was to regard ethnically-based nationalisms as silly and a waste of time, a dangerous remnant of the traditional attitudes that had so much burdened the "old world."[12] The greatest disappointment for Americans is thus objectified in the fact that Sarajevo was the site of the Winter Olympics in 1984 and the site of bitter ethnic strife ten years later. How Americans are to react to such strife, how they are to tell the difference between a Bosnian Muslim and a Serb or a Croat, or between an Armenian and an Azeri, opens up some very major questions of American foreign policy. Rather than being the exception to the rule, the pattern of the Arab–Israeli or Northern Irish conflicts may now look much more like the normal pattern. Americans may find it easier to identify with the Israelis in their conflict with the Arabs (although even here the more normal American attitude is to blame *both* sides for a conflict based on such outmoded ideas of what is important in life); they would find it much harder to identify with either side in most of the other new ethnic conflicts that have emerged.

RELIGIOUS FUNDAMENTALISM AND OTHER INTOLERANCE

Explaining a portion of such ethnic nationalist rivalries, but amounting to an even larger phenomenon, was the growing visibility at the beginning of the 1990s of Islamic fundamentalism, and of some parallel leanings toward a religious intolerance in various strands of Christianity and also Judaism.

In the Cold War, religion had typically been seen as an ally by Western liberals in the struggle against "godless communism." The Marxists had made containment easier by alienating Christians and Muslims alike, and other religious groups as well (the Buddhists in Vietnam, for example). Indeed, if the United States had not been a strong supporter of Israel, it would have been very difficult for the Soviet Union to win friends and allies in the Islamic world, because of the way it had repressed Islamic religious practice within its own Asian Republics. Americans saw themselves as defending religion against such total anti-religious persecution, and also as protecting religions against each other, in systems of separation of church and state and guarantees of tolerance. The end of the Cold War would thus be seen as a victory for religious liberty, but at heart, for most Americans, the emphasis would be on the "liberty," rather than the "religious." If the final defeat of communism was now to be accompanied by victories of those who cared much more about the "religious" than about "liberty," with major upsurges of Islamic fundamentalism across the Arab world and also inside the former Soviet Union and in non-Arab "secularized" places like Turkey or Malaysia, this amounts to another *surprise* for most Americans, and not a welcome surprise.[13]

The news reaching Americans at the start of the 1990s would now include the bombing of the World Trade Center in Manhattan by Islamic fundamentalists, and the killings in Hebron by an ultra-Orthodox Jewish West Bank settler who had emigrated from Brooklyn, and regular citings of a threat of "Islamic fundamentalism" as an excuse by Orthodox Serbs or Roman Catholic Croatians trying to seize the land of Bosnian Muslims. Just like the ethnic disputes discussed above, such conflicts of religion would be confusing for Americans, who pride themselves (in effect, without thinking about it) on never taking their religion so seriously that they would kill anyone over it.

But, apart from being confusing, this kind of motivation for violent conflict is disturbing because it seems so much to be on the upsurge all around the globe, another disappointment of the 1990s.

Equally disheartening for most Americans, albeit without any basis in *religion*, was the appearance, most noticeably in Germany, but also elsewhere around Europe, of the "skinhead" variety of neo-Fascist and neo-Nazi sentiment.[14] While the West German educational system had been fairly forthright about acknowledging Nazi attrocities, the East German system had done very little of this, since everything evil in the world was to be blamed on capitalism (and the Austrian educational process had also somewhat glossed over Austria's role in the Nazi period, comparable to the way Japanese schoolbooks had failed to address Japanese barbarism during the Second World War).

For Americans, the "skinheads" of Eastern Europe were like the "Islamic fundamentalists" of Central Asia, a disappointing exercise of the freedom that had been won from communist rule, a disappointing sign that communism had repressed, but had not at all succeeded in educating; it was a sign that the trend toward modernity was not necessarily assured, as some very disturbing negative "traditions" of the past were returning.

RESURGENCE AND DISAPPOINTMENTS ON INTERNATIONAL LAW

The Bush administration's effort to put together an international coalition against Iraq's occupation of Kuwait was a clear success. In part, this was because Saddam Hussein amounted to the perfect villain. He had blatantly invaded a neighboring country, the primary reason for action (by the somewhat paradoxical nature of "collective security" reasoning outlined above). He had killed large numbers of his own citizens, utilizing poison gas. He had used such chemical weapons in warfare against the Iranians earlier. If Saddam Hussein would be allowed to retain Kuwait, his Iraq would hold a menacingly large percentage of the world's oil supplies. And Saddam Hussein was rumored to be reaching for nuclear weapons, despite Iraq's prior signature and ratification of the Nuclear Non-Proliferation Treaty (NPT).

At American prodding, the United Nations Security Council made the juridically clever move in its resolutions of declaring that Iraq had to divest itself of all equipment designed for the production of nuclear weapons, not just because it was already a party to the NPT, but because any such move by a nation like Iraq was *ipso facto* a threat to peace, and thus already more broadly banned by the United Nations Charter.[15] In the domestic constitutional law of the United States, this is what is sometimes styled an *obiter dicta* finding, an unnecessary additional ruling where simpler principles would have sufficed, a foot in the door for a whole range of subsequent assertions of authority.

At the beginning of the 1990s, Americans and others were thus inclined to be optimistic about an expansion of "customary international law," such that even nations that had not agreed to adhere to the NPT and thus to renounce nuclear weapons would have to abstain anyway, such that even nations that had never acknowledged the paramountcy of human rights in their domestic political practices would now have to accept international standards.

By the vision of UN Secretary-General Boutros Ghali, shared by at least some Americans, the UN Charter mandate to preserve peace would now become quite elastic, as there would be a "threat to peace" in shooting at fellow Yugoslavs, or in allowing Somalis to starve because warlords are seizing their food, or even in acquiring nuclear weapons and chemical weapons. By an earlier standard, the fighting in Yugoslavia might simply have been an internal "civil war"; because Slovenia and Croatia, and then Bosnia, were quickly admitted to membership in the United Nations, this fighting became an international war and thus a "threat to peace."

If Americans were very proud of what they had done for Kuwait, the glow of this faded very fast, however, in part because of a disappointment afterward that the problems with Saddam Hussein had not ceased, and because of sour feelings about what was being accomplished, at what cost, in the intervention in Somalia, set against the frustrations of other members of NATO in their intervention in the former Yugoslavia. Within a year, Clinton was able to defeat Bush for reelection on a general theme that Bush had devoted too much attention to foreign policy; and within another year the American enthusiasm for a much more active United Nations, and for a greatly expanded "customary international law" had been reined in.[16]

Just as each of the other predictions implicitly generated by the end of the Cold War were now being followed by disappointment, such disappointment characterized the situation here as well. In this case, one might indeed see a mixture of disappointment *of* Americans, and disappointment *about* Americans, as what seemed to be an eagerness to terminate international involvements took hold, just at the point where such involvements might be crucial to a "new world order."

THE FADING OF COMMUNISM

As noted, the defeat of communism in Eastern Europe, and in the Soviet Union itself, came as a glorious surprise for those who had opposed its political and economic manifestations for so long. Even where this was not achieved explicitly, as in the People's Republic of China and in Vietnam, one saw a marked liberalization of economic practices, followed by a slower relaxation also of the political straightjacket.

The leaders of the Chinese Communist Party were now talking of "Socialism with Chinese characteristiscs," which basically meant that people were free to make as much money as market skills would win them.[17] Vietnam had stubbornly stuck longer to the Marxist visions of Ho Chi Minh, until the middle of the 1980s when the country actually experienced a rice shortage because of the misdirection of incentives this had produced. If nothing else could do it, this had to be a "moment of truth" for the dictatorship in Hanoi. In a dramatic surrender to market principles and return to effective private use of the land, Vietnam went within a single year back to the status of being a major rice exporter and has since then allowed the practices of Saigon to come north to Hanoi, rather than persisting with the reverse.[18]

The defeat of communism had been a dramatic confirmation of "domino theory," but in reverse. Yet, if the outside world, and the United States in particular, now were expecting that *every* communist regime would fall, they were to be disappointed about two countries, Cuba and North Korea, with the second of these survivals posing very serious problems.

The Cuban emigrés living in Miami were dancing in the streets at the prospect of the fall of Fidel Castro, feeling that he deserved the same fate as Ceaucescu and Honecker. As Cubans continue to flee the island, and as Russian and other communist country subsidies have been cut off, the delay in the termination of communist rule there is very hard on the Cubans and perplexing for those on the outside who identify with them, but it poses no great threats or strategic problems for the American people.[19]

Many might feel that the rulers of North Korea also deserve the fate of Ceaucescu, for having oppressed their citizens for more than four decades now in one of the most rigid dictatorships the world has seen, and for having invaded South Korea in 1950, launching a war that took millions of lives.

Yet a most important difference has already been alluded to, in that Fidel Castro has no plausible way to acquire nuclear weapons, while the Koreans are accused of having accumulated plutonium for the production of such atomic bombs. Such nuclear weapons might only be intended as a last-gasp deterrent to ensure the regime against being deposed in the fashion of the other communist rulers.

Or such atomic bombs might be viewed as an accessory to one more attempt to "unify" Korea by conquering the south. The mere possibility of such weapons had already under the Bush administration, supplied some leverage to induce the withdrawal of the *American* nuclear weapons deployed in South Korea. Since North Korea still maintains an army quantitatively much larger (albeit qualitatively inferior in equipment) than that of South Korea, and since the South Korean capital at Seoul is less than 50 kilometers from the border with the North, the risk remains of a sudden *conventional* attack on the South, with the absence of U.S. forward-deployed nuclear weapons making it all the less likely that a nuclear escalation would come in response.[20]

The disappointing end of the trail on this sector of analysis might thus be, for South Koreans and for their American friends, that "the Cold War is not over" for the Korean peninsula, as the military problems remain the same or have actually gotten worse. Perhaps there is a "new world order" elsewhere that has often become "disorder"; but the situation in Korea offers a lot that is "old" rather than "new." What was "new" here was indeed the disorder of seeing neither Moscow nor Beijing have much influence anymore in Pyongyang. Americans and South Koreans had once denounced Kim Il-sung as being merely the puppet of the Russians and Chinese; one now can only wish that this was so.

ECONOMIC UPS AND DOWNS

Most Americans expected that the territories that had been subjected to doctrinaire Marxist rule would prosper economically, once such rule was lifted. Just as West Germany took off on the "economic miracle" in the summer of 1948, after the Deutschmark was introduced and price controls were lifted, producing a period of sustained economic growth in West Germany and Western Europe exceding anything that had been seen in history, so the lifting of the command-economy central controls in the communist countries could have been expected to achieve similar results. One (as noted) could see a similar upsurge of economic prosperity in communist China, once Deng Xiaoping had decided to junk the egalitarian central management system that Mao and Marx had stood for, and then also in Vietnam, as soon as the peasants were told that the old system of personal profit was back for their work on the land. One had indeed seen an earlier example of the same liberation of producers and consumers in Lenin's desperate introduction of the NEP in 1921, when, just as in Germany in 1948, goods miraculously reappeared in the shops over a weekend.[21]

Yet the pattern in Eastern Europe and in the former Soviet Union has been much more uneven, producing a widespread sentiment that the economic side of de-communization has somehow been a failure, or that "shock therapy" was a mistake. While goods have reappeared in the stores, and people no longer have to waste enormous amounts of time waiting in line for their shopping, unemployment has been higher than hoped for in many sectors, and people on fixed salaries or pensions have seen their living standard go down.

The tendency to grumble is widespread in democracies, so that there will always be less open comment about the positive aspects of the change than about the negative. The actual overall "bottom line" on the degree of economic improvement or worsening is something that can be debated among economists or between competing parties in election campaigns. Yet the economic picture is certainly another *disappointment*, for Americans as well as for the people directly involved, a disappointment compared to what happened in China, a disappointment compared to what Americans would have guessed would happen.[22]

SOME MISCELLANY IN ORDER AND DISORDER

Just as it looked for a time as if there would be a remarkable direct improvement in relations between North Korea and South Korea, the period in which the Cold War came to an end saw encouraging possibilities emerge on several persistant *non-Cold War* confrontations, but with each of these also posing risks of disappointment.

One such confrontation was always less serious than the outside press commentary tended to paint it, the "historical rivalry" between Brazil and Argentina, which (since neither country was ready to sign the Nuclear Non-Proliferation Treaty renouncing nuclear weapons) might now become a nuclear rivalry. Yet the same symmetry of nuclear potential may now have been turned around to head off nuclear proliferation, as each of these Latin American states might have liked to be the *only* state in the region with nuclear weapons (for the prestige and stature this can convey), but where each has realized that there is little gained, and much lost, if *two* such countries get atomic bombs. The logic between the two countries has thus become an implicit, and at times explicit, kind of mutual deterrence: "we won't produce nuclear weapons as long as you don't, and we will if you do."[23]

Americans have always cared more about the Western hemisphere than about other regions of the globe, and the Latin Americans have often resented this special care. The United States has been committed to discouraging nuclear proliferation around the globe, and has pushed the NPT. The opposition of Brazilians and Argentines to the NPT has importantly thus stemmed from the feeling that this was being pushed by the United States, that the NPT was an unfair and one-sided dictate of the superpowers.

The United States has also been committed to encouraging democracy and human rights, around Latin America and around the globe, with this sometimes also becoming counterproductive when the Latin American right-wing and military could paint such a commitment as Yankee imperialism. Yet democracy has spread remarkably in Latin America in the 1980s, in part due to U.S. pressure, and the emergence of democratic instead of military regimes in Brazil and Argentina is a part of the explanation for the movement away from nuclear proliferation.[24]

This linkage makes the good news here again somewhat prone to disorder and disappointment, of course. If the elected presidents of these countries perform poorly, if the military takes it into its head to establish juntas again, the joint arrangements intended to prevent nuclear proliferation could fall apart.

Latin America is interestingly different from the rest of the world, for having produced very few wars or international crises. It is not a continent from which writers like Hans Morgenthau could extract illustrative examples. The armies and navies of Latin America have been a major problem for over-throwing democratically-elected governments, but not for planning or fighting wars with each other.

Yet it surely was possible that the introduction of nuclear weapons to this continent could have changed this, pulling Latin America into the discussion of mutual deterrence and counterforce threats. A desire to avoid this "normalcy" of outside world military confrontation may have been an important part of what led the two countries now to keep their distance from nuclear weapons.

A much more serious confrontation, also surprising in the way it was unwravelling as the world entered the 1990s, was the struggle between the black African majority in South Africa and the white minority regime that had imposed the system of apartheid. Here there was also a nuclear element involved, with rumors that the Pretoria regime was secretly enriching uranium and assembling nuclear warheads, perhaps as a veto over any attempts to terminate white rule.

Rather than forcing things to a last-gasp desperation scenario, the government of South African President DeKlerk instead surprised the world by releasing the head of the African National Congress, Nelson Mandela, initiating and concluding negotiations toward the establishment of a political system where all South Africans would have the vote. In the process South Africa also stunned the world by announcing that it had indeed produced nuclear weapons but had then dismantled them, and was now submitting to the NPT and the IAEA international safeguards designed to guarantee that there would be no nuclear weapons in the country.[25]

Even more than in the Brazil-Argentina "confrontation," there is still a great deal that can go wrong in the South African case, in the extreme scenario seeing the white minority subjected to physical attack and having to flee, producing situations requiring international intervention just as much as in Yugoslavia. The possibility also remains that rumors will circulate that South Africa cannot account for, and did not totally give up, all the fissionable material it possessed, so that it may be holding some nuclear warheads in reserve, in case the current move toward a peaceful transition to majority rule should break down.[26]

In short, the news from South Africa is very good by the yardsticks Americans would apply to justice and self-determination around the world, as almost all Americans had come to condemn apartheid; yet the net of what has happened might easily add again to what would have to be called disorder, rather than order, and what could produce yet another disappointment.

Direct negotiations between the Israeli government and the Palestine Liberation Organization (PLO) amounted to another very positive surprise in the afterglow of the end of the Cold War, although there might not be very much of a direct connection. Given how deep the hostility between Israelis and Arabs had seemed to be, ever since the 1920s, very few analysts would have dared to predict that the PLO would renounce violence, or renounce its dreams of reacquiring *all* of Palestine, and that Israel would give up its refusal to negotiate with the PLO.[27]

This was the kind of ethnically-based conflict that was, happily, so exceptional during the Cold War. As noted above, the end of the Cold War held the major disappointment that so much more of this kind of ethnic conflict was unleashed. The standard ideological conflict of the East-West Cold War had seen each side genuinely pursuing what it regarded as the good of all, with the problem that the visions of "good" were so often so opposite. By comparison, ethnic conflict lacks this concern for the welfare of the opposite ethnic group.

As we shift now to what all of this means for the future of American role in the post-Cold War world, a new world of either order or disorder, it suffices to note that this is another arena where there may be disappointments, or where, since the predictable relationships of hostility have been altered, a new kind of uncertainty and lack of order may emerge.

U.S. POLICY IN THE FUTURE: CONFLICTING INTERPRETATIONS

Through the bulk of the Cold War, three major interpretations of American foreign policy contended for the acceptance of Americans.

A first is what could be called a "realist" (realpolitik) or "power-politics" interpretation, by which the United States was just an ordinary country, interested like all other countries in maintaining its independence, and thus in assembling the military and other power for such independence interested like all other countries in accumulating power beyond this, because the search for power, in a world of international anarchy, is a natural attribute of sovereignty. By this analysis, the Cold War was no one's fault in particular. It was rather the inevitable result of the defeat of Nazi Germany. Once a common enemy was eliminated, allies would become adversaries. This has been a central theme of how international relations has been taught at American (and many other) universities since the Second World War, reflecting the new insights brought to bear from Europe by writers like Hans Morgenthau.[28]

A second interpretation (what could be called the "liberal" perspective, in the broader and more worldly sense of the word) was what most Americans had instead grown up with, a belief that the United States was an unusually good country, never starting wars but only fighting when first attacked by another, a country which had succeeded at home in the implementation of a pluralistic free society and a political democracy, and would be happy to share this with other countries, at least by example, perhaps by major contributions of economic or military effort.[29]

This kind of interpretation would differ from the first in attaching strong significance, for the future of international peace, to whether democracy was the system governing the powers involved. A good political arrangement at home produces good results in foreign policy, as democracies are very unlikely to get into wars with each other. This was an interpretation in which the United States in its foreign policy would be seen by Americans, and by many others, as much better than most powers as altruistic and generous, and inclined to peace, defending itself only when dictators like Hitler or Stalin made peace impossible. The Cold War, in this view, was the fault of the world communist movement directed from Moscow.

A third interpretation captured a great deal of following on American campuses during the Vietnam War, what could be called a Marxist or radical interpretation, by which the United States, being one of the most capitalist countries in the world, would be driven thereby into imperialism and militarism. Rather than the Cold War being the fault of Stalin, this produced a "revisionist" interpretation by which it had been the fault of Truman and Acheson, just as the Vietnam War was the fault of American imperialism, with Ho Chi Minh becoming a hero. This was thus an overall interpretation by which the United States was a worse country than the average, rather than being "ordinary" or "better than average."[30]

The end of the Cold War *may* shed greater light on which of these theories most plausibly accounts for the events of the 1940s or 1960s or 1980s. And, such alternative theories may offer us a tool for guessing the future American commitment to world activism, after the Cold War had ended.

U.S. POLICY IN THE FUTURE: AMERICAN MILITARY POWER TRIUMPHANT?

A power-politics interpretation of what has happened since 1989 would surely have to see this as an American victory in the Cold War. It was a victory for American military power, as Ronald Reagan matched the challenge of Soviet military expenditures and drove the Soviets into quitting a race they could not win. And it was also a victory for the strength and resiliency of the American economic system.

The Americans and Russians never used nuclear weapons against each other, and almost never even shot at each other, working through their proxies in "limited war," but the Cold War was a military conflict nonetheless, and if it is over, the winner was the United States.

This is an interpretation then, that in power-politics terms begins speaking of a "unipolar world," since the United States will now be the only "superpower." Some Indian and Chinese analyses of the post-1989 international political scene have sounded warnings about American hegemony, as the Americans, like other war-winners in the past, might now seek to dominate and dictate to the entire globe. The United States will see itself as the "world policeman." Just as Henry Luce wrote in 1945 of the "American Century,"[31] George Bush exulted in a "new world order," as American forces effectively dominated the decisions and the execution of the military operations against Iraq.[32]

Yet this theory flies in the face of the fact that George Bush lost the election to Bill Clinton, with Clinton again and again accusing Bush of paying too much attention to foreign policy. If any American General or Admiral were to use the phrase "world policeman" when trying to get Congress to forego cutting the budgets of the U.S. military, he would not only lose his case, but would probably quickly lose his job.

The current American reluctance to become engaged, from Somalia to Haiti to Bosnia, surely does not support the over-arching "realist" theories of international politics that ascribe to every country an endless thirst for power. Rather than wanting to exercise power over others, and wanting to compound upon and increase their national power, a great many Americans and their elected representatives are showing a thirst instead for a "peace dividend" and a respite from international concerns.

Those who argued, all through the Cold War, that Americans were only responding to the unignorable geopolitical threat posed by Moscow's control over the bulk of Eurasia, surely have some ammunition now for their case. As the Soviet *conventional* threat of traditional military power and geopolitical position has been trimmed back (while the thermonuclear threats posed by the enormous former Soviet arsenal of missiles remain), most Americans are showing no signs of being so triumphant and hegemonic, or interested in foreign policy, but rather of being *relieved* that more domestic problems can be turned to.

U.S. POLICY IN THE FUTURE: THE AMERICAN MODEL TRIUMPHANT?

If the Cold War ended with a sort of "military" victory or power victory for the United States, many would thus see it as a victory more broadly for the American model, a model of political freedom and pluralism coupled with the free choice of free markets, with all the economic growth and prosperity this brings, as compared with the dismal results where Marxism imposes a command economy.

There were periods, as during the Vietnam War, where many Americans had lost confidence in their role as a model for the world, and when some of them had come to adopt a Marxist or other "revisionist" or "radical" interpretation of what the Cold War had been all about. The entirety of Americans, for much of the Cold War, had been inclined to respond that they were "losing" this contest, when the question was posed in opinion polls.[33] This could have been because of superior nuclear and conventional, and sub-conventional, military tools being imputed to the communist powers, and/or because of doubts about whether the world would really now prefer political democracy and liberal freedoms over the "economic democracy" and "socialism" that the communist powers were offering.

In the nineteenth and early twentieth centuries, the United States had looked to one and all like "the new world"; but in the nomenclature of the 1960s and 1970s it became common to refer to Africa and Asia and Latin America as the "Third World," which obviously then meant that the communist countries were the "Second World," with the United States being lumped in with traditional Western Europe into a "First World."

But the rapid collapse of the communist model across Europe and the Soviet Union, and the adoption of non-Marxist market approaches in China and Vietnam, and the great success of such approaches across non-communist East Asia, and the shift away from socialist approaches in places like India and Africa and Latin America, all now have restored the status of the U.S. as the model for the future.[34]

Applying this interpretation of the roots of American attitudes toward the outside world, the events since 1989 have been a magnificent reconfirmation of the rightness of the Western and American cause through all the Cold War, a confirmation that the U.S. was on the right side in Europe and Korea and Vietnam. By this interpretation, the U.S. has not been out to seek power, but to seek to spread democracy and free market-choice. By this interpretation, the U.S. might be very enthusiastic now about completing the application of its model, as not only all the former communist countries except for Cuba and North Korea, but also a great number of "Third World" countries, are swinging toward either the economic example of the U.S., or the political example, or both.[35]

But here we also encounter a variety of discouragements to American international activism. First of all, Americans have always faced a quandary on whether they could be more than a *model* for the world, whether they would not compromise their own democracy as a model by being too involved in helping others to adopt it. Just as in 1919, Americans may celebrate the end of a conflict by endorsing a new world order, but also by hankering after a "normalcy."

Beyond this, as a second major problem, the enormity of the success in defeating Communism, in *so many* places, might now strike Americans as daunting. The U.S. after the Second World War managed to bring constitutional democracy to West Germany and to Japan; but this was a much shorter list than the number of ex-communist countries that have appeared after the Cold War.

Beyond this simple glut of success – such that there is so much to celebrate that the average American is not even capable of remembering all the countries' names – a third, still more profound, problem for an American willingness to "keep order" stems from all the disappointments noted above, disappointments about the end of military requirements, disappointments about the return of ethnic hatreds, disappointments about the speed of economic recovery.

We will, at the end, have to contemplate how much of this "disappointment" is simply based on premature expectations or on misleading signals of setbacks that have not really occurred, and how much of this disappointment is real, real enough to inject doubt again about the American model for, and role in, the world.

U.S. POLICY IN THE FUTURE: RADICAL THEORIES CONFIRMED?

The disappointments with events since the fall of communism will, here and there, nourish the Marxist view again, the view of those who see extensive government intervention and regulation as the solution to problems, rather than as their cause. One has thus seen renamed communist parties winning votes in Poland and East Germany and the former Soviet Union. And one will find American Marxists and other "radicals" drawing some satisfaction, that their view of the Cold War has thus not been totally undermined.

Yet a failure of the U.S. to play a major role in the post-Cold War world would hardly seem to support the view that the U.S. economy lives off of miltarism and interventionism, and is desperate to win entry into markets. The leftists saw Soviet military preparations as the necessary response to American threats. Now that the Soviet Union has collapsed, where is the American advance that so much needed to be headed off?

The average Chinese and Russian and Vietnamese indeed wants *more* U.S. investment now, rather than less.[36] And the majority of such people still aspire to being allowed to copy the economic and political model of the United States. Despite the disappointments and setbacks noted in the post-Communist world, the Marxist view of American post-1945 foreign policy (as taught as the official catechism of communist country universities, and also as taught in the free atmosphere of western universities) is hardly plausible to most of these people.

DISCOUNTING FOR DISAPPOINTMENT: THE BOTTOM LINE

We began by noting how few of us had predicted the end of the Cold War, and the opportunity and need for a "new world order." What might one dare to predict now?

The disappointments with the *economic* side of the termination of communism are indeed still likely to pass soon enough, with East Germans ten years from now wondering why they had ever grumbled about the first years of the merger with West Germany, with Poland and Czechslovakia, and even the republics of the former Soviet Union getting growth rates underway more comparable to those of the United States and Western Europe, if not China and the "Asian tigers."

But the disappointments about whether liberal free speech will be free of ethnic hatred, and about whether the interactions of constitutional democracies will be free of arms races and threats of war, may last longer. And, above all, a basic disappointment may remain about whether a world's expressed love of peace will help to produce peace, or instead set up opportunities for some to exploit threats of war.

For most of the reasons cited, Americans will be joined by the other nationalities mentioned in welcoming the end of the Cold War, even if a tinge of disappointment causes some to forget what the benchmark for comparison is (of the people who vote for neo-communist parties in Eastern Europe, how many would really prefer a return to the system of the 1970s?). But if the new world is welcomed here, this may not be because it is more "orderly" than the old. And it will probably not be, except only most indirectly, an "American century."

NOTES

1. John Lewis Gaddis, "International Relations Theory and the End of the Cold War", *International Security*, Vol.17, No.3 (Winter, 1992/1993) pp.5–58.
2. For this author's more extended analysis of the earlier debate about the sources of American foreign policy, see George H. Quester, *American Foreign Policy: The Lost Consensus* (New York: Praeger, 1982).
3. Josef Joffe, "Collective Security and the Future of Europe", *Survival*, Vol.34 No.1 (Spring, 1992), pp.36–52.
4. Karl Von Clausewitz, *On War* (Princeton, New Jersey: Princeton University Press

translation, 1976), p.370.

5. David Gates, *Non-Offensive Defense: An Alternative Strategy for NATO?* (New York: St. Martin's Press, 1991).

6. See chapters by Alexei Arbatov in *Disarmament and Security* (Moscow: IMEMO yearbook, 1987).

7. For longer analyses by the author on these themes, see George H. Quester, *Offense and Defense in the International System* (New York: John Wiley, 1977), and "Some Barriers to Thinking about Conventional Defense", in Elmar Schmaling (ed.), *Life Beyond the Bomb* (Oxford: Berg, 1990), pp.105–116.

8. Bruce Blair, *The Logic of Accidental Nuclear War* (Washington: Brookings, 1993).

9. Ian Anthony, *Arms Export Regulation* (Oxford: Oxford University Press, 1991).

10. Christopher Paine and Thomas Cochran, "So Little Time, So Many Weapons, So Much to Do", *Bulletin of the Atomic Scientists* Vol.48, No.1 (January/February, 1992), pp.12–16.

11. Nicholas Eberstadt, "Can the Two Koreas Be One?", *Foreign Affairs*, Vol.71, No.5 (Winter 1992–93), pp.150–65.

12. John Mearsheimer, "Back to the Future: Instability in Europe After the Cold War" ,*International Security*, Vol.15, No.1 (Summer, 1990), pp.5–56.

13. Richard W. Bulliet, "The Future of the Islamic Movement", *Foreign Affairs*, Vol.72, No.5 (November/December, 1993), pp.38–44.

14. Charles William Maynes, "Containing Ethnic Conclict", *Foreign Policy*, No.90 (Spring, 1993), pp.3–21.

15. A very key Security Council Resolution is #687, adopted April 3, 1991.

16. John R. Bolton, "Wrong Turn in Somalia", *Foreign Affairs*, Vol.73, No.1 (January/February, 1994) pp.56–66.

17. Nicholas D. Kristof, "The Rise of China", *Foreign Affairs*, Vol.72, No.5 (November/December, 1993) pp.59–74.

18. George C. Herring, "America and Vietnam", *Foreign Affairs*, Vol.70, No.5 (Winter 1991/92) pp.104–120.

19. Jorge Dominguez, "Secrets of Castro's Staying Power", *Foreign Affairs*, Vol.72, No.2 (Spring, 1993), pp.97–107.

20. Peter Hayes, "The Realpolitik of the DPRK-IAEA Standoff", *Pacific Research*, Vol.7, No.1 (February, 1994), pp.25–9.

21. Armand Hammer (with Neil Lyon), *Hammer* (New York: Perigee Books, 1987), pp.112–113.

22. Ronald I. McKinnon, *The Order of Economic Liberalization* (Baltimore: Johns Hopkins University Pres, 1993).

23. John Redick, *Argentina and Brazil: An Evolving Nuclear Relationship* (Southhampton: Programme for Promoting Nuclear Non-Proliferation Occasional Paper No.7, 1990).

24. Robert Pastor, "The Latin American Option", *Foreign Policy*, No.88 (Fall, 1992) pp.107–125.

25. J.W. De Villiers, Roger Jardine and Mitchell Reiss, "Why South Africa Gave Up the Bomb", *Foreign Affairs*, Vol.72, No.5 (November/December, 1993) pp.98–109.

26. J. Daniel O'Flaherty, "Holding Together South Africa", *Foreign Affairs*, Vol.72, No.4 (September/October, 1993), pp.126–37.

27. Ian S. Lustick, "Reinventing Jerusalem", *Foreign Policy*, No.93 (Winter, 1993–94) pp.41–59.

28. Hans Morgenthau, *Politics Among Nations* (New York: Alfred Knopf, 1948).

29. Philip Quigg, *America the Dutiful* (New York: Simon and Schuster, 1971).

30. Gabriel Kolko, *The Roots of American Foreign Policy* (Boston: Beacon Press, 1969).

31. Henry Luce, *The American Century* (New York: Farrar and Rinehart, 1941).

32. Charles Krauthammer, "The Unipolar Moment", *Foreign Affairs* Vol.70, No.1 ('American and the World 1990/1991), pp.23–33.

33. Helen Gaudet Erskine, "The Cold War: Report from the Polls", *Public Opinion Quarterly*, Vol.XXV, No.2 (Summer, 1961) pp.300–15.

34. Gregory Fossedal, *The Democratic Imperative* (New York: Basic Books, 1989).

35. Barber J. Conable and David M. Lampton, "China: The Coming Power", *Foreign Affairs*, Vol.71, No.5 (Winter 1992–93), pp.133–49; James Lilley, "Freedom Through Trade", *Foreign Policy*, No.94 (Spring, 1994) pp.37–42.

36. Keith Richberg, "Back to Vietnam", *Foreign Affairs*, Vol.70, No.4 (Fall, 1991), pp.111–31.

Psychological Dimensions of Post-Cold War Foreign Policy

RICHARD NED LEBOW

> We are engaged in the kind of crusade that Lincoln foresaw when he said, of our Declaration of Independence, that it promised "liberty, not alone to the people of this country, but hope for the world for all future time."
>
> John Foster Dulles, July 1950

The Cold War is over and the international system is in a state of flux. The threat of superpower nuclear war has receded and has been replaced by new and more diffuse threats about the stability of the post-Cold War world order. The momentous structural changes of the past few years have reshaped the psychological context in which leaders and peoples make foreign and domestic policy. As in the past, this context can be expected to influence the nature of the problems that engage public attention, the solutions seen as appropriate, and the ways in which leadership is won and held.

Among the many changes in the post-Cold War psychological context, two in particular stand out: the absence – at least for the time being – of an external enemy and the shifting nature of domestic constraints on foreign policy. I examine these changes and their implications for American foreign policy. My treatment is of necessity speculative. The post-Cold War world is still taking shape, and there is only fragmentary evidence on which to base an analysis.

ENEMIES

The Cold War was fought against powerful and seemingly ruthless communist enemies: the Soviet Union, which ruled an empire stretching from the Elbe to the Pacific, and "Red" China, a totalitarian behemoth almost one billion strong that fought the West to a standstill in Korea by repeated human wave assaults.

Powerful enemies are dangerous, but they also confer advantages. They permit leaders to organize the world into simple "them" and

Richard Ned Lebow is Director of the Mershon Center and Professor of political science, history and psychology at The Ohio State University.

"us" dichotomies, with all the advantages this has for the formulation of foreign policy, the co-ordination of bureaucracies charged with its implementation, and the mobilization of public support needed to sustain and pay for an active role in world affairs. It seems unlikely, for example, that the American people would have supported Marshall Plan aid for Europe or the permanent deployment of U.S. forces in Europe and Asia in the absence of a perceived communist threat.[1]

Powerful enemies also allow leaders to mobilize populations in support of domestic goals. The "Red Scare" of the 1920s provided the cover for a war against organized labor. The Cold War spawned McCarthyism and its decade-long suppression of liberal-left nonconformists. The 1950s also saw the rise of "the military-industrial complex," with its cozy relationships between corporations in search of lucrative government contracts and politicians in search of contributions to government expenditure in the districts. This vast and often wasteful expenditure was justified in the name of national security.

Powerful enemies are useful in explaining away failures. The "loss of China" and vilification of Americans throughout the Third World were blamed by many on the betrayal and subversion by communists at home and abroad. So, too, were rock'n roll, the civil rights movement, marijuana, cohabitation, feminism, and, for the far far Right, fluoridation of the reservoirs. Psychologists have long observed that such explanations are appealing because they exonerate the values and policies of those who resort to them.

Powerful enemies legitimate otherwise repugnant foreign and domestic policies. There is always some discrepancy between a country's declared goals and its policies. In the United States, where foreign policy has always been justified with reference to its moral content, the disparity between theory and practice has at times been acute. The cognitive dissonance this generates can be reduced by assertions to oneself and to others that unsavory means are sometimes necessary to achieve a larger, worthwhile end. During the Cold War, the allegedly life-or-death struggle against the evil of communism was repeatedly invoked to justify American support of corrupt and repressive regimes. In 1961 Vice President Lyndon Johnson brushed off a question about what he really thought about South Vietnamese strongman Ngo Dinh Diem with the reply, "Shit, man, he's the only boy we got out there."[2] In the 1980s Oliver North and other members of the Reagan administration justified their illegal transfer of laundered funds to the Nicaraguan Contras as essential to protect the hemisphere from communist penetration.

From the vantage point of the United States, the most striking feature of the post-Cold War world is the absence of powerful adversaries. To be sure, there are Saddam Hussein, Muhammar

Gaddafi, and fundamentalist Iran, but they are small fry in comparison to Joseph Stalin's Soviet Union or even Mao Zedong's China. At best, they provide the Defense Department with some justification for its budget. Six months before Saddam Hussein's invasion of Kuwait, U.S. forces had staged an exercise that entailed the expulsion of Iraqi forces from Kuwait. The exercise was not the result of political foresight – the Iraqi invasion took the State Department and intelligence community by surprise – but a response to the Defense Department's need to find an enemy. Military planners were instructed to invent a scenario, any scenario, that would justify a large and diverse force structure. Iraq was picked on the basis of its military capabilities.[3]

Attempts are under way to bestow the mantle of enemy on Japan. Japan bashing was on the upswing even before the end of the Cold War, and there has been a noticeable attempt to hold that Asian colossus responsible for some of America's economic problems. A recent bestseller describes a future war with Japan.[4] Elite opinion has begun to contemplate the possibility of a hostile People's Republic of China.[5] A nuclear power that is run with an iron hand by the butchers of Tiananmen Square, that swamps American markets with the products of prison camp labor, that keeps Tibet in thralldom, and that seems on the verge of snuffing out the political liberties of the residents of Hong Kong has lots of adversarial potential.

Enemy images of either Japan or China could also draw on residual racial prejudices and memories of Pearl Harbor or Korea, the latter fought with a communist regime that still hangs on to power. These are still distant forebodings, and in the case of Japan, there is reason to believe that there is enough goodwill and common sense in both the US and Japan to weather whatever economic conflicts strain their relationship. Whatever the long-term relationship with either country, for the foreseeable future neither is likely to fill the size fourteen extrawide jackboots vacated by the Soviet Union.

Without powerful enemies leaders confront fewer external constraints. This apparent advantage also has its drawbacks. A comparison of Hungary and Bosnia indicates that in a world without powerful enemies, contradictions between policies and values can become painfully evident.

In the 1952 presidential campaign, the Republicans made political capital over the alleged failure of the Democrats to keep Eastern Europe from falling under Soviet control. In an appeal for the white ethnic vote, Dwight Eisenhower promised to "roll back" Soviet influence in Eastern Europe. However, when workers rioted in East Germany in 1953 and Hungarians overturned their Stalinist regime in 1956, the Eisenhower administration made it clear to Moscow that it would not intervene. Eisenhower was very careful to do nothing that could provoke a military confrontation with the Soviet Union. In

1992 candidate Bill Clinton was openly critical of the Bush administration's failure to come to the aid of Bosnia. Once in the White House, President Clinton found it in his interest to remain just as detached from Bosnia.

Hungary and Bosnia confronted presidents with different kinds of political-psychological dilemmas. In 1956, President Eisenhower and Secretary of State John Foster Dulles felt enormous frustration at not being able to come to the aid of Hungary's freedom fighters. They were further embarrassed by their prior public commitment to roll back communism in Eastern Europe. We can surmise that the contradiction between their campaign promises and foreign policy created dissonance for both men. They could reduce this dissonance by convincing themselves that American intervention in either East Germany or Hungary would have provoked a war-threatening confrontation with the Soviet Union, and that anything short of intervention would not have been effective. Faced with the reality of Soviet power, Eisenhower and Dulles believed that they had no choice but to exercise restraint, and this must have made it easier for them to live with their failure to honor their pledge. Many conservative Republicans and voters of Eastern European ancestry felt betrayed. Their anguish was deep and not so easily assuaged.

A much smaller constituency demanded intervention in Bosnia, and Clinton had never made the same kind of promises as Eisenhower. The president and some of his advisers nevertheless felt themselves on the horns of a political and moral dilemma. They were troubled by the atrocities committed in Bosnia but were reluctant to intervene because the European allies were unenthusiastic and the American military establishment and secretary of defense were opposed. Any prolonged foreign entanglement would threaten the success of the administration's domestic legislative agenda. In the absence of the Soviet threat, they had to face up to their responsibility for making the choice for nonintervention or conjure up constraints that would justify inaction to the American people and themselves.

The administration chose to conjure. Secretary of State Warren Christopher was sent to Europe to sound out the Europeans on the possibility of intervention and returned to report that they were opposed. Subsequent leaks indicated that the real purpose of his trip had been to elicit an expression of opposition to intervention that the administration could then use to justify its reluctance to proceed. The Pentagon provided another justification. The Joint Chiefs of Staff insisted that intervention would encounter serious resistance and lead to an open-ended and costly commitment. Some experts questioned this self-serving estimate, but Clinton accepted it uncritically and used it to buttress his decision not to intervene.

The debate on Bosnia reflected two different conceptions of

American interests. Former Cold Warriors, on the whole hostile to intervention, maintained that nothing that happened in the former Yugoslavia directly threatened American security. Together with other opponents to intervention, they were prone to portray the civil war in Yugoslavia as the latest episode in a historical struggle among hostile ethnic groups that could not be resolved or significantly ameliorated by third parties. Many of the Americans who favored a more interventionist policy by then had been active in or were generally sympathetic to the goals of the peace movement. They believed that it was imperative for the United States and its European allies to prevent "ethnic cleansing" and uphold the most basic principles of international justice. They maintained that Bosnia was the test case of the post-Cold War order, the same claim made by many former Cold Warriors to justify intervention in Kuwait.

The Cold War and its larger-than-life communist enemies helped create a consensus about foreign policy that endured until America's failure in Vietnam. The American response to Bosnia, Somalia, and other major international issues revealed widely varying opinions among elite and public opinion. There is no consensus about America's role in the world, how and where its influence should be expressed or sought, the nature and gravity of the threats the country faces, or the appropriate strategies for dealing with them. In the absence of the Cold War, there is no obvious frame of reference for ordering the world.

Congress mirrors the wider public confusion. It has swung wildly between support and opposition to foreign deployments of U.S. forces. Thomas Mann, a noted congressional scholar at the Brookings Institution, observed that members of Congress are absolutely without anchor here. They find themselves responding on an ad hoc basis, responding to public opinion and pictures on television screens, and also influenced by short-term ideological considerations, such that responsible members end up embracing extraordinary inconsistent imperatives on foreign policy.[6]

Such uncertainty and vacillation reflect a deeper contradiction. The American people and their leaders cling to a belief that they are the chosen people and have a god-given mission to export their liberties and way of life to the rest of the world. But they are increasingly reluctant to expend the lives and money such responsibility entails. Most Americans seem unprepared to renounce their country's putative mission. They want to believe that they are morally superior to everyone else – and more courageous. No other nation has bumper stickers of the national flag with the slogan "These Colors Don't Run." So American leaders vainly search for some way to exercise influence on the cheap. Their frustration will continue until such time as they and the American people are willing to come to terms with themselves and, by extension, the world.

DOMESTIC CONSTRAINTS

Cold War commitments could sometimes be exploited for domestic ends. On other occasions, perceived strategic imperatives threatened important domestic goals and confronted leaders with difficult choices. Lyndon Johnson agonized over military intervention in Vietnam, fearful that it would consume the funds required by the Great Society. The post-Cold War political environment confronts presidents with choices more reminiscent of Vietnam.

In his first year in office, Bill Clinton repeatedly shied away from international involvements that put American lives and his domestic legislative agenda at risk. The consensus among Washington insiders is that Bosnia was sacrificed for health care. Clinton's reluctance to pursue a more active policy in Bosnia was also a response to public opinion. In the early 1960s, Lyndon Johnson worried that the loss of Vietnam to the communists could lead to the loss of the presidency to the Republicans. Clinton recognized that his administration could easily survive the loss of Bosnia to the Serbs but not the loss of the American lives that it might take to prevent this outcome. Bosnia is indicative of a broad shift in public attitudes toward foreign commitments. During the Cold War, Congress appropriated billions for military assistance. Today it is reluctant to vote funds to help revitalize the Soviet economy. Congress and the American people have also become increasingly antagonistic to military intervention.

The Gulf War, the country's first post-Cold War military action, was preceded by a massive allied military buildup and diplomatic effort designed to bring about an Iraqi withdrawal from Kuwait. Most Americans supported the president, but a significant minority opposed the use of force; some urged the adoption of economic sanctions instead. When war broke out, public opinion rallied to the troops. Support for the president remained high throughout the conflict because it was short, ended in victory, and entailed remarkably few American casualties. This support waned considerably over the next few months as it became apparent that Saddam Hussein retained his grip on power and that the United States and its allies could do little short of direct involvement to halt his murderous campaigns against the Shiites and the Kurds.

In Somalia, another Bush administration initiative, Americans were initially supportive of intervention because of its humanitarian motive. Subsequent firefights in Mogadishu between American soldiers and the irregular forces of warlord Mohammed Farah Aidid rapidly shifted opinion against the operation. Voicing a widely shared feeling, one concerned citizen interviewed by ABC news explained that he would rather see starving Somalis on television every night than the dead bodies of American soldiers. In October 1993 Congress began debating the wisdom of the intervention, and the president, to head off criticism, committed himself to a date for the withdrawal of all American troops.

In Haiti, President Clinton took the lead in organizing international pressure on the military to allow the return to power of exiled President Jean-Bertrand Aristide. To compel the obviously reluctant Haitian military to step down from power, the administration convinced the United Nations to authorize the dispatch of peacekeeping forces to that country. In October 1993 as blue-helmeted soldiers prepared to disembark at Port au Prince, "attachés" in the pay of Haiti's generals conducted a reign of terror in the country's capital and murdered a prominent member of the opposition. The crescendo of violence in Haiti prompted Republican senator Robert Dole to declare that "restoring Jean-Bertrand Aristide to power was not worth a single American life and that the American people wanted more restraint on the use of troops abroad."[7] Concerned that this policy would alienate public opinion, the Clinton administration ordered American ships and the forces they carried to return to American ports.

The general reluctance of the American people and their elected representatives to support military intervention in Europe, Africa, and the Caribbean is in the first instance attributable to the end of the Cold War and the collapse of the Soviet Union. Without a powerful enemy to deter and prevent from exploiting instability, there was no compelling strategic need to act.

Congress and the public have also come to doubt the efficacy of military intervention in situations of civil war or breakdown. In the Gulf, military intervention succeeded in expelling Iraqi forces from Kuwait but failed to remove Hussein from power, protect the Shiite minorities in Iraq or encourage greater democracy in liberated Kuwait. Somalia was even more of a watershed. Foreign military forces were welcomed at first as providers and liberators by a starving and terrified population. They gradually became the enemy to at least one clan, whose influence they threatened. Unable to restore civil authority but unable to leave in its absence, and handicapped by squabbles among their governments and between them and the United Nations, these forces seemed trapped and vulnerable in a situation not of their own making.

The Somali experience made Americans more cautious about intervention in Bosnia and Haiti. Even for thoughtful people not easily seduced by superficial analogies, the experience in Somalia seemed to highlight the difficulty of using military means to resolve complex and sometimes poorly understood local antagonisms. The failure of compulsion in Haiti and the suffering caused to the local population – but not the military junta – by the subsequent economic blockade will most likely reinforce the general conclusion that it is very difficult for outsiders to ameliorate civil conflicts in developing countries.

One important respect in which Haiti was different from Somalia was motive. Intervention in Somalia was prompted by largely humanitarian concerns. This sentiment was not absent in Haiti, but it took a second seat to a more practical consideration: stemming the flow of boat people to the United States. The administration sought to do this by restoring a popularly elected but avowedly left-wing government to Haiti but changed its mind when it concluded that the political costs of intervention were almost certain to exceed those of illegal emigration, detention camps, and deportations.

More practical considerations were also apparent in the public's reaction to Somalia and Haiti. In Congress and the media, many voices urged the administration to focus its attention and resources on domestic problems. They drew attention to "domestic Haitis" where impoverished and underfed inner-city residents were terrorized by criminal elements armed with automatic weapons.

Greater public interest in domestic versus foreign problems is nothing new. But it has become more pronounced in recent years in response to the recession and its aggravation of many pre-existing social ills. The political agenda has been dominated by unemployment, drugs, crime, corruption, and how to respond to them. There are interesting parallels between the domestic and international debates, just as there were during the heyday of the Cold War.

The 1960s witnessed activist policies at home and abroad. The Johnson administration conducted a war on poverty in the United States while it waged war on communism in Vietnam. Both struggles were rooted in the premise that an enlightened, committed, and well-funded government could reshape unpleasant and threatening social realities and had a responsibility to do so. The 1990s is characterized by widespread pessimism about social engineering at home or abroad and by lack of faith in government at all levels. Almost everybody recognizes the need to do something about the national debt, unemployment, crime, drugs, and international instability, but few people believe that government can do much about them. The combination of grave social problems and a seemingly helpless government constitutes the political crisis of the late twentieth century.

How do leaders respond to this dilemma? One approach, adopted by Ronald Reagan and George Bush, is to do nothing and to claim that nothing is something. Both presidents promised that deep cuts in expensive social programs and lower taxes for upper income brackets would create tickle-down prosperity. Another approach, characteristic of Bill Clinton and his administration, might be called half-hearted activism. Clinton announced a series of reforms (for example, homosexuals' rights, the environment, taxation, health care) but accepted major compromises when his proposals encountered opposition.

The Reagan and Clinton strategies reflect at least in part the different class bases of the presidents' parties. Many more Republicans are well-to-do and untouched by the recession. They live and often work in the suburbs, send their children to private schools, and may never set foot in dangerous neighborhoods. They confront social problems in their tax bills, and many deeply resent the sacrifice this entails. By denying the efficacy and value of government programs and proclaiming that individual greed had beneficial social consequences, Reagan and Bush rewarded their supporters financially while at the same time legitimizing their avarice.

Democrats have a more diverse constituency, at least some of which demands government intervention on behalf of the minorities, the underprivileged, and the average citizen who is the victim of well-organized special interests. Many of these constituents have contradictory desires. Compelling the military to accept homosexuals antagonizes many officers and enlisted personnel; banning logging in certain tracts in the Cascades threatens the livelihood of entire communities; and higher taxes on gasoline adversely affect the poor. Reluctant to choose between competing constituencies, the president has sought to placate all of them by introducing reforms and then backing away from them to varying degrees.

THE CITY ON THE HILL

The French, the Germans, and the Japanese know who they are because of their language, culture, and ancestry. For the United States, where immigration has been the national rite of passage, it has been necessary to forge an identify from an idea. Being American means being committed to "the American way of life" and its belief in the perfectibility of the individual through democratic institutions, economic progress and tolerance.

The American ideology has always had universalist pretensions. The American dream was for export, and Americans saw themselves as a modern-day chosen people with a divine mission to carry their ideas, products, and way of life to the far corners of the globe. American power and influence were a means to this end and a validation of the nation's mission.

For two centuries American foreign policy struggled under the burden of two masters. It had to be pragmatic and safeguard the security and economic interests, first, of a fledgling power and, ultimately, of a world power with all its attendant interests and responsibilities. Foreign policy had to advance the American ideology and its political, economic, and social values. From the time of the French Revolution on, Americans have been divided over the respective primacy of these missions. In our time this struggle has been acute and complex. Cold Warriors described their policies as pragmatic. They defended American support of authoritarian regimes and intervention in Third World struggles as unpleasant necessities vital to the struggle against communism. Their critics, often referred to as peaceniks, accused the national security establishment of conducting a crusade that sacrificed the real interests of the nation to ill-conceived ideological goals. Cold Warriors in turn bitterly derided the efforts of the Carter administration to make a country's respect for human rights a litmus paper test for American support. Such ideological objectives, they insisted, could be pursued only at the expense of America's real interests.

Cold Warriors and peaceniks represented different blends of ideology and pragmatism. Their competing conceptions of foreign policy reflected different understandings of the national interest. For Cold Warriors, all other considerations were secondary to the containment of the Soviet Union and its allies. For peaceniks, the preservation of American liberties required a foreign policy that did not trample on those liberties and nourished their development in other parts of the world. Both groups claimed to be pragmatic in their approach to foreign policy but justified that approach with reference to their broader moral purpose.

Throughout the twentieth century, American military commitments – and opposition to them – has always been justified in terms of moral and even altruistic goals. The First World War was sold to the American people as the war to end all wars, the Second World War was fought to make the world safe for democracy, and the Vietnam War was a struggle to keep Southeast Asia from communist enslavement. Opposition to Vietnam was a crusade to maintain constitutional liberties within the United States.

Since the end of the Cold War, there has been a noticeable change in the rhetoric of the foreign policy debate. One increasingly hears arguments devoid of ideological packaging. Opponents of intervention in Somalia and Haiti suggested that the absolute benchmark for assessing foreign policy should be the possible loss of American life. Opponents and proponents of NAFTA made direct, unvarnished appeals to the pocketbook. In the past, appeals to naked, individual self-interest would have been regarded as embarrassing and unpersuasive. Presumably, those making such arguments today do so in the expectation that it will enhance the effectiveness of their appeals.

This rhetorical evolution suggests that self-interest is coming out of the closet in American public life. This is most apparent in domestic politics, where private greed was more or less portrayed as a public virtue by Ronald Reagan. Throughout the 1980s, economic self-interest was legitimized as the standard for assessing the merits of any policy proposal. It has even affected the world of scholarship, where rational choice, which identifies the individual as the unit of analysis and self-interest as the motive for behavior, has increasingly come to dominate the social sciences.

This emphasis on self-interest may reflect the triumph of materialist values and another assault on what remains of our civic culture. It may also be a sign that Americans feel more comfortable with their national identity. American foreign policy has always been harnessed to build, shape, and strengthen that identity. The demystification of that policy and its partial retreat from the pretension of divine mission have been paralleled on the domestic front by the demise of that other great myth: the melting pot. It is gradually giving way to a conception of the United States as a salad bowl composed of different ethnic and religious groups that retain their distinctive cultures. For better or worse, America may be on its way to becoming a normal nation.

NOTES

1. See Melvyn Leffler, *A Preponderance of Power: National Security, the Truman Administration, and the Cold War* (Stanford: Stanford University Press, 1992).
2. Quoted in David Halberstam, *The Best and the Brightest* (New York: Random House, 1969), p.135.
3. Interviews with US Army planners.
4. George Freedman and Meredith LeBard, *The Coming War with Japan* (New York: St. Martin's Press, 1991).
5. On November 10, 1993, Richard H. Solomon, president of the United States Institute of Peace, gave a lecture at the Council on Foreign Relations entitled "China and the United States: The Next Cold War?"
6. Quoted in Adam Clymer, "Foreign Policy Tug-of-War: Latest in a Long String of Battles," *New York Times*, October 19, 1995, p.A4.
7. Thomas L. Friedman, "Dole Plans Bill to Bar the Use of G.I.'s in Haiti," *New York Times*, 18 October 1993, p.A1.

The Clinton Administration and Regional Security: The First Two Years

SAMUEL F. WELLS, JR.

THE EVOLUTION OF REGIONAL SECURITY POLICY

Today's disorderly world poses great difficulties for international relations theorists and policy analysts alike. Many policymakers must secretly yearn for the stability of the bipolar world and the superpower competition which functioned in a reasonably predictable manner from roughly 1950 until 1989. But today, absent the superpower rivalry, old disputes have revived and new problems develop and are quickly vented.

The field of regional security has suffered more than most from this transition which renders old paradigms obsolete. Regional security came to life as a recognized field of analysis and a subset of the field of international security about 1980 when analysts and policymakers began to realize the full implications of Soviet policy for the Third World under the pressure of the invasion of Afghanistan. They constructed a set of policies for regional conflict which dealt with the different types of Soviet activity in the Horn of Africa, Angola, Cuba, Nicaragua, and Afghanistan. Analysts at several institutes, primarily at the International Institute for Strategic Studies, began to create special groups to work on regional security issues that were emerging as alternative areas of superpower competition under a general nuclear stalemate.

Even before 1980, the issues that came to be called regional security had a history that is worth recalling. During the high Cold War, roughly 1950–68, the United States relied on regional alliances to deal with the Soviet challenge. In the early years of detente, roughly 1969–80, the United States explored variations of the

Samuel F. Wells, Jr., has been Deputy Director of the Woodrow Wilson Center, Washington, DC, since 1988. Prior to this he was Founder and Director of the Canter's International Security Studies Program and Associate Director and Head of the European Institute.

"Nixon Doctrine" of training allied forces to provide much of their own security. This continued in the Carter administration with support for the "twin pillars" of Israel and Iran.

With the election of Ronald Reagan, a new phase of regional security began and it is in many ways the high point of the field. The Reagan administration provided widespread support to what were called the forces of freedom with the general objective of countering Soviet advances and supporting freedom fighters from Afghanistan to Nicaragua. Despite numerous complications with human rights and undemocratic governments, the policy achieved some success at the political-military level.

As the Cold War was beginning to come to an end, the Bush administration had the opportunity to apply what was the ultimate, and in some ways the final, application of regional security in the Gulf War against Iraq. Iraq's egregious violation of international law, along with its suspected nuclear program and its threat to the free movement of oil, combined to create a broad-based coalition for a United Nations mandate under which the war could be conducted. Within the limited objectives that it set for itself, the Bush administration was highly successful. But it should be noted that this same administration, which took such bold steps in the Gulf and earlier in the diplomacy for the unification of Germany, chose to take no meaningful action in the former Yugoslavia at a time when, in the view of many analysts, a limited demonstration of force might have had a significant effect.

THE CLINTON ADMINISTRATION AND INTERNATIONAL AFFAIRS

Bill Clinton entered the White House having campaigned on a platform of focusing the attention of a new generation on domestic issues and relying to the highest degree possible on multilateral institutions for the conduct of foreign policy. He was extremely concerned about global issues such as the quality of the environment, the protection of human rights, limiting the drug trade, containing the spread of weapons of mass destruction, and attacking the AIDS epidemic through both national and international means. After a year in office and a chance to deal with many difficult issues, Clinton's foreign policy team produced a draft national security strategy paper which reiterated many of these abstract principles. In addition to a significant commitment to global issues, the paper, which was leaked to the press in February 1994, stated that the United States has "no higher priority than revitalizing its economy" and becoming fully competitive. It also emphasized the importance of "enlargement" of the democratic community of nations through diplomacy, economic incentives, and the work of non-governmental organizations. On the military side, the draft paper restate the goal of retaining enough military power to fight two regional wars of roughly the size of Desert Storm nearly simultaneously. This military force structure was the result of the Department of Defense's Bottom-Up review conducted by Les Aspin.[1]

In the first two years of the Clinton administration, events in Somalia, Haiti, and Bosnia showed the complications of dealing with multinational institutions for peacekeeping. As a result, the administration substantially altered a draft policy paper on peacekeeping to provide significant constraints on U.S. involvement in multilateral peacekeeping ventures.

The new peacekeeping policy was announced on 5 May 1994, by press briefings from a new Presidential Decision Directive 25 (PDD 25). The basic message of PDD 25 was that the United States acknowledged that it could not resolve a large number of the conflicts around the world but did not believe that the United Nations was capable of making peace when hostilities still existed among the parties.[2]

PDD 25 specified certain strict conditions that should be met before the United States agrees to participate with troops in a new international peacekeeping operation. These conditions included: the operation should advance American interests; personnel and funds adequate to do the job should be available; American participation should be essential to the success of the operation; Congress should be in support of the operation; and there should be clear objectives, an established exit strategy, and acceptable command and control arrangements. Among other points, the directive stated that the United States did not support the creation of a standing United Nations army, nor would it contribute American troops to such a force. After significant debate and intense Congressional criticism, the directive was revised to state that American combat forces would never be put under foreign commanders.

By May 1994, frequent policy changes and noticeable failures in Bosnia, China, and North Korea had produced widespread comment by foreign policy analysts and media pundits over the disarray in foreign policy. While it was true that the public was not very interested in foreign policy, they were concerned about competence in government, and taken along with staff difficulties in the White House, lingering problems about the President's personal behavior and family finances, this issue of competence and ultimately of legitimacy to govern was one that stimulated increasing concern among those who wished to see the United States move ahead to address its problems, both domestic and international.[3]

By the end of 1994, a sophisticated poll sponsored by the Chicago Council on Foreign Relations showed an increased interest in foreign policy issues and a desire for stronger leadership in this area by the president. But the results showed a substantial decline since 1990 in support for protecting weaker countries against external attack, for promoting human rights overseas, and for providing developmental assistance.[4]

CLINTON AND THE WORLD'S REGIONS

Senior officials of the Clinton administration rarely mention regional security per se, yet the basic approach of regional security survives as an effort to coordinate approaches to the policy challenges of each region. We should examine each of the principal regions of American policy concern briefly to indicate those policies that are of greatest salience.

Western Hemisphere

In Latin America, there is a significant attempt to redefine the type of threat that existed since the 1930s when there was always a possibility of external great power involvement to ally with various Latin American states against the United States. The threats are now different, and the focus of U.S. policy is on containing arms sales, persuading the Latin Americans to involve themselves in international peacekeeping, seeking cooperation in high technology research and development, and developing extensive economic integration with all countries that are interested in doing so. The United States has placed particular emphasis in Latin America on increased multilateral cooperation in combatting drug trafficking, and this policy receives mixed responses from the various states of South and Central America.

The largest threat to United States security in the Western Hemisphere stems from floods of refugees coming from Haiti and later from Cuba. U.S. policy has vacillated between trying to turn them back, intercepting them and taking them to the U.S. naval base at Guantanamo Bay, Cuba, increasing the sanctions on the government and people of Haiti, and finally sending them immediately back to Haiti itself. As the Clinton administration struggled with the best way of dealing with the Haitian refugees, Fidel Castro announced that his government would no longer prevent Cuban refugees from leaving. This led to waves of Cuban refugees on rafts and small boats of every description. Urged on by the hardline Cuban-American community in Florida, as well as by the democratic governor of Florida, the Clinton administration reversed the U.S. asylum policy of 28 years standing and began to send Cuban refugees to Guantanamo, holding them in camps separate from the Haitians. Sharper economic sanctions were also imposed on Cuba to discourage the policy of allowing or even encouraging refugees to leave. Subsequently the administration worked out arrangements by which some of the Cuban refugees would be held at U.S. bases in Panama and housed by other countries in the Caribbean. By the early autumn of 1994 the problem of Cuban refugees eased.

But the Haitian situation seemed intractable. Sanctions seemed to have no effect on the regime of Lt. General Raoul Cédras, and threats of force were not taken seriously. There was continuing pressure from the Congressional Black Caucus and from liberals and human rights advocates for the administration to take some action to restore democracy in Haiti. After numerous meetings to develop a new strategy, the administration began to move steadily toward the use of force in Haiti. Most national security experts opposed the use of force, and many conservatives such as Karen Elliott House of *The Wall Street Journal* felt that Cuba would be a much more justifiable place for military intervention if it had to be used.[5]

As the United States moved steadily toward intervention, the offer of mediation by former President Jimmy Carter provided the basis for a remarkable solution. Accompanied by Senator Sam Nunn of Georgia and General Colin Powell, Carter went to Haiti over the weekend of September 17–18, 1994. He negotiated an arrangement with General Cédras and his two top lieutenants for them to resign and for the legislature of Haiti to be called into session to provide a general amnesty for Cédras and his top officials. Carter returned to Washington, and on September 19 he and President Clinton announced the deal which led to Cédras' resignation. That same day U.S. troops began to land without opposition in Haiti. Later, after receiving amnesty, Cédras and his colleagues sought exile in Panama. The Carter mission was a last-ditch episode of unconventional diplomacy. After getting trapped in factional warfare in Somalia, the United States took a narrow view of its mission in Haiti. It restored President Jean-Bertrand Aristide to power and maintained relative calm. But when President Clinton turned over command of the operation to United Nations officials on March 31, 1995, the economy was at a standstill and the country lacked a functioning police force and judiciary system. The whole range of policy toward Haiti through March 1995 shows a high level of domestic political involvement in foreign policy decisionmaking, the administration's lack of any long-term strategy, and the operation of an unusually large quantity of good luck.[6]

The administration's most successful policies in the Western Hemisphere lay in the area of trade liberalization. President Clinton and his trade officials invested a great deal of political capital in the passage of the North American Free Trade Act (NAFTA), approved by the Congress and signed by the President in December 1993. During its first year of operation it was viewed as a big success, as U.S. exports to Mexico substantially increased and all of the three countries showed signs of an economic revival. In December 1994 the United States hosted in Miami the Summit of the Americas, where thirty-three countries joined the United States in celebrating democracy and liberalizing trade. One of the key steps announced at the summit was the agreement with Chile to begin negotiations to add a fourth nation to NAFTA. But just at the end of 1994, darker clouds began to develop as the crisis with the Mexican peso led to an over-thirty percent devaluation of the peso, a real crisis of confidence in the Mexican economy accompanied by a panic in the stock market. In January 1995, the Clinton administration committed itself to a major financial bailout of the Mexican treasury, a move that was resisted by Congress but implemented by executive action.[7]

Europe

In relations with Western Europe, the United States shows a welcome change of policy toward European integration and is now advocating significant support for the closer integration of the states of the European Union and the addition of new states from the European Free Trade Association and from the Visegrad Group of Four to the European Union as they negotiate terms of membership. The United States has also stopped its steadfast opposition to the creation of an autonomous European security entity, and as a result of negotiations in the fall of 1993 which culminated in the January 1994 NATO summit in Brussels, the United States has agreed to terms under which it can support European peacekeeping efforts outside the NATO area through the use of combined joint task forces. This provides a means by which a European security entity can grow, most likely from the Western European Union, and become a full-fledged European pillar of the North Atlantic Alliance. Relations between France and the United States have significantly improved over collaboration within NATO and possible cooperation on peace-keeping.

In February 1995 important leaders of Britain, France, and Germany spoke of creating new mechanisms to coordinate trade and monetary policies to parallel the security links between Europe and North America.[8]

All major attempts to shape new European security structures have fallen victim to the disagreements and recriminations flowing from failed West European and American efforts to limit the conflict in the former Yugoslavia. Everyone admits that the conflict came at a bad time, but it was not a coincidence that Serbian, Croatian, and Slovenian leaders acted in different ways to break up the federal structure of Yugoslavia at a time when Western Europe and the United States were preoccupied during the fall of 1991 with a contest against Iraq in the Gulf, the breakup of the Soviet Union, the problems of German unification, and a sustained economic recession in Europe and Japan that was spreading to North America. Western responses suffered from a number of mistaken assumptions. Europeans believed their political and economic pressure would influence the behavior of the contending parties more than was the case. The Bush administration hoped that the federal system of Yugoslavia could be preserved and desperately wished to avoid U.S. involvement in any case. Western leaders did not understand that the Serbian government had a dangerous if poorly developed plan to create a "greater Serbia" and had the strong support of the Yugoslav federal army in this effort.

Having seen atrocities, hatred, and mendacity from all parties in the subsequent civil war initiated by Serbian aggression, most policymakers conclude that no outside intervention could have prevented the violent breakup of Yugoslavia. Many believe that the casualties and destruction could have been limited by a coordinated Western intervention at the time of the attack by the Yugoslav federal army on Dubrovnik in October 1991. But at that time no one recognized the gravity of the situation and there was no will in any Western nation to intervene with the level of force that could have been effective.[9]

The Clinton administration inherited a near-desperate situation when it took office in January 1993. A loose ceasefire patrolled by United Nations peacekeepers existed in Croatia, with the Serbs controlling roughly one-fourth of the newly independent republic's territory. The Bosnian government had been under attack since March 1992 by Bosnian Serb forces, led by marauding bands from Serbia and supported by officers and equipment from the Yugoslav federal army. The Serb offensive used artillery attacks on largely Muslim cities and towns along with mass rapes, concentration camps, and group executions. Serbian forces were well on their way to control of seventy percent of Bosnian land. There were numerous claims of Croatian and Muslim atrocities in the Serb press and Western officials talked often about the conflict being a civil war. But a recently disclosed CIA report charges the Serbs with ninety percent of the acts of ethnic cleansing, and the basis for this analysis almost certainly was presented to President Clinton and the senior officials of his administration when they entered office.[10] The United Nations had taken a number of steps to limit the violence and aid the victims, but these actions were ineffective in blunting the Serb aggression.

Finding himself in this unpromising situation, President Clinton was unable to make a policy decision and enforce it on his divided administration. He clearly wanted to avoid allowing Bosnia to distract him from the domestic agenda which he saw as his electoral mandate. This led him to accept willingly two elements of Bush administration policy – no U.S. ground troops would be sent into this area of conflict, and policy for Bosnia would be closely co-ordinated with Boris Yeltsin in order to avoid disputes with Russia. Very few administration officials outside the Pentagon and few members of Congress who supported the position understood the immense implications of refusing to send U.S. ground forces to Bosnia. This refusal eliminated the possibility of effective bombing without forward air controllers or infantry to follow the air attacks; it limited Washington's ability to influence its allies who had troops on the ground; and, most seriously, it unmistakably signaled to the Serb leadership that the United States would not back up its all-too-frequent threats. The new administration soon retreated from its campaign rhetoric about being more active in Bosnia than the Bush administration had been. The Serb leadership played a clever cat-and-mouse game that effectively denied Western governments any easy or low-cost policy options. A pattern of action-reaction developed over months of sporadic fighting. Serb leaders used the UN peacekeepers and aid workers as hostages to protect their forces from retaliatory air strikes, and there were cases when Serbs and Muslims were each believed to have fired on their own people to create an incident that could be used as a provocation to further violence.

The mortar attack on a Sarajevo marketplace on 5 February 1994, in which 68 people were killed, seemed to change this pattern. Western outrage led the United Nations to create an exclusion zone extending 20 kilometers from the center of Sarajevo in which heavy artillery and mortars were prohibited. A subsequent ceasefire around the city was largely effective in improving conditions for the beleaguered population of that multi-racial Bosnian capital, but military pressure soon shifted to Gorazde. Despite its status as a United Nations-designated "safe area," the United States declined to use air strikes to retaliate, then reversed course to authorize two strikes on symbolic targets, and ultimately failed to lift the siege of the city. Just before Christmas 1994, Jimmy Carter engaged in negotiations with the Bosnian Serbs and won a ceasefire of four months that only reflected the desire of all parties to halt fighting during the harshest months of the winter.[11]

The Western governments used the Sarajevo mortar attack to launch another diplomatic initiative, sponsored by a new five-nation "contact group" consisting of the United States, Russia, France, Britain, and Germany. In July 1994, this contact group proposed a new loose federation for Bosnia, with Serbs controlling forty-nine percent of the territory (a reduction from the seventy percent they then dominated) and the Muslim-Croat federation controlling fifty-one percent. The Bosnian Serbs rejected this plan, and new fighting soon broke out around Sarajevo. Early in 1995 Western strategy shifted again in an attempt to split Serbia from the Bosnian Serbs by offering to lift the sanctions against Belgrade if it would recognize Bosnia and Croatia. The prospects for this initiative were complicated by the intensification of Bosnian Serb attacks on Sarajevo and eastern "safe areas" in April and May. United Nations forces responded in late May with two bombing raids against an ammunition dump near Pale, and the Bosnian Serbs then retaliated by taking over 370 UN troops hostage, chaining some to potential bombing targets, and by shelling five of the six U.N.-designated "safe areas," killing seventy-one people in a crowded cafe in Tuzla. Although Britain and France sent up to ten thousand additional troops to Bosnia and formed a rapid reaction force that would use U.S. equipment, the stage appeared to be set for a withdrawal of UN forces if a settlement among all sides was not agreed by the early autumn of 1995.[12]

The vacillating policy of the Clinton administration is easy to criticize, but we should recognize that the administration had to operate within the context of a series of harsh realities. The Bush administration had urged the Europeans to take the lead on the problems stemming from the breakup of Yugoslavia, had set the limitation on U.S. involvement of no ground troops, and had won widespread public endorsement of this approach. The United Nations had committed itself to do more than it could manage and had thoroughly confused the missions of providing humanitarian assistance and peacekeeping in circumstances where no set of agreed peace terms ever existed among all the parties. The United States' European partners had different views on the nature of the conflict and the responsibility for the violence in Bosnia, but they were united with the United States in wanting to avoid any significant number of casualties that might be involved in imposing a solution on the warring factions. Within these circumstances, it has proved impossible to move Serbian forces off territory they have conquered by any combination of diplomatic pledges and economic sanctions. It is a serious analytical error to blame this tragic set of failed Western policies on either the United Nations or NATO. Both institutions only reflect the political will of their constituent governments, and these governments are clearly supported in their limited commitments by the voters who have put them in office. The brutal conclusion is that the major industrial democracies did not feel that Serbian aggression in Yugoslavia was sufficiently important or clear-cut for them to intervene.[13]

Yet some things have been accomplished. Serbian aggrandizement and brutality have been illuminated. There are hopeful signs that, with renewed U.S. support and extended UN mandates, Croatia and Macedonia can remain independent, and the Western policies have bought some time for those who can leave Bosnia to seek a better life elsewhere.

Russia, Central Europe, and NATO

When he entered office in January 1993, Bill Clinton found Boris Yeltsin struggling to implement a broad program of reform against resistant institutions and a wide range of political opposition, and he was confronted with the leaders of Russia's former Warsaw Pact allies in Central and Southeastern Europe all clamoring for membership in NATO. The administration's initial policy, shaped mainly by Ambassador-at-Large Strobe Talbott, was to support Yeltsin and reform in Russia to the fullest extent possible. This included giving strong endorsement to Yeltsin throughout 1993 as he fought with rivals in parliament, escaped a vote of impeachment, got a new constitution passed by referendum, and asserted Russian authority over separatist republics in Siberia and Transcaucasia. At the Vancouver summit in April 1993, Clinton pledged $1.6 billion in economic aid to Moscow, and the administration continued to give assistance to Russia – and to Ukraine – a high priority in its programs before Congress. But U.S. officials had difficulty finding good projects for investment, and at the end of 1994 less than $500 million had been spent of the $2 billion in aid pledged to Russia over the preceding two years.[14]

On the question of NATO expansion, the administration found itself in a dilemma. Officials in Washington wanted to support democratization and economic reform in Eastern Europe, and they understood that reform advocates in the region were under popular pressure to show benefits in the form of ties with the West in return for the sacrifices demanded by the economics of shock therapy. Since the leaders of the European Community had declared that membership in their privileged group could only come many years in the future, the nations of Central and Southeastern Europe had fixed their hopes on early membership in NATO. Early expansion of the alliance posed several problems. None of the aspirants were prepared for the responsibilities of membership in terms of having civilian control of military institutions or modernized forces capable of operating with alliance units; Congress and the American public were not ready to extend a defensive guarantee to fledgling democracies in Eastern Europe; and, most serious, Russia strongly opposed any extension of NATO to its western border.

The administration resolved its dilemma by creating the Partnership for Peace. The partnership concept was proposed by Secretary of Defense Les Aspin on 20 October 1993, at a meeting of NATO defense ministers at Travemuende, Germany. Under individual partnership programs, each member would develop a range of activities to coordinate its defense with the North Atlantic alliance. Activities could include staff consultations on equipment, budgets, tactics, and civil-military relations as well as joint planning and exercises. The Partnership for Peace would not extend the alliance's defense guarantees to its members, but NATO would pledge to consult with a partner if its territorial integrity were threatened. The activities of partners could prepare them for eventual membership in NATO, but were not a guarantee of alliance membership. The NATO summit meeting in Brussels in January 1994 adopted the Partnership for Peace program and made the commitment in principle to expand the alliance after appropriate evaluation and preparation of new members. In his visit to Warsaw the following 7 July, President Clinton declared to the Polish parliament that expansion of the North Atlantic Treaty Organization "is no longer a question of whether, but when and how" and expressed confidence that "a democratic Poland" would be among the new alliance members.[15]

The process of NATO expansion took another step at the foreign ministers meeting in Brussels in December 1994. The ministers agreed that the first half of the year 1995 would be spent discussing the "why" and "how" of alliance expansion, and the second half presenting the conclusions to those of the twenty-four Partnership for Peace participants that have expressed an interest in alliance membership. The foreign ministers will meet again in December 1995 to decide how to proceed.[16]

While Russia joined the Partnership for Peace on 22 June 1994, it did so in a manner that signaled problems ahead. A month earlier Defense Minister Pavel Grachev had put a range of demands and assertions to NATO defense ministers that made it clear that Russia intended to be a "senior partner" in the new alliance partnership. He and other Russian officials insisted that, in return for its cooperation, Moscow must have Western recognition of its predominate influence within the Commonwealth of Independent States, especially in the three republics of Transcaucasia and the five of Central Asia.[17]

During the last four months of 1994, Yeltsin's shift to nationalistic and anti-reform policies and his erratic personal behavior diminished Western support for his government. He removed the last remaining reformers from top positions and made deals with the military on numerous issues. A variety of officials made statements strongly opposing NATO expansion and attacked elements of the Partnership for Peace program that Russian representatives had already negotiated. The government completed negotiations to sell nuclear reactors to Iran, a step vigorously opposed by the United States. The Yeltsin government launched an assertive policy in republics along the southern border culminating in the brutal suppression of an independence movement in Chechnya.[18]

Faced with these problems with Moscow, the Clinton administration shifted its policy from all-out support of Yeltsin to a more pragmatic basis. After some awkward statements about the movement for Chechen independence being "an internal Russian matter," the administration first moved to criticize the brutal Russian tactics in Chechnya on December 29. Three weeks later in a speech at Harvard University, Secretary Christopher spoke of the administration's "unwavering... support for Russian reform" but made no mention of Yeltsin. Early in April the United States engaged in a full-scale campaign to persuade Russia to cancel the reactor sale to Iran, even going to the extent of sharing intelligence reports on the suspected Iranian nuclear weapons program. Clinton pressed the case further during the Moscow summit of May 9–10, 1995, but received only a minor concession from Yeltsin. A modest advance on another issue came on May 31 in Brussels when Foreign Minister Andrei Kozyrev signed a program of activities for Russian participation in the Partnership for Peace. Policymakers and analysts did not take this as a turning point, for it was clear by mid-1995 that the Clinton administration would no longer put Russia first in its policies for Europe.[19]

Middle East and the Gulf

In the Middle East and the Gulf, the United States has had its most coherent and consistent set of regional policies. The Clinton administration has shown steadfast support for Israel and for the Middle East peace process. It is perhaps not a coincidence that the major Israeli–Palestinian breakthrough came under auspices other than the United States. The unintended "benign neglect" shown during the first months of the Clinton administration allowed skillful Norwegian mediation to achieve what the United States might not have been able to do. President Clinton did host the ceremony in Washington for the formal signing of the Oslo Declaration of Principles on September 13, 1993, and he successfully brokered the famous handshake between Israeli Prime Minister Yitzhak Rabin and PLO Chairman Yasser Arafat. Since that event the United States has taken a more active role in Israeli–PLO discussions, especially in raising funds to build Palestinian infrastructure, and Washington help set a positive context for the Israeli-Jordanian agreement of October 1994.

The United States has played its most vital role in the peace negotiations with Syria. Secretary of State Christopher has taken the role of mediator in this complex set of talks and has traveled numerous times to Damascus to meet with President Hafiz al-Asad and his ministers. President Clinton also met twice with Asad during 1994, in Geneva in January and in Damascus in October. Since mid-1994, the Clinton administration sponsored a series of over two dozen private negotiations in Washington between the Israeli Ambassador Itamar Rabinovich and the Syrian Ambassador Walid al-Moualem with senior administration officials usually joining the principals, and late in December President Clinton hosted an unprecedented session that included the army chiefs of staff of Syria and Israel. These negotiations have dealt with a wide range of issues including the return of the entire Golan Heights to Syria and the possible stationing on the Golan of a multi-national peacekeeping force including about 1,000 U.S. troops and civilians to provide reassurance to both sides. After a lapse of over five months, Syria agreed to resume the high-level military negotiations at the end of June 1995.[20]

For the Gulf, the United States has pursued a policy of "dual containment" which seeks to limit the capacity of both Iran and Iraq to acquire new technology for weapons of mass destruction, to pursue terrorism, to intimidate their neighbors, or to foment revolution.[21]

With regard to Iraq, the main objectives of dual containment were to maintain the sanctions imposed by United Nations resolutions stemming from the Gulf War in order to insure the elimination of capabilities to manufacture weapons of mass destruction and to permit permanent inspections of military installations. The Iraqi regime posed an early challenge to the Clinton administration through an attempt to assassinate former President George Bush with a car bomb during his visit to Kuwait in mid-April 1993. The plan was discovered and investigators traced evidence directly to Iraqi intelligence officers. Once the investigation was completed, the Clinton administration moved quickly to respond by firing Tomahawk missiles from U.S. ships in the Gulf during the night of June 26 and destroying a major intelligence center in downtown Baghdad. When UN reports in early 1995 indicated that Iraq had concealed evidence of a biological weapons program, both the President and Secretary Christopher strongly restated their desire to maintain full sanctions on Iraq.[22]

By February 1994, Iran had become "international Public Enemy No.1 for the Clinton administration," according to a leading journalist.[23] This position was a result of accumulated evidence of Teheran's support for terrorism in Lebanon and North Africa, its funding of the suspects arrested in the World Trade Center bombing, and its widespread efforts to build up its conventional military forces. American analysts also identified efforts to advance a nuclear weapons program and were suspicious of Iranian negotiations to purchase Russian nuclear power reactors. The policies pursued by the Clinton administration included international embargoes on high technology sales to Iran, forcing the cancellation of a Conoco contract to refine and market Iranian oil, and pressure against the Russian sale of nuclear reactors. In April 1995 the administration launched a campaign against a pending Chinese contract to build two nuclear reactors in Iran and train technicians to operate them. After

Secretary of State Christopher failed to persuade the Chinese Foreign Minister to suspend the nuclear agreements with Teheran, President Clinton in a speech before the World Jewish Congress in New York on April 30 announced a ban on all trade with Iran. The administration's assaults on Iran won strong backing among the new Republican majorities in Congress. Although most U.S. allies disliked the trade and investment restrictions advocated by Washington, there is every reason to believe that a strong enforcement of dual containment will remain a Clinton policy for the Gulf.[24]

East Asia

The administration's regional policies for East Asia had clear objectives and direct ties to the overall global agenda. These policies focused different global priorities on differing countries with a nonproliferation emphasis being applied to North Korea, a human rights policy invoked for China, and a very tough trade negotiating posture taken with Japan. Arching over many of these issues was the U.S. support for the new multilateral economic institution APEC (Asia Pacific Economic Community). As the policies were applied, problems developed when leverage was not used effectively, when incentives did not change behavior, and when allies pursued their own agendas.

In relations with North Korea, the Clinton administration inherited a nuclear nonproliferation problem that deteriorated almost daily. By late 1992, U.S. intelligence and the International Atomic Energy Agency (IAEA) uncovered clear evidence of North Korean cheating on its nuclear commitments. Confronted with increasing international pressure, North Korea rejected on February 13, 1993 an emergency inspection request from the IAEA and a month later stunned the world with an announcement that it would withdraw from the Nonproliferation Treaty (NPT) after the required three months' notice.[25]

The Clinton administration spent much of 1993 exploring the limits of U.S. leverage in the nonproliferation policy. The United States had to defend the nonproliferation regime which the North Koreans had accepted and subsequently violated, and Washington had to keep the confidence and support of Japan and South Korea and needed to win the cooperation of China. The administration also had to work closely with the IAEA, whose reputation had been badly tarnished by the disclosures of an extensive, clandestine Iraqi nuclear program that had escaped discovery during repeated agency inspections. There were differences of strategy and objectives within the U.S. government, where the military and some Asian specialists felt a tough approach was all North Korea would understand while others wanted to be conciliatory.

The administration and South Korea finally agreed at the end of March to accept some of Pyongyang's demands in an effort to win cooperation. The United States opened what turned out to be four rounds of direct talks with North Korea, and on June 11 North Korea announced it had "decided unilaterally to suspend" its withdrawal from the NPT. Pyongyang still refused to allow inspection of two suspected nuclear sites and over the next year resorted to bluster, threats, and broken promises to prevent progress in the talks. The United States, for its part, had difficulty developing a unified government position and gaining full cooperation on strategy from South Korea and the IAEA. On April 1, 1994, North Korea forced another crisis by shutting down the reactor at Yongbyon and beginning to remove the fuel rods on May 12. These steps made available enough plutonium to manufacture four to six bombs and at the same time destroyed the evidence of any earlier diversion of nuclear fuel for weapons fabrication. On June 13, North Korea intensified the crisis by withdrawing from the IAEA.[26]

As the United States was completing negotiations with the permanent members of the Security Council for UN sanctions against North Korea, Jimmy Carter arrived in Pyongyang for a visit in mid-June. Kim Il Sung welcomed the former U.S. president with concessions that represented nothing more than promising not to violate his nation's international commitments. Convinced that he should explore new options to break a dangerous deadlock, Carter praised the North Koreans for their flexibility and misrepresented U.S. policy in an effort to win further cooperation. Despite embarrassing the Clinton administration and undercutting the IAEA and potential UN sanctions efforts, Carter's unconventional diplomacy began a process that led to a freeze of the North Korean nuclear program and a resumption of high-level negotiations between Washington and Pyongyang early in July.[27]

After a delay caused by the sudden death of Kim Il Sung on 9 July, the talks resumed in Geneva and eventually produced an "Agreed Framework" signed on October 21, 1994. The agreement called for closing all North Korean nuclear facilities and their eventual elimination. In return the United States, Japan, South Korea, and other nations would provide heavy oil for electricity generation and two light-water nuclear power reactors which would not produce spent fuel that could be used for weapons manufacture. The terms specified a twelve year step-by-step approach so that North Korea had to shut down its nuclear facilities and be subject to IAEA safeguards before the construction of the light-water reactors began. The oil shipments could be terminated if any evidence of North Korean violation of the agreement were found. The cost of this agreement would be shared roughly seventy percent by South Korea, twenty-five percent by Japan, and the other five percent by the United States and other nations.[28]

The North Korean nuclear agreement was a significant achievement for the Clinton administration. Many Republicans criticized the agreement for rewarding the North Koreans for launching a secret nuclear weapons program, but almost all of the critics who studied the alternatives to this pact have acknowledged that the agreement allows the United States and the South Koreans to lift the veil of the formerly closed society in North Korea, stop the nuclear program that is already underway, and facilitate improved relations between North and South Korea. No one thinks the task of implementing the agreement will be easy or smooth, and the North Koreans quickly objected that they did not want reactors built by their arch enemy South Korea. Complicated negotiations followed, with the South Koreans wanting to ensure that they received full credit for providing the technology and paying most of the cost of the two power reactors. On 12 June 1995 the United States won agreement from both North and South Korea to the terms for the reactor design and construction, and the road appears open for the gradual resolution of the nuclear crisis with North Korea.[29]

The administration did not coordinate its North Korean policy very well with its policies toward China and Japan. In China, Clinton's retreat on the policy of linking improvement in human rights to the renewal of Most Favored Nation (MFN) trading status was a widely-discussed defeat. Not only did the administration fail in its human rights effort, it continued to talk about it until the last minute when it had to give in and support renewal of Most Favored Nation status for China. The Most Favored Nation designation was quietly renewed again in June 1995. But at no point did the administration, in exchange for its capitulation on human rights, gain support from Beijing for its nonproliferation policies toward North Korea. Through much of the negotiations with North and South Korea, when Washington needed Japanese political support and financial backing for an agreement, the U.S. Trade Representative was attacking Japan for failure to open its markets to American automobiles and auto parts. President Clinton ordered punitive one-hundred percent tariffs applied to Japanese luxury cars imported into the United States if an agreement was not reached by the end of June. This acrimonious trade war could disrupt the more significant attempts to terminate a serious case of nuclear proliferation on the Korean peninsula.

THE CLINTON ADMINISTRATION AND REGIONAL SECURITY

On the basis of this review of the important regions in U.S. policy, one must say that without the overarching calculus of the superpower competition, regional security policy in the United States lacks coherence and tends to reflect shifting definitions of national interest.

Regional security is still a useful way for analysts and policymakers to examine the relationship of issues within a region and to analyze tradeoffs among national priorities. It should be able to tell us what the impact of U.S. policies in China may have on relations with North Korea and Japan, although the lessons do not appear to have been taken fully to heart by this administration.

The complications of regional politics are further exacerbated by other factors peculiar to the Clinton administration. The foreign policy team assembled by Bill Clinton has been unusual in enunciating most of its most strongly held foreign policy objectives in the form of abstract principles. The administration calls for expanding democracy and free markets, for stopping the spread of weapons of mass destruction and their means of delivery, for improving the global environment, for reducing the drug trade and the spread of AIDS. These abstract principles do not sit very well with another characteristic of the administration, which is to treat foreign policy as if it were domestic policy and to engage in a bargaining process with domestic and foreign interest groups. An example of this is the way in which Bosnian policy has been negotiated among U.S. military leaders, human rights activists, outspoken members of Congress, the United Nations Secretary General, the governments of Bosnia, France, Britain, Russia, and leaders of Serbia and the Bosnian Serbs. When solutions are offered, then modified, and finally withdrawn, the type of politics that may be successful in White House bargaining with the Congress appear to our foreign policy partners to be in total disarray.

Then there is the Jimmy Carter phenomenon. It is hard to imagine Ronald Reagan or George Bush allowing Richard Nixon or Gerald Ford to be a self-appointed negotiator in international crises, but this is exactly what Bill Clinton did three times during 1994 when former president Carter put himself in the middle of complex foreign policy negotiations. In North Korea in June, something positive emerged from the Carter discussions, although no one has adequately explained how it happened. In Haiti in September, Carter made a genuine contribution and helped prevent a dangerous landing of U.S. military forces in the face of armed groups and a hostile government. And in Bosnia in December, the peripatetic statesman from Plains, Georgia, helped both sides get what they wanted, a negotiated cessation of hostilities during the Winter months. In baseball as in politics, one solid hit in three attempts at bat is a good average. Yet in international affairs, it does not inspire confidence in the quality of Washington's leadership when outside interventions occur repeatedly.

Since the November 1994 elections, the conduct of foreign policy has become more difficult for the Clinton team. The new Republican majorities in Congress differ with the administration on a number of critical points, and they will have greatest effect in those areas where Senate approval of agreements and nominations is required and where Congressional appropriation of funds is necessary. As an example of things to come, the House of Representatives on June 8, 1995, approved by a significant majority a foreign affairs bill that cut foreign aid sharply, reduced funding for United Nations agencies, put restrictions on peacekeeping activities under UN auspices, and specified a number of changes in policies toward Russia, China, and Bosnia.[30]

When in addition to these principles, procedures, and Congressional politics, one adds an indecisive and frequently disinterested President, the American foreign policy process has concocted a recipe for delay, reaction, and inconsistency.

NOTES

1. Quoted in John Lancaster and Barton Gellman, "National Security Strategy Paper Arouses Pentagon, State Department Debate," *The Washington Post*, March 3, 1994.
2. Quoted in Elaine Sciolino, "New U.S. Peacekeeping Policy De-emphasizes Role of the U.N.," *New York Times*, May 6, 1994.
3. Karen Elliott House, "Clinton Speaks Loudly and Carries a Twig," *Wall Street Journal*, May 4, 1994; Jim Hoagland, "Image Isn't Everything," *Washington Post*, May 31, 1994; "Cornered by His Past," *Economist*, June 6, 1994.
4. John E. Rielly, "The Public Mood at Mid-Decade," *Foreign Policy*, 98 (Spring 1995), pp.76–93.
5. Karen Elliott House, "The Wrong Mission," *Wall Street Journal*, September 8, 1994.
6. David Broder, "Hostage to Haiti," *Washington Post*, September 20, 1994; Douglas Farah, "To Clinton, Mission Accomplished; to Haitians, Hopes Dashed," *Washington Post*, March 30, 1995.
7. John M. Berry, "U.S. Plan to Aid Mexico Calms Financial Markets," and Clay Chandler and Martha M. Hamilton, "Loan Guarantees Get Cautious Hill Backing," *Washington Post*, January 14, 1995; Hobart Rowen, "Administration Ignored Peso Warnings," *Washington Post*, February 5, 1995.
8. Joseph Fitchett, "Western Europe Proposes New Trans-Atlantic Pact," *International Herald Tribune*, February 7, 1995.
9. Warren Zimmermann, "The Last Ambassador: A Memoir of the Collapse of Yugoslavia," *Foreign Affairs*, Vol.74 (March/April 1995), pp.2–20.
10. Roger Cohen, "C.I.A. Report Finds Serbs Guilty in Majority of Bosnia War Crimes," *New York Times*, March 9, 1995; Lawrence Freedman, "Why the West Failed," *Foreign Policy*, 97 (Winter 1994-95), pp.53–69, and Richard K. Betts, "The Delusion of Impartial Intervention," *Foreign Affairs*, Vol.73 (November/December 1994), pp.20–33.
11. David Binder, "Anatomy of a Massacre," *Foreign Policy*, Vol.97 (Winter 1994–95), pp.70–78; Daniel Williams, "Carter Provides Cover for Another U.S. Shift," *Washington Post*, December 21, 1994; John Pomfret, "Carter's Down-Home Style Eased Way for Accord," *Washington Post*, December 22, 1994.
12. Elizabeth Drew, *On the Edge: The Clinton Presidency* (New York, 1994), pp.429–30; Roger Cohen, "Allies Agree on a Proposal To Belgrade," *New York Times*, February 15, 1995; Jim Hoagland, "End Sanctions on Serbia? Desperate Diplomacy at Work," *International Herald Tribune*, February 20, 1995; Roger Cohen, "NATO Jets Bomb Arms Depot at Bosnian Serb Headquarters," *New York Times*, May 20, 1995; Joel Brand, "Serbs Take Hostages After Airstrike," *Washington Post*, May 27, 1995; Christine Spolar, "Freed U.N. Soldiers 'In Good Spirits,'" *Washington Post*, June 4, 1995.
13. Noel Malcolm, "Bosnia and the West: A Study in Failure," *The National Interest*, Vol.39 (Spring 1995), pp.3–14.

14. Carla Anne Robbins, "Kentucky Senator, Handed Keys to Foreign Aid, To Be Most Potent Foe of Clinton's Russia Policy," *Wall Street Journal*, December 13, 1994.
15. Steve Vogel, "U.S. Proposes NATO 'Partnerships' for Former Warsaw Pact Nations," *Washington Post*, October 26, 1993; Richard Holbrooke, "America, A European Power," *Foreign Affairs*, Vol.74 (March/April 1995), pp.43–44; Clinton quoted in Ruth Marcus, "Clinton Assures Poles of NATO Membership, Eventually," *Washington Post*, July 8, 1994.
16. Holbrooke, "America, A European Power," pp.44–5.
17. Daniel Williams, "Russia Joins NATO Plan," *Washington Post*, June 23, 1994; Bruce Clark, "Old Enemies Make Tricky Friends," *Financial Times*, June 9, 1994.
18. Lee Hockstader, "Ex-Allies See Yeltsin Jumping Democracy's Foundering Ship," *Washington Post*, January 1, 1995.
19. Michael Gordon, "U.S. Warns Russia: Stop Attacking Chechen Civilians," *New York Times*, December 30, 1994; Warren Christopher, "Principles and Opportunities for American Foreign Policy," Address at Harvard University, January 20, 1995; Steven Greenhouse, "U.S.-Russian Intersection: The Romance is Gone," *New York Times*, March 27, 1995; Steven Greenhouse, "U.S. Gives Russia Secret Data on Iran To Fight Atom Deal," *New York Times*, April 3, 1995; Steven Erlanger, "Russia Says Sale of Atom Reactors to Iran Is Still On," *New York Times*, April 4, 1995; Steven Erlanger, "Clinton and Yeltsin Find Way to Ease Strains at Least a Bit," *New York Times*, May 11, 1995; Michael Dobbs, "NATO Has Initial Talks with Russia," *Washington Post*, June 1, 1995.
20. John Lancaster, "Assad: Threatened by Peace?," *Washington Post*, October 25, 1994; Elaine Sciolino, "Syria and Israel Said to Conduct Talks in Private," *New York Times*, December 31, 1994; Richard N. Haass, "1,000 Americans on the Golan," *New York Times*, November 21, 1994; Barton Gellman, "Assad Agrees to Resume Golan Talks," *Washington Post*, June 11, 1995.
21. R. Jeffrey Smith and Daniel Williams, "White House to Step Up Plans to Isolate Iran, Iraq," *Washington Post*, May 23, 1993; Douglas Jehl, "Fearing More Hostility from Iran, U.S. Considers Moves to Isolate It," *New York Times*, May 27, 1993; Anthony Lake, "Confronting Backlash States," *Foreign Affairs*, Vol.73 (March/April 1994), p.49.
22. Drew, *On The Edge*, pp.229–30; Elaine Sciolino, "U.S. Pressure Put on Iran and Iraq," *New York Times*, April 5, 1995.
23. Thomas W. Lippman, "White House Sees Iran as Worst 'Outlaw,' " *Washington Post*, February 27, 1994.
24. Sciolino, "U.S. Pressure," *New York Times*, April 5, 1995; Elaine Sciolino, "Beijing Rebuffs U.S. on Halting Iran Atom Deal," *New York Times*, April 18, 1995; Ann Devroy, "President Will Ban All Trade with Iran," *Washington Post*, May 1, 1995; for a critique of "dual containment" widely shared by Middle East specialists, see Shibley Telhami, "How to Lose Friends in the Persian Gulf," *Los Angeles Times*, June 4, 1995.
25. Mitchell Reiss, *Bridled Ambition: Why Countries Constrain Their Nuclear Capabilities* (Washington, D.C., 1995), pp.231–51.
26. R. Jeffrey Smith, "North Korea Broke Nuclear Agreement, Inspectors Conclude," *Washington Post*, May 20, 1994; Reiss, *Bridled Ambition*, pp.248–71.
27. R. Jeffrey Smith and Ann Devroy, "U.S. Debates Shift on North Korea," *Washington Post*, June 20, 1994; Ruth Marcus and R. Jeffrey Smith, "North Korea Confirms Freeze: U.S. Agrees to Resume Talks," *Washington Post*, June 23, 1994; Reiss, *Bridled Ambition*, pp.271–3.
28. The text of the Agreed Framework is published in the *Newsbrief* (Number 28, 4th Quarter 1994) of the Programme for Promoting Nuclear Non-Proliferation of the University of Southhampton, U.K., pp.27–8; see also Reiss, *Bridled Ambition*, pp.276–80.
29. R. Jeffrey Smith, "U.S., N. Korea Reach Tentative Nuclear Deal," *Washington Post*, June 13, 1995; T.R. Reid and Lee Keumhyun, "S. Korea Accepts Deal with North on A-Power," *Washington Post*, June 14, 1995.
30. Kenneth J. Cooper and Dan Morgan, "House Votes to Restructure Foreign Affairs," *Washington Post*, June 9, 1995.

Israel, the United States, and the World Order Crisis: Fuzzy Logic and Conflicting Principles

ROBERT L. ROTHSTEIN

MOURNING FOR THE CLARITY OF THE COLD WAR

The Cold War tended to be system-driven. The great conflict between East and West stretched across and influenced perceptions of virtually all dimensions of international relations. As such, it was a wonderful, if dangerous, simplifying device, resembling in its more extreme variations Aristotle's world of the excluded middle: You were either A or B, East or West, for us or against us. These days disaster myopia and the frustrations of dealing with the complexities of the post-Cold War world may be inducing a kind of premature nostalgia for the "good old days" and a kind of premature amnesia about the dangers and costs of that period. One hardly needs to emphasize that system-driven security conflicts with Russia, China, or Japan may begin to dominate calculations of national interests once again. Still, the prospects for such developments or other unanticipated systemic shocks are unclear and, one hopes, relatively long-term and preventable. For the near term, the world that we have to try to understand is the world of fuzzy logic, where categories are partial and overlapping, risk and uncertainty are inordinately high, and the system itself seems to be moving in two or more conflicting directions at once. It has become a cliche to note that the velocity of change has escalated and that distance and time have shrunk and narrowed because of technological innovations. This means that the trends we confront link together very rapidly and affect different states in widely divergent ways. It is also very important to emphasize that all of the trends that we shall discuss have counter trends and patterns of resistance. One should not simply assume or take it on faith that the latter are inferior or irrational. In what follows, therefore, I shall discuss some major trends that we shall have to understand and

Robert L. Rothstein is the Harvey Picker Distinguished Professor of International Relations at Colgate University.

manage and indicate various patterns and problems that may emerge from the interaction between global trends and local circumstances. I will conclude with a discussion of the principles that might provide some guidance through these complexities.

Because of limitations on space, I will discuss only two trends in some detail and merely mention several others. I will also not be able to comment in depth on the interaction among the trends and the possible responses to these interactions.

EMERGING TRENDS AND THE QUEST FOR A ROLLING EQUILIBRIUM

What do we mean when we denote the existence of a particular world order or, more prosaically, a particular international system? One presumably refers to a relatively stable balance of power among the major actors, values and principles that are widely shared or are at least in a relatively stable pattern of conflict, an institutional structure that performs mutually agreed tasks and legitimates interstate (and perhaps some state) patterns of behavior, and some principle of authority that links together different levels and types of governance. Any world order thus presumes a large degree of stability and predictability amidst change, but stability and predictability of a particular kind. The basic belief structure, the principles and norms that define a distinct order, must remain intact but the other elements can vary and adjust to new developments – much as a constitution can be amended but not restructured in its fundamental principles.

Any new world order must rest on some means of establishing a rolling equilibrium that maintains and sustains basic values and structures by containing threats and challenges within acceptable limits. The task of policymaking is to manage major trends and conflicts well enough to keep the equilibrium intact. The task is obviously inordinately difficult when some of the trends are contradictory or unclear. The rolling equilibrium can very rapidly thus become a rolling disequilibrium, especially in a system where communications technology can link and spread crises very quickly. In any case, an equilibrium must rest on perceptions of self-interest, which may be somewhat easier now with the commitment to shared norms – although the depth of commitment will surely vary across issues and actors. There are also other factors that may help in establishing an equilibrium that can survive the next crisis, including an effective learning process, an explicit effort to generate consensual knowledge about common problems, a resistance to extreme or radical solutions to complex problems, a willingness to abide by a rule-based system, and a willingness to pool risks and to share costs equitably.

THE META-TREND: GLOBAL INTEGRATION, LOCAL DISINTEGRATION

One trend appears like a leitmotif in virtually all discussions of the post-Cold War world. It is the contrast between the forces propelling us toward global integration (globalization of markets, the spread of communications, rising interdependence, weakening of sovereignty) and the forces propelling us toward localism or, in its worst forms, local disintegration (hypernationalism, the reassertion of sovereignty, the disintegration of large states, the erosion of support for a liberal, rule-based system). One should emphasize that the movement toward integration does not rest only on technological developments. There have been equally consequential changes in the emergence of shared norms (democracy, the market) and governmental policy shifts.

It is worth emphasizing that a simple dichotomy between the "good" forces of integration and the "bad" forces of disintegration may be dangerously misleading. The conflict itself is not new, even if strikingly salient at the moment, and has usually been tentatively resolved by compromises on rules and timing. Even local nationalists need or will benefit greatly from some forms of economic and political cooperation and global co-operation, in a world still dominated by sovereign states, requires compromise with national interests and needs. Moreover, it is not always or necessarily true that global integration should or must triumph over local resistance in any particular time period: integration is preferable only if its costs and benefits are equitably shared and if it does not generate dangerous patterns of instability and disequilibrium.

Given the obvious need to cooperate, why has the conflict between these trends become so bitter and apparently insoluble? The forces propelling toward greater global integration are rational, orderly, and predictable. They are strongly supported by technocratic elites, multinational corporations, and states that think they will prosper in a competitive environment. The presumed aggregate benefits are especially great over the long run, but they are also distributed asymmetrically and depoliticized in the sense that national interests and ideological preferences are meant to yield to the logic of the market, and national boundaries are largely irrelevant and sometimes hard to discern because of the long-run focus. In addition, as with many trade problems, the losers from integration are concentrated and the losses immediate while the winners are diffuse and unclear. All of these characteristics, needless to say, intersect badly with the political logic of weak and heavily stressed sovereign states.

The forces propelling local reactions and local resistance are to some extent the mirror images of the forces propelling global integration. That is, they are short-run, heavily politicized, politically but not technocratically rational, and unpredictable and disorderly. At best, local leadership seeks to select and determine the terms of integration with the wider world, at worst there can be desperate Luddite reactions or an attempt – as with religious fundamentalists – to reject modernization entirely and to return to some mythical state of purity and autonomy. There are also important differences in the pattern of change that emerges from these trends: Integration tends to generate continuous, orderly change while local changes tend to be discontinuous, disorderly, and harder to foresee. As noted earlier, while the tensions between these two sets of trends is potentially severe and at the extremes unrelenting, there are many possible compromises that may dilute the conflict. But they require a willingness to compromise, some painful trade-offs between equally valuable goals, and institutions to facilitate and legitimize the negotiating process.

We can easily see the dangers of either trend dominating or overwhelming the other. Global integration may proceed too rapidly, thus leaving behind and alienating both poorer countries and poorer citizens, setting the stage for an inevitable backlash. The nation-state, already weakened by the loss of autonomy attendant on increased interdependence, but still pressured by demands for improved short-run performance, may respond by seeking to regain control of national policymaking. This may be done by a variety of means, all of which are a threat to global welfare as one self-interested, short-run policy generates another. Thus the attempt to regulate or reregulate markets to contain unwanted external linkages or to export problems (for example, via social or environmental "dumping") are bound to elicit countervailing reactions from injured parties. In addition, integration also increases the possibility of linked and escalating crises. Various means have been devised to contain these linkages (firebreaks in the stock market and financial markets, emergency funds, consultative mechanisms), but these are prudential responsive measures rather than a genuine reassertion of control. Perhaps the above suggests another meta-trend or meta-theme: the nature of the problems that appear in the process of global integration and the need to respond to them quickly and efficaciously fit badly, if at all, with the national and international institutions that are required to deal with the problems. The failure to respond quickly may worsen problems beyond repair, but existing institutions tend to foster delay, muddling through, and lowest common denominator policy responses. This problem may well be exacerbated if more countries become democratic, or more policy responses must be devised by existing international institutions.

The dangers of letting some of the more negative aspects of localism prevail are too obvious to require much comment. We have already witnessed some of the worst effects of hypernationalism and the revival of ancient ethnic conflicts and border disputes. However these are resolved or left to fester, there are other long-term consequences that may be even more dangerous. There may be a loss of global welfare as some states or regions withdraw into themselves and perhaps even seek to undermine or thwart the movement toward a more liberal and integrated global system. The danger is even greater to the states themselves since they will be consigning themselves to more or less permanent inferiority and an inability to improve the quality of life for their citizens. One implication is an increasingly unequal international system, which is certainly morally repellent and practically problematic with the escalation of the dangers from terrorism, rising numbers of refugees, local wars with horrific weapons, and the export of drugs. Another implication may be a sharp decline in the movement toward democracy in many areas of the world.

All of this has some relevance for the Middle East and indeed for other Third World regions that must adjust to powerful global trends. The severity of regional conflicts, the difficulties of establishing patterns of co-operation, the emergence of powerful movements of religious fundamentalism, the skewed structure of most regional economies, the heavy burden of military expenditures, the looming resource crises over water and arable land, persisting patterns of inequality, and the continued dominance in some critical states of brutal and corrupt regimes – all of these taken together suggest a strong likelihood that the Middle Eastern response to the forces of global integration will be particularly dysfunctional and destructive. What ought to be done, insofar as we can discern it, is likely to be impossible to do. This implies that euphoria about the peace process may be premature because the hard tasks of establishing stable and prosperous democratic regimes may take decades to accomplish.

CONFIGURATIONS OF POWER AND THE REDEFINITION OF SECURITY

The configuration of power has always been the defining characteristic of any international system. It reflects not only the "relationship of major tension" but also the basic normative conflict and the definition of interests and goals. But the end of the Cold War, the relative decline of US power, and the emergence of new issues on the international agenda have created a kind of conceptual vacuum. The interpretation of national interests, the priorities to be attached to different threats, and indeed the very nature of security in the current confusion are unclear and ambiguous. Criticism of the fits and starts of various foreign policy initiatives, whether by the Clinton administration or others, is thus easy grist for the mill of the critics; suggesting viable alternatives that take account of complexity and the limits of choice is an entirely different matter. We are in the age of reluctant commitments, diminished expectations, and "uncertain trumpets."

Perhaps we can begin sorting through some of the complexities if we seek to provide tentative answers to four questions. The first of these, the most abstract and amorphous, is about the very nature of power in the post-Cold War environment.

Begin with the simplest proposition. The end of the Cold War has compelled a redefinition of national interests, thus accelerating a shift that had begun to emerge earlier because of rising levels of interdependence and the appearance of new issues on the international agenda. The security issue has hardly disappeared because it is obvious that there are circumstances in which a new or revised system-threatening security threat might arise, the destruction of the old rules of the game has seemed to free ancient enemies to resume ancient conflicts with widely available and not-so-ancient weapons, and the absence of a new conceptual framework and the usual lag in abandoning sunk intellectual capital has meant a continuing need to treat security seriously. In effect, the post-Cold War security environment is clearly different but not clearly better.

Still, while there are and will be some very salient continuities with the past, there are also some very salient discontinuities that need to be considered. While it oversimplifies to assert, as some have, that only economic power now matters and that foreign policy has become commercial policy, it is also obviously true that economic power – in the sense of the capacity to provide citizens with a rising standard of living and to protect against threats to vital economic interests – has become more consequential. Declining growth rates and a turbulent international economic environment, increasing demands on governments to perform more effectively, and rising expectations (or the fear of losing benefits) among relatively more educated and more aware citizens have turned "the struggle for the world product" into a major battleground.

Several points seem to follow from the enhanced prominence of economic power in the new international environment. One simple point, of course, is that economic power is more widely dispersed and multipolar, as several states may be weak militarily but powerful economically, others may possess valuable economic resources, and yet others may be potentially important as markets. Furthermore, economic power is becoming increasingly privatized, that is, under the control of banks, multinational corporations, and financial markets. This implies a great deal of economic instability, especially for poor and weak countries, because private investors and lenders can and will move rapidly to take advantage of new opportunities or to react against new threats to investments and loans. More importantly, the state itself loses power and leverage as private power increases, further threatening stability and making it more difficult for any state or group of states to exert control over economic developments. In effect, the emerging world order is likely to be less hierarchical because governments have lost legitimacy because of poor performance, citizen demands "from the bottom up" become more consequential, and the spread of various kinds of regional economic arrangements further erodes sovereignty and autonomy.

One likely result of these changes is that security decisions will increasingly be affected (note: *not* determined) by economic calculations about costs and interests: Who is going to pay and how will action affect domestic budgets and calculations of interests? Power that is diffused and that has a large domestic component thus implies an international security environment that is slow to react to external conflicts, that seeks non-military (and thus less costly) solutions to military conflicts, and that seeks to pass responsibility for action or reaction to regional organizations that are usually poor, ineffectual, and divided about what to do – as in Bosnia and Rwanda. In short, there is confusion not only about who is powerful on what issues but also about who is willing to use power – whose interests are sufficiently engaged – all of which generates disorder, risk, and uncertainty. The unwillingness to use force against aggression will presumably grow if one or more of the participants in a local conflict has acquired nuclear, chemical, or biological weapons or seems in such a state of chaos that intervention becomes equivalent to long-term trusteeship. Insofar as this is true, the notion of the indivisibility of security, that great staple of collective security, may shortly sink without trace.

The end of the Cold War, the growing importance of economic power, and the continued erosion of the power of the state have thus combined to create a situation in which conflicts in the Third World and perhaps elsewhere are likely to be both more frequent and more horrific. In particular, the end of the Cold War, which has seemingly delinked most local conflicts from central Great Power concerns (the Middle East may be an exception), may mean that rules of restraint are no longer in force at a time when the local desire to control population and territory is increasing (more about this below) and the need to buy or manufacture the most advanced and horrific arms seems to be growing. The willingness of outside powers to sell the arms and to stand by and watch them be used seems assured. The moral ambiguity of many of these conflicts also implies that it will be difficult to develop a consensus for external intervention, that norms will be applied inconsistently – thus generating cynicism – and that delay and buckpassing will dominate decisionmaking. We are thus likely to see a pattern of too little, too late, of grudging commitments hastily withdrawn. One sees this, for example, in the conditions set by the Clinton administration for involvement in peacekeeping activities. In short, while there is an obvious need to co-operate in a world of diffused power and ambiguous interests, a slow and uncertain decision-making process implies much less ability to achieve co-operative outcomes.

There has also been a very important change in the nature of nuclear power, not only in how it might be used but also in terms of who might be seeking a nuclear (or chemical and biological) option. The major nuclear powers may no longer need or want nuclear weapons to deter each other, although prudence suggests the need for some kind of deterrent force to deal with surprises or threats from smaller nuclear states. By contrast, the incentives to acquire nuclear weapons by currently non-nuclear powers may be gaining strength. These weapons might deter outside powers from intervening in local conflicts, they might be insurance against dominance by local enemies, and they might be used as bargaining chips to extract foreign aid and assistance (as in the case of North Korea or Ukraine). This is despite the fact that the development of such weapons is very costly and diverts scarce resources from economic development (especially foreign exchange); that discovery of the effort could lead to sharp cuts in foreign aid and other external assistance; and that it could generate a local nuclear arms race and/or preventive or preemptive war with neighbors.

Nevertheless, the weakness of the non-proliferation regime and the multiple sources of potential conflict in the developing world will certainly generate fears about enemy capabilities and intentions, especially if and when tensions increase and a crisis occurs. Timing and context will be crucial in trying to deal with this issue. While some countries are obviously far along in the effort to acquire nuclear weapons, most developing countries are either unwilling or unable to pursue the nuclear option, and even those who do will require a minimum of a decade or more of intensive effort. Context will also be significant in terms of such matters as the bitterness of local conflicts and the stability and rationality of local leaders. One central point of this is that in certain regions – the Middle East, South and East Asia – nuclear fears are inevitable, doubts about sufficient or timely support from external allies are bound to grow, and the result is likely to be a sustained period of tension and instability. In effect, security concerns both internally and externally will dominate socioeconomic concerns, and expenditures on conventional and unconventional weapons will drive out development expenditures. Thus, the general point about the increasing importance of economic power has to be sharply qualified in certain regions. By the same token, however, the definition of the security threat will itself be increasingly affected, even in these regions, by the increasing costs of buying or developing advanced weapons and by the need to compete effectively in economic terms and thus to meet citizen needs.

Since internal and external conflicts in parts of the developing world are likely to be prevalent and the willingness to intervene militarily to resolve these conflicts is likely to be minimal, the search for non-military forms of conflict resolution or abatement is likely to become an important focus of the post-Cold War security environment. The continuation of aid and trade sanctions, the prosecution of war criminals, and ostracism from international society might be useful mechanisms even against aggressors who are convinced that external military intervention is unlikely, especially if these actions are in fact taken against some of the most evil transgressors in recent conflicts. If few are willing to pay the costs of military intervention, many may be willing to inflict the punishment of international isolation for aggressors.

While the security dilemma and realpolitik are likely to reign supreme in some parts of the Third World, if more leavened by economic pressures than in the past, one might also ask whether the increasing emphasis on economic power might have a relatively beneficial effect on the nature of conflict in the years ahead. Some have argued, for example, that economic conflicts will be easier to resolve than many other kinds of conflict because they are usually less emotional and symbolic, there may seem to be less at stake, and it may be more possible to calculate gains, losses, and potential compromises. This issue intersects with the issue of redefining security, which I shall discuss below. Here I would only say that it would be dangerous to assume that economic disputes will be more easily resolvable. As the economic dimension grows in importance, it also begins to appear more and more like the political and security dimensions. That is, something of an economic security dilemma may be emerging: the issues at stake may be system-threatening and/or nation-threatening, as with the debt crisis in the 1980s; actions taken to protect national interests may generate reactions that leave everyone worse off; and the construction of coalitions against potential threats may generate counter-coalitions that increase the rigidity and diminish the welfare of the emerging order.

What relevance does this have for the Middle East? This is an area, of course, where traditional interpretations of the need for military power still dominate. Nevertheless, two aspects of the shifting nature of power seem likely to be important. The decline of the Soviet Union and the inward-turning trend of the United States will obviously complicate regional patron–client relationships. The inability of Russia to support Syria has already had an effect on Syria"s reluctant participation in the peace process but whether the regional arms race will continue, both through the purchase of arms and the development of even larger domestic arms industries, is unclear. Much will depend on the availability of financial resources and whether domestic pressures to improve standards of living require shifting military expenditures to meet citizen needs.

It is inherently difficult to predict whether the turn inward by the United States, continued economic difficulties, and an increasing focus on the Pacific Basin will have a significant effect on US–Israel relations. The United States is bound to remain closely involved in the Middle East, because of the importance of oil and the continuing threat to the major oil producers, the potential effects of the spread of nuclear weapons, and longstanding patterns of cooperation with Israel. But those ties may become increasingly frayed, especially if the peace process fails, if the radical right in Israel thwarts the resolution of critical issues (especially about the settlers) or initiates more terrorist actions, and if the decline in the US military and foreign aid budgets makes helping Israel increasingly costly. In short, the window of opportunity opened by the peace process, however risky and perilous, may need to be grasped before other developments threaten a relationship that remains crucial for Israel's security and prosperity.

The second aspect of the shifting nature of power that concerns the Middle East relates to domestic developments in the region. I do not believe that the region will be able to isolate itself, except at great cost, from external pressures to democratize and to convert to a market economy.[1] Moreover, the increasingly complex nature of the world economy will require a degree of flexibility, a commitment to a high quality educational system, and an openness to the telecommunications revolution that may very well threaten authoritarian governments. If the regimes resist external pressures, there will be domestic turmoil and a growing gap with countries that are adapting successfully. Conversely, if the regimes seek to respond to external pressures by liberalizing both politically and economically, there will also be turmoil as the costs of adjustment will be severe. In short, one is likely to see a great deal of domestic turmoil in the years ahead, turmoil that is likely to make stable peace in the region more difficult in the short run but may also may make it more likely (or possible) in the long run. The transition period may well be bloody and violent, the new and weak democratic regimes may not act as peacefully as rich and stable democracies, and regimes dominated by the need to propitiate mass demands may be even more likely to resist peace with Israel.

The second major question about the nature of the power configuration that concerns us relates to the major conflicts that have the possibility of defining the emerging world order or generating system-threatening crises. This is an area in which different levels and kinds of threats – political, economic, military – may coalesce to generate a defining confrontation, the whole being greater than the sum of its parts. Whether this grand confrontation will reflect a "clash of civilizations" is unclear and, given certain widely shared values and interests, it is not foreordained that the confrontation will occur or, if underway, will escalate to the system-threatening level.[2] By the same token, we should not assume that the fact that the nature of conflict is (or may be) shifting away from military and ideological conflicts between the major powers to economic and social conflicts means that the ensuing conflicts will be less severe or less capable of evolving into violent conflict. The complexities are vast, not least in the sense that we do not even know the identity of the major protagonists. Or perhaps one should say that one of the protagonists is bound to be the developed, market-oriented democracies, but who might have the power and a plausible alternative vision to raise a serious challenge is unclear or debatable.

One threat might arise from the failure of the United States, Western Europe, and Japan to remain unified. This is most likely from trade wars that would destroy the liberal, rule-based trading and financial regimes and thus the possibility of a mutually beneficial extension of the process of global integration. So much is at stake, however, that the more likely pattern is frequent crises and incremental compromises to step back from the brink – as with the conclusion of the Uruguay Round. But a retreat into spheres of interest and regional blocs that are closed and potentially hostile is also possible, especially if the pattern of winners and losers from global integration begins to rigidify.

Given the weakness of Russia, the most dangerous threat might well be a revival of the alliance with China but with one very important difference: Russia would probably be the junior partner. China's rejection of democracy and its limited cooperation in enforcing the rules of the existing international system may make it an attractive partner for a right-wing regime in Russia. Even more crucially, China's booming economy and its relatively low level of technological development suggest that it might be a good economic partner for Russia in a number of areas. The economic fit is far from perfect because both partners need massive amounts of help from economically more advanced countries: aid, investment, access to markets, and so on. It is thus unsurprising, although somewhat disturbing, that trading ties between the two countries have grown rapidly in the last few years and that China has nearly displaced Germany as Russia's key trading partner. There is a real danger here if this relationship deepens and if both become increasingly authoritarian and hostile to an international order dominated by the West.[3] It must also be noted, however, that it might not only be Russia that is a weak and problematic partner. China's GNP has grown impressively in the last decade but at great cost: Inflation is up, bankruptcies are frequent, law and order are eroding, poverty and inequality are rampant, and central control of economy and society is weakening. There is consequently a significant danger of great turmoil in China, particularly after Deng dies.[4]

Still, it does not seem likely that any of these potential threats are likely to come to fruition in the next decade. This suggests, in terms of the Middle East, that the most important external influences are likely to come from the developments already noted: pressures from abroad to democratize and move toward the market and pressures from within to improve standards of living and to provide citizens with more freedom to express themselves and to pursue goals of individual self-fulfillment. If history is any guide, system-threatening crises are likely to arise eventually as new patterns of winners and losers emerge and as unanticipated problems surface, but the gap in power between the currently dominant powers and the potential challengers and the manifest failures of alternative visions and ideologies suggest that the major short-run challenges will be within-system challenges.

What are the implications of the answers we have given, however tentatively, to the first two questions for the security situation in the Third World? This is the third question that we need to consider, although we must keep in mind the fact that many economic and technological trends are very negative for many Third World countries. These trends suggest that many of these countries, whether they accept or reject the conversion to democracy and a market orientation, will find it increasingly difficult to meet citizen needs, improve standards of living, and establish a degree of political stability. Ethnic and other internal conflicts could become violent and perhaps insoluble. These factors will make the security issue, rather than the development issue, the central focus of Third World politics in the decade ahead. One factor that will persist across periods is a concern with elite survival. In what follows here we shall look only at the more general factors that are likely to affect the definition of the security *problematique* in many Third World countries.

A number of authors have argued that the characteristics of the developed world (plus a few Third World success stories) and the developing world will vary across virtually all dimensions in the post-Cold War world: the former will be essentially democratic, peaceful, and cooperative; the latter will still be in the realm of realpolitik, violent, unstable, and increasingly poor.[5] This kind of dichotomous, mirror-image picture is oversimplified because it misses important differences in prospects and behaviors within the developing world and because it ignores linkages and ties between the two worlds that imply joint losses if the Third World does deteriorate into violence and chaos. Thus, foreign aid in various forms may be provided to avoid some of these outcomes and some of the trends that are emerging (democracy, the market) may gradually improve prospects in some countries. Still, in relative terms the argument that much of the Third World is likely to be increasingly violent and unstable in the years ahead seems all too plausible. Resource conflicts (water, land, minerals) will be severe, population pressures are pervasive, unemployment and underemployment are massive, conflicts over the allocation of ever scarcer resources between ethnic and other groups are growing, arms are widely available, the end of the Cold War has freed local leaders to pursue their own ends, and the unwillingness of the rich countries and the inability of the UN to intervene is apparent – the list could go on. The reluctance of the rich countries to intervene but their willingness to sell virtually any arms means that the pressure to reduce defense spending in the Third World – strongly advocated by all aid organizations – is not likely to have much success. Even the continued movement toward democracy may generate increased conflict, not only because of resistance by the old regime but also because democracy may increase support for national self-determination among discontented ethnic or religious groups, which threatens territorial integrity. In some cases, where the masses are less risk-averse and more viscerally hostile to ancient enemies, democratic regimes may actually be more prone to violence than non-democratic regimes.

A variety of analysts and practitioners have made this point in regard to the Middle East. They contend that mass-dominated regimes, filled with a visceral hatred of Israel and in need of a scapegoat for domestic failures, will be more aggressive than the (supposedly) risk-averse autocrats of the region. There may or may not be much truth to this in the short run – there are too many unknowns to take this argument on assertion alone – but it should also be said that not all of the autocrats seem quite so risk-averse, as Saddam's attacks on Iran and Kuwait might suggest. Note that the general point here about the possible aggressiveness of some new democracies also raises doubt about the automatic assumption that more democracies means more peace.[6]

One clear implication is that conflicts over land, water, and other territorial resources are likely to become increasingly prevalent.[7] Border stability in certain regions, especially Africa and the Middle East, may become increasingly tenuous and fears about real or potential threats to territorial stability may generate a very dangerous security dilemma, as well as some preemptive or preventive wars. Since it is extremely unlikely that economic success from conversion to the market, increases in worldwide growth rates, or increases in foreign aid, foreign lending, or foreign investment will bring these governments enough gains to diminish the need to protect and/or acquire more territorial resources, the outlook for peaceful settlement looks bleak. It should come as no surprise that the Middle East may suffer the worst violence from these trends not only because resource shortages are severe, boundaries not always settled, and ancient conflicts still unresolved but also because arms spending on all kinds of weapons systems is so high.

If we look at security in a traditional sense – that is, in relationship to threats to territorial integrity and political independence, balances of power, and military spending – the prognosis for many parts of the

Third World is grim. But suppose we redefine security so that it includes or incorporates many of the new issues that have become part of the international agenda. Ecological issues, economic conflicts, the migration of peoples, drugs, terrorism, the sharing of resources – these and other problems and conflicts have been suggested as part of the new meaning or definition of security. The fourth question I want to consider briefly is whether redefining security in this fashion might have a beneficial effect on the security problems of the Third World.[8]

For the developed countries, the universe of threats has shifted. The Soviet Union has disintegrated and its empire is long gone, conflicts within the Western bloc are likely to be resolved peacefully, and most Third World (and Eastern European?) conflicts do not seem worth the risks and costs of war. The real threats now seem to be issues that do not threaten political independence and territorial integrity, that cannot effectively be resolved by the use of military force or the construction of a balance of power, that are heavily affected by the play of domestic politics, and that – above all – seem to threaten life styles or quality of life characteristics. One problem with this argument is that almost anything can become a security issue because almost anything can have some effect on the well-being of a country. Having so many issues defined as security issues may generate both analytical and practical confusion.

There is an even greater problem. Defining quality of life and other such issues in terms of security may force these issues into an inappropriate conceptual framework. Security issues have traditionally been considered from a zero sum, relativistic, conflictual perspective. This may make it more difficult to resolve issues that require cooperation, a consensus on rules, trade-offs between short-run costs and long-run benefits, and a focus on systemic benefits that are widely shared. Many of these issues cannot be effectively resolved unilaterally or in small groups of the powerful. But it is equally true that trying to resolve them globally or multilaterally is likely to generate delay, lowest-common denominator responses, and a great deal of free-ridership. Consequently, it seems more appropriate to think of them in terms of international collective goods or, where this is not feasible, at least as international club goods that will be shared by all those willing to accept the club's principles and rules.

The new transnational threats will surely benefit from and may require immediate policy responses to avert escalating deterioration and long-run insolubility. Nevertheless, these threats are also diffuse and long-term in impact, do not always have agreed solutions, and generate widely varying short-run patterns of costs and benefits. In the short run they also intersect with traditional security threats, thus conflating "old" threats to territorial integrity and political independence with "new" threats to the quality of life nationally and internationally. Treating these very different kinds of issues as part of the same "security dilemma" is not always wrong or misleading because some of the new threats do indeed have potential implications in terms of domestic instability or conflict with neighbors. But not all of the new threats are of this nature and treating them as if they are security issues risks increased conflict over intervention and a misconceived conceptual focus for problems that may at some point become security problems but may also be worsened by thinking about them primarily from a security perspective. One implication of this argument is that we need to begin with a mapping exercise that delineates which of the new issues might or might not benefit from thinking about them as security issues. One presumes here that those issues that can be most effectively resolved by getting domestic politics "right" (say, in trade, or energy, or drugs) ought not to be considered security issues and only those that seem likely to generate inter-state conflict ought to be thought about in a security context.[9] This mapping exercise thus avoids the double danger of misperceiving the nature of some issues and of increasing pressures on a weak international security framework to provide solutions to problems that are in fact best handled at another level entirely.

One might also note that redefining many transnational issues as either national or international security issues could be especially problematic in large parts of the Third World. On the one hand, there are some potential benefits for the Third World from such a redefinition. Some of these new issues are directly or indirectly related to security in the sense that failure to resolve them will make it much more difficult for governments to meet citizen needs, to act fairly, to sustain either democracy or the market, and to reduce military expenditures. And raising the salience of these issues and emphasizing the need for cooperative policy responses may make it easier to generate greater benefits, more aid, and special compensation for poor countries. On the other hand, as noted earlier, traditional security issues, both internal and external, will still dominate calculations in many parts of the Third World. Thus interpreting these issues as security issues might force them into a particularly dangerous conceptual framework where relative gains dominate absolute or joint gains, zero sum outcomes are the norm, and the effort to acquire and defend territory becomes a central concern. Consequently, on the margin and especially in areas of conflict, it seems more prudent to try to *narrow* the meaning of security and to think about the new or newer issues in a framework that emphasizes co-operation, mutual benefits, and a shared interest in a less conflictual world order.

PRINCIPLES OF GUIDANCE

The principles of guidance reflect several critical points that emerge from the earlier analysis. Perhaps the most salient point is the need for, and lack of, effective intermediary institutions and ordering principles that help to diminish the conflict between global trends and developments and local or national reactions and needs. A related point, which we cannot pursue here, is the need to rethink what we need and want from the international system itself. We need to get beyond thinking of the latter as primarily a diplomatic system concerned with the great issues of war and peace – which may still be a crucial function in a few cases – and begin thinking of it as a policymaking system with some elements of sovereignty formally ceded to reformed institutions and some characteristics (bargaining, compromises, trade-offs) that we normally associate with democratic political systems. Another point that emerges clearly concerns the escalating problems of a large part of the Third World. No world order is likely to be stable without a principle of equity that provides some compensation to those who cannot compete effectively. It has been inordinately difficult to devise a practical, politically feasible principle of distributive justice in the past and it is unlikely to be much easier in the future with rising domestic needs and "aid fatigue." Nevertheless, as more countries move toward democracy and the market, the moral obligation to help them increases and so too may the practical benefits of doing so. Finally, since governments will increasingly be judged by performance, since fear of losing in a competitive environment is widespread, and since the gap between expectations and achievements may grow rapidly, one likely outcome may be an emphasis on seeking to regain control of the policy process and trying to limit the effects of global trends. This may imply a slower liberalization of the system, an emphasis on cooperation among smaller groups of the like-minded, and an attempt to build carefully from local cooperation upwards and not from grand designs downward.

In these circumstances guiding principles might include the following:

1. A principle of subsidarity, adapted from the European community. The issue here concerns the proper level at which decisions should be made. Higher level institutions should act only where "objectives cannot be sufficiently achieved" by members acting alone, or can be better achieved by acting in concert.[10] In the abstract, most decisions are probably best done in concert but the difficulties of achieving consensus may make smaller arenas or groups a reasonable second-best option. The principle implies a bias toward seeking initially to establish effective domestic policies and to rely on international institutions only when this does not suffice. There will

be much need for the latter but one needs to set priorities carefully and to be parsimonious in what one asks international institutions to do – and more generous toward them when they are asked. And of course where regional institutions or other intermediate institutions are able to function effectively they too ought to be used to diminish the burden on international institutions, but only if their actions are consonant with broader principles and seen as building blocs toward a more cooperative world order. Multilateralism surely matters, but if states seek to make it matter too much or matter only when they want to pass the buck, it will soon matter not at all.

2. Who sits at the decisionmaking table? There are obvious costs in increasing the number of participants (delays, watered-down policies, free riders) but equally obvious dangers of not doing so when more is necessary, not merely desirable. One option, again borrowing from the Europeans, is the idea of "variable geometry," that is, cooperation among sub-groups willing and able to accept certain obligations. This increases flexibility in the policy process and has the virtue of encouraging agreements that move as many as possible as quickly as possible toward shared goals. There is a rough parallel to the idea of club goods in economics, that is, goods from which non-payers can be excluded (as with toll roads or licensing fees). This is again a second-best option but a useful option if within-club rules are observed and clear and fair criteria for admission of new members are established. Less talk about globalism and more talk about whose interests are most engaged and who is willing to accept obligations and pay costs would be appropriate.

3. A principle of justice is especially necessary now because so many trends work against large parts of the Third World and gaps within and between countries are large and growing. One needs here not abstract lectures on principles of distributive justice or compensation for earlier exploitations but rather practical schemes that stand some chance of being effectively implemented and improving standards of living quickly and fairly. As noted earlier, the obligation to help through a prolong transition period is stronger now because so many countries have been urged and are seeking to convert to democracy and the market. Self-interest is also at stake for the rich countries as they will obviously benefit from new economic opportunities and a reduction in a number of dangers (terrorism, mass emigration, nuclear and other arms races).

While I cannot set forth details here, what I have in mind as a kind of model of what needs to be done is reflected in the co-ordinated effort to help the new Palestinian entity. All the potential donors have come together to work out a plan of action with local experts, they have set out principles for disbursing resources, and have established controls to avoid the misallocations and corruption that have undermined the effectiveness of so much foreign aid. If there is some flexibility in the application of the rules in the early years of implementation and if the Palestinian leadership begins to understand that the rules are in fact useful – both politically and economically – the prospects for peace and stability will surely increase.

NOTES

1. For extensive comments on this complex issue, see my two chapters in Edy Kaufman, Shukri B. Abed, and Robert L. Rothstein (eds.), *Democracy, Peace, and the Israeli-Palestinian Conflict* (Boulder, Colorado: Lynne Rienner Publishers, 1993).
2. On the clash of civilizations, see Samuel P. Huntington, "The Clash of Civilizations?" *Foreign Affairs*, Vol.72, No.3 (Summer 1993), pp.22–49.
3. See Chalmers Johnson, "Shape Up and Stay Influential in Asia," *International Herald Tribune*, 26 May 1994, p.6; *New York Times*, September 4, 1994.
4. See the comments by Professor Thomas Homer-Dixon, quoted in the New York Times, April 5, 1994, p.C8.
5. See Robert Jervis, "The Future of World Politics – Will It Resemble the Past?" *International Security*, Vol.16, No.3 (Winter 1991/92), pp.39–46, at p.47ff; James Goldgeier and Michael McFaul, "A Tale of Two Worlds: Core and Periphery in the Post-Cold War Era," *International Organization*, Vol.46, No.2 (Spring 1992), pp.467–91.
6. For a detailed consideration, see my works cited in note 1.
7. On this issue, see Thomas F. Homer-Dixon, Jeffrey H. Boutwell, and George W. Rathgens, "Environmental Change and Violent Conflict," *Scientific American*, Vol.268, No.2 (February 1993), pp.38–45.
8. For a useful overview of this issue, see Joseph J. Romm, *Defining National Security: The Nonmilitary Aspects* (New York: Council on Foreign Relations, 1993).
9. Romm, *Defining National Security*, pp.81–90.
10. The quotation is from the Maastrict Treaty, summarized in the *New York Times*, September 20, 1992, p.12.

The Continuing Importance of American Interests in the Middle East after the Cold War

STEVEN R. DAVID

There is no question that the principal American interest in the Middle East during the Cold War was its role in the US–Soviet competition. During the 1950s, the Middle East assumed importance as the locale of the Baghdad Pact in which Arab states were expected to provide bases for the United States to threaten the Soviet Union. The beginnings of a significant strategic partnership between Israel and the United States in 1970 followed Israel's seeming protection of a pro-Western Jordan from a pro-Soviet Syrian invasion. During the Reagan era, strategic cooperation between the United States and Israel reached record levels largely because of Israel's assumed importance as a bulwark against Soviet expansionism. There is also no question that with the demise of the Soviet Union this central interest in containing Moscow no longer exists.

But the end of the Cold War will not end American interests in the Middle East. In fact, in a world in which many regions will see their significance to the United States diminish, the overall level of importance of the Middle East to American interests will remain roughly where it was during the Cold War. This will be so for three principal reasons (each of which will be considered in detail). First, instability and warfare will continue to characterize much of the Middle East. Second, this turmoil will threaten key American interests including access to oil and concerns about the spread of nuclear weapons. Finally, American ties with Israel will be maintained regardless of security considerations.

Not only will the end of the Cold War not undermine these interests, in many respects it will enhance them.

Steven R. David is Professor of Political Science at the Johns Hopkins University.

WHY CONFLICT AND INSTABILITY WILL PREVAIL IN THE MIDDLE EAST

It is no great revelation to identify the Middle East as an unstable region. Since the establishment of Israel there have been at least six Arab–Israeli wars, several inter-Arab conflicts, and countless assassinations, coups, insurgencies and civil wars. This is in marked contrast to the "developed" world (North America, Western Europe, Japan, Australia and New Zealand) where there has been no major conflict since the end of the Second World War.

To understand why the developed world has been so peaceful and the Middle East so unstable, it is first necessary to look at the characteristics of Middle Eastern states. Most of these states are relatively young. Instead of the four or five centuries of development that countries of Western Europe had, they measure their independence in decades or less.[1] Virtually all are wrestling with problems of political and economic development. Most have experienced the legacy of colonialism with its imposition of arbitrary borders and the exacerbation of ethnic and religious rivalry by colonial leaders. The great majority of Middle Eastern states are led by authoritarian leaders who place their own interests over those of the people they purport to lead. The result has been the emergence of Middle Eastern states with internationally recognized borders, but without the ability (or sometimes the will) to control ethnic and religious conflicts that all to often rage within those borders.

Along with domestic instability, we can expect wars between states to persist in the Middle East. Internal instability itself promotes interstate warfare in several ways. Internal disorder provokes international conflict as neighboring states act to prevent instability from spreading to them, as Iraq did when it invaded Iran in 1980. Domestic instability might leave a country too weak to suppress sub-national groups who are left free to provoke attacks from bordering states, with such results as the Israeli invasion of Lebanon in 1982 and continuing strife on the Israeli–Lebanese border. Internal instability can create the impression that a foe has been so weakened that a "window of opportunity" for attack has been opened, as seen again in Iraq's 1980 invasion of Iran.[2]

Interstate warfare is also likely because the factors that explain the "long peace" of the developed world do not apply to the Middle East. With the exception of Israel, there are no democratic countries in the Middle East, removing the peace-inducing effects that democracy is alleged to provide among democratic states.[3] In the developed world, the benefits of conquest have declined, because emphasis on knowledge-producing forms of wealth has lessened the importance of territory as a source of power.[4] In the Middle East, land is still critical for security and wealth. As the political scientist John Mueller argues, developed states may be moving toward a realization that war, like slavery and dueling, is an indefensible form of behavior that is rapidly becoming obsolete.[5] Among some Middle Eastern regimes (Iran, Iraq, Libya), however, militarism and warfare are still celebrated. The prevalence of revolutionary states in the Middle East – Libya, Iraq, and Iran – also enhances the prospects for war. Revolutionary states are more prone to war because they are more likely to seek to impose their ideological beliefs on other countries (as Libya tried to do with Chad), or neighboring states preemptively attack out of fear that such expansion is imminent (as Iraq did with Iran).

The religious beliefs of many Middle Eastern states may make them more prone to conflict. The chief concern of the United States and the West lies with extremist Islamic regimes. This is not because Islam is any more warlike than other religions such as Judaism or Christianity. Rather, the concern is that extremists of any religion might pursue radical policies leading to war. Islamic extremists are a particular worry because they have already come to power in two states (Iran and Sudan), nearly came to power in a third (Algeria), and potentially can come to power in many more. Since Islamic extremists share a belief that the West is immoral and corrupt, and are prepared to act to spread their beliefs, their gaining control of states raises legitimate concerns that Islam will be selectively interpreted by some Third World leaders in order to mobilize their populations for war.[6]

Many Middle Eastern leaders are not restrained from going to war even when public support for war is weak. Since most Middle Eastern countries are not democratic, the leadership does not depend on the people's support for war. Equally important, Middle Eastern leaders no longer need to fear that a loss in war will inevitably mean a loss of power. Improved capabilities for suppression have made Middle Eastern leaders less vulnerable to the uprisings, coups, or revolutions that often follow military setbacks. Whereas defeat in the 1967 Middle East war helped bring about the downfall of the leader of Syria, defeat in the 1973 war did little to threaten Asad's rule. Saddam Hussein is vivid proof that a ruthless leader can survive eight years of ruinous stalemate with one adversary and a crushing defeat by another. Egypt's Anwar Sadat and Iran's Ayatollah Khomeini are further examples of Middle Eastern leaders whose military losses did little to shake their hold on power.

The absence of constraints on going to war for many Middle Eastern leaders is critical because most Middle Eastern states are led by a narrow elite. This elite tends to be alienated from the population at large and focused on meeting its own narrow interests, the most important of which is remaining in power. If a Middle Eastern leadership judges that going to war will enhance its prospects of remaining in power (by, for example, increasing the wealth available for distribution to key domestic groups), it is likely that it will choose war.[7] This will be so even if war might not be in the broader national interest. Since it is more likely that war will serve some narrow group than the society at large, basing the decision to go to war on the interests of a small elite makes that decision more likely.[8]

The contemporary Middle Eastern situation is supportive of war. Most of the Middle Eastern states have severe economic problems. Egyptian unemployment is over 20 per cent, Jordan is in recession, and even oil-rich Saudi Arabia and Kuwait are running huge deficits. While Western states are cutting defense expenditures, they are rising dramatically in the Middle East. Since the Gulf War, Saudi Arabia alone has ordered over $25 billion worth of defense equipment.[9] Syria and Egypt are also in the midst of major rearmament drives. Most Middle Eastern countries face additional pressures stemming from population increases and concern over scarce water resources.[10] The potential growth of Islamic extremism feeding on economic despair and the disruptions of modernization threaten moderate states such as Egypt and Jordan.[11]

The Israeli-Palestinian peace process will not end instability in the Middle East. If the negotiations are not successful, anger over unfulfilled promises and hopes on both sides can lead to conflict. If the peace process does lead to the establishment of a Palestinian state, war can still erupt. An unstable Palestine may lead to war by provoking Israeli or Arab intervention or a takeover by radical Palestinian groups not committed to peace. A strong, cohesive Palestine can also bring about war through the temptation of finally satisfying its irredentist aims.[12] If a Palestinian–Israeli peace proves enduring, other sources of tension in the Middle East may lead to war. The Iraqi invasions of Iran and Kuwait, and the recent civil war in Yemen, are just some examples of Middle East conflict that do not stem from the Arab-Israeli dispute.

Nor will the end of the Cold War usher in a new era of peace. To be sure, the superpowers have exacerbated conflict through their profligate arms sales and (as especially was the case with Nasser's Egypt) by dragging countries into an East–West dispute that they just as soon would have preferred to avoid. But the source of Middle Eastern conflicts are indigenous and will not go away with the absence of great power involvement. Moreover, it was never in the interests of the United States or the Soviet Union to provoke war in the Middle East, since to do so would have raised the risk of losing a client or, even worse, of a superpower confrontation. Consequently, the United States and the Soviet Union frequently acted to prevent the outbreak of war as seen in Moscow's restraint of Egypt's Anwar Sadat from 1970 to 1973.[13] If armed conflict nevertheless did occur, the superpowers often attempted to bring it to a halt as they did in the 1956, 1967, and 1973 Middle Eastern wars. Perhaps if the Soviet

Union had maintained influence over Iraq, Baghdad's 1990 invasion of Kuwait would never have happened. This superpower-induced restraint is now gone.

WHY CONFLICT AND INSTABILITY IN THE MIDDLE EAST THREATENS US INTERESTS

Conflict and instability in the Middle East are of concern to the United States because their presence threatens key American interests. Nowhere is this clearer than in the United States dependence on importer oil. The United States imports half of its petroleum needs. American allies are even worse off, with foreign oil accounting for more than 60 per cent of West European requirements and almost all of Japan's needs. The demand for oil will in all probability rise due to the rapidly expanding economies of Asia and the decrease in energy efficiency after more than a decade of low energy prices. The supply of oil to meet this rising demand will almost surely fall over time; no new big oil fields are waiting to be exploited, and former major oil producers such as the United States (which has seen a 25 per cent decline in production since 1986) and the former Soviet Union (which has seen its production collapse with the demise of the empire) cannot make up the difference. Major foreign investment in the former Soviet Union may result in increases of production, but no one knows if large deposits exist to be exploited or, if such deposits exist, whether the political climate will allow production to take place. A major portion of the shortfall will have to be made up by the Persian Gulf states that possess nearly 70 per cent of the world's excess production capacity and are the likely locale of any new major oil finds.[14]

Those who argue that this dependence on Persian Gulf oil does not threaten American interests maintain that market forces will protect American concerns. They reason that whoever owns the oil will have to sell it to reap the profits. Boycotting a single state or group of states is no longer possible as the International Energy Agency mandates sharing. Large price increases could also not be sustained, they argue, since that would drive the importers to different suppliers, energy alternatives and conservation. With oil at its lowest price in decades, they assert there is little reason for worry.[15]

This view is mistaken. Precisely because there is so much instability in the Persian Gulf, oil production may be cut off regardless of the economic costs. There have been 16 disruptions in the Middle East since 1950, and as the 1991 Gulf War so vividly demonstrated, interruptions in supply are not dependent on the Cold War. Internal instability prevails in the Gulf. Saudi Arabia, which possesses the world's largest oil reserves, faces a multiplicity of domestic threats, any one of which could disrupt production for long periods of time. They include a potential revolt by the 400,000 Saudi Shiites, a takeover of the government by Muslim zealots similar to the 1979 insurrection, or a civil war between rival Saudi clans. Similar vulnerabilities exist within the other Gulf states as well. The Iraqi invasions of Iran and Kuwait are clear illustrations of the threat posed by external war. Another Arab–Israeli conflict or renewed efforts by Iran or Iraq to establish its hegemony could also threaten the stability of the Gulf. A protracted war within or among states could destroy pumping stations, pipelines and refineries that could cripple production for months or even years.[16]

Economic logic might not work in the Persian Gulf because of the impact of culture and religion. Those who minimize the threat posed by American dependence on Persian Gulf oil assume that whoever controls the oil will behave in an economically rational (that is, profit maximizing) manner. But what rationality or desire for economic gain underlay Saddam Hussein's torching of the Kuwaiti oil fields when defeat for the Iraqi forces was imminent? In Saudi Arabia, the religious extremists who took over the Grand Mosque emphasized the need to prevent Saudi Arabia's moral collapse by removing the corrupting influences of the West. If similar insurgents were to gain power, they might seek to recreate a state along the lines of the society idealized by the Prophet Muhammad in the seventh century and might attempt to eliminate all the corrupting influences of the West, including those involved with the production and sale of oil. Religious extremists, of course, might behave according to Western precepts with regard to the sale of oil if they seized power, but then again they might not. To assume that their cultural and religious beliefs would have no effect on economic behavior is as dangerous as it is foolhardy.

If Persian Gulf oil is cut off for a protracted period of time, it would have a disastrous effect on American interests. There could well be an intense scramble for remaining supplies. With the United States committed to sharing oil, huge price increases and shortages are likely. The possibility of worldwide depression or at least recession could not be ruled out. Perhaps over the long term (more than a year) the crisis could be defused. But that would not negate the tangible and psychological damage inflicted on the importing states in the interim.

The second major threat to American interests from the Middle East stems from nuclear proliferation. Middle Eastern states seeking to develop nuclear weapons include such avowed enemies of the United States as Libya, Iraq, and Iran.[17] As the near development of nuclear weapons by Iraq and the probable development of nuclear arms by North Korea has illustrated, international inspection in a country and formal adherence to the Non-Proliferation Treaty is not enough to prevent it from acquiring a nuclear capability. A nuclear attack represents the principal threat to the physical security of the United States and its allies. Far from allaying U.S. fears, the disintegration of the USSR has exacerbated concerns about nuclear proliferation. Not only has the restraining influence of the USSR on global proliferation been lost, there are also thousands of nuclear scientists from the former Soviet Union now out of work who may be tempted to offer their services to Middle Eastern bidders. The breakup of the Soviet Union has also raised fears that nuclear weapons will be transferred to Middle Eastern countries.[18]

There are those who argue that nuclear proliferation should not be a major concern to the United States. They assert that Middle Eastern states will behave essentially like the existing nuclear powers in their use or non-use of nuclear weapons. Since nuclear weapons have induced caution and reduced the margin for miscalculation among the great powers, there is no reason to believe it will be different for the minor powers. Even radical Middle Eastern states, they say, would not use nuclear weapons recklessly because their leaders would recognize the price of doing so. Even heads of state assumed to be irrational (at least by Western standards) are still sensitive to costs. Accidents, unauthorized launching, or theft of nuclear weapons would not be more likely in the Third World, it is asserted, since the leaders of the countries would have every incentive not to allow their nuclear arms to fall out of their control. Even if a Middle Eastern nuclear war broke out, they argue that American interests might be best served by remaining aloof. In sum, this view asserts, Middle Eastern states are no more likely to use nuclear weapons than the major powers, and if they do the result would not threaten American interests.[19]

These are all valid points, but precisely because Middle Eastern states are more likely to engage in internal and external warfare, nuclear weapons are more likely to be used and American interests are more likely to be endangered than if such weapons were deployed by more stable states. Internal conflict in the Middle East heightens the likelihood of nuclear use in several ways. Widespread domestic turmoil may prevent a state from exercising control over its nuclear weapons despite its best efforts to do so, and nuclear weapons could thus fall into the hands of terrorists. That terrorist groups are so prevalent and powerful in the Middle East is not reassuring, especially since terrorist groups are likely to have fewer inhibitions about launching nuclear strikes. Nuclear weapons might also fall into the hands of insurgents in a civil conflict; because civil wars are often more brutal and destructive than interstate wars, the intensity of feelings could overcome any inhibitions that threats of retaliation would engender. It is doubtful that nuclear deterrence could have been relied upon to keep the peace if a Lebanese faction had gained control of nuclear arms during that country's civil war.

The large number of Middle Eastern states that may potentially develop nuclear weapons can also undermine deterrence. For deterrence to work, a state needs to be able to identify its adversary. But in the Middle East, there may be many nuclear powers, most of which face many enemies. With nuclear weapons able to be launched from sea, air, and even from trucks, it might be difficult if not impossible to determine the origin of a nuclear strike. If Israel is attacked in a Middle East where Iran, Iraq, Libya, Syria, and Saudi Arabia all maintain nuclear weapons, against whom should it retaliate? Middle Eastern countries might also use terrorist groups to launch nuclear strikes in an effort to avoid responsibility and thus retaliation.

The intensity of the conflict faced by many Third World states also makes nuclear war more likely than among the great powers. The United States and the Soviet Union have never experienced the degree of hostility that characterizes the Middle East. Moreover, because the very existence of some Middle East states is threatened, their resort to nuclear weapons becomes all the more probable. Israel, for example, was reported to consider the use of nuclear weapons against invading Arab forces during the October 1973 War on at least two occasions,[20] and may have been prepared to use nuclear weapons in response to an Iraqi chemical weapons strike during the Gulf War.[21] The problems of preempting another state's nuclear capability did not prevent Israel from attacking Iraq's nuclear reactor in 1981. As more Middle Eastern states seek nuclear weapons, attacks of this kind and retaliations, some of which might be nuclear, cannot be ruled out.

Because the threat of war is so high, the possibilities of accidental or unauthorized launchings will also be greater in the Middle East than elsewhere. The need to prevent preemption of small nuclear forces could force Middle Eastern nuclear states to adopt a "hair-trigger" response to conventional or nuclear attacks. Such a response combined with primitive radar and command and control capabilities might lead to inadvertent nuclear strikes. In addition, it is likely that Middle Eastern regimes would disperse nuclear weapons and move them from place to place to enhance their protection from attack. These steps might also increase the chances that lower-ranking officers could launch nuclear weapons without authority from the government, and that the nuclear weapons themselves would be more vulnerable to sub-national and terrorist groups. The sorry record of command and control of American nuclear weapons does not lend confidence that Middle Eastern nuclear arms will be free from accident or theft.[22]

American interests will be hurt if nuclear weapons are used in the Middle East. Even if confined to the Middle East, nuclear conflict could make subsequent nuclear use more likely, while encouraging the proliferation of nuclear weapons to still more countries. A Middle Eastern nuclear conflict could produce severe environmental damage, and if it occurs in the Persian Gulf, would cause great economic distress to the United States. American allies such as Israel and Egypt are potential targets of a nuclear strike. The possession of nuclear arms by an enemy of the United States could deter Washington from acting to defend its interests. It is difficult to believe that the United States would have intervened against Saddam Hussein by placing some half a million troops in a relatively small area if Washington had believed that Iraq had nuclear weapons. Indeed, a major lesson of the U.S.–Iraqi war for would-be Middle Eastern hegemons is not to refrain from attacking American interests, but to wait to acquire a nuclear weapons capability before doing so. The United States might also be deterred from taking action against states engaged in terrorist activities. As Libyan Leader Mu'amar Gadaffi reportedly remarked, "If at the time of the U.S. raid on Tripoli [1986] we had possessed a deterrent-missile that could reach New York, we could have hit it at the same moment."[23]

Most alarmingly, nuclear weapons might be directed against the United States itself. There is no shortage of Middle Eastern countries and groups with grievances against the United States. In the coming years, Middle Eastern states and other actors will be able to deliver nuclear weapons against the United States by using aircraft, cruise missiles, ships, and conceivably even suitcases. One has only to imagine the damage that would have occurred if instead of conventional explosives, Middle Eastern terrorists were able to plant a nuclear device under the World Trade Center in New York to appreciate the threat to American interests that the proliferation of nuclear weapons to the Middle East entails.

Aside from the threat to Persian Gulf oil and concerns over proliferation, the United States maintains a wide range of interests that are endangered by Middle Eastern instability. The United States is committed to protecting the lives and property of American citizens both of which may be jeopardized by disorder in the Middle East. Concerns over drug smuggling, much of which originates in the Middle East, will continue to focus American policymakers' attention on this region. The spread of biological and chemical weapons to Middle Eastern states, while less worrisome than nuclear arms, nevertheless poses a challenge to American security and that of its allies. Finally, the disproportionate role the Middle East plays in sponsoring terrorism will threaten American interests both throughout the world and in the United States itself. None of these problems are likely to improve – and some may get worse – in the wake of the end of the Cold War.

Regardless of specifics, it is crucial for the United States to be prepared to be engaged in the Middle East because it is impossible to identity far in advance which countries and interests are likely to be important. When Secretary of State Dean Acheson excluded South Korea from the range of American vital interests, he did so because South Korea lacked intrinsic importance to the United States. The subsequent invasion by North Korea (probably encouraged by Acheson's action) demonstrated that countries of seemingly small significance can gain in importance when threatened (even indirectly) by a hostile power because the threat calls into question America's credibility as an ally. During the 1980s, few would have predicted that America's budding friendship with Iraq would end in war between the two countries just as few foresaw the budding Israeli–Palestinian peace that emerged in the early 1990s. In a region as volatile as the Middle East, it is not surprising that prognosticators have such a poor record.

Nevertheless, as uncertain as the future may be, the Middle East will almost surely be a region of major importance to the United States. This is not because vital interests are at stake, but because U.S. interests in the Middle East are more *likely* to be threatened. During the Cold War, the United States has focused its efforts on interests of high intrinsic worth that confront relatively small risks: defending Western Europe and avoiding superpower nuclear war. American interests in the Middle East cannot match these in importance, but there is a far greater probability they will be threatened. When determining the value of interests, the greater likelihood of risk to American interests from Middle Eastern developments must be given weight.

THE UNITED STATES AND ISRAEL

American interests will continue to be engaged by Middle Eastern developments because the United States will continue to be concerned about Israel. This is so principally for three reasons. First are the values shared by Israel and the United States. Both Israel and the United States are democracies with a commitment to basic freedoms. The Clinton administration has demonstrated a strong willingness to support democratic regimes because of its oft stated beliefs that democracies are more peaceable and make better allies than other types of government. With Israel the only democracy in the Middle East, it will benefit from this approach. Moreover, many senior officials of the Clinton administration appear to genuinely admire Israel. Given the threats to Israeli security that are likely to remain regardless of the outcome of the peace process, continued American backing of Israel will almost certainly persist in the Middle East for the foreseeable future.

Secondly, the pro-Israeli lobby is widely believed to be among the most effective in the United States. Its effectiveness stems in part from the high concentration of Jewish voters in key states and the funding given to pro-Israeli candidates. Most important, the pro-Israeli lobby is powerful because it mobilizes support for Israel that already exists among the American electorate. This is demonstrated by the consistency of American support for Israel despite major changes in the level of funding provided to key decision makers by pro-Israeli groups. Although tensions between Israel and the United States and even between Israel and Jewish lobbying groups can be expected to surface from time to time, the strength of the American–Israeli relationship is likely to endure.[24]

Finally, as discussed in this essay, the United States will continue to maintain strategic interests with Israel. To be sure, the demise of the Soviet Union has lessened the importance of these interests. But American interests will continue be engaged by concerns over the supply of oil, the spread of weapons of mass destruction, the appeal of Islamic radicalism, and the impact of terrorism. In addition, the end of the Cold War has brought about an increased American reliance on dependable allies. The decline in the United States defense budget has meant more emphasis on utilizing facilities and forces of friendly states. Israel is an obvious component of this "less is more" strategy. Finally, the peace process itself will enhance American interests and engagement in the Middle East. The United States is the key outside power in the peace negotiations and could well be called upon to provide peacekeeping forces to assist the implementation of an agreement. Insuring the continued success of the agreement and concerns over the fate of American forces might well engage American interests for years to come.

CONCLUSIONS

In absolute terms, the importance of the Middle East to American interests may have declined. But in a world without the Soviet Union, virtually every security related interest has become less salient to the United States. This includes Western Europe whose protection from the former Soviet Union absorbed over half of the American defense budget and the lion's share of American foreign policy concerns. With the need to protect Western Europe (and to contest the Soviet Union throughout the Third World) largely gone, space has been created to focus on other areas of interest. With its oil, threat of nuclear proliferation, and instability, the Middle East stands out as a region that is likely to absorb much of this displaced interest. In relative terms, therefore, one can expect to see a Middle East that will account for a much larger share of a diminished American foreign policy pie. The central driving force of American policy in the Middle East may have disappeared with the Soviet Union, but American interests and commitment to this troubled region will remain.

NOTES

1. For an examination of the European experience in state-building, see Charles Tilly, "Reflections of European State-Making," in Charles Tilly (ed.), *The Formation of National States in Western Europe* (Princeton: Princeton University Press, 1975), pp.3–83. For a contrasting look at the Third World experience that has much relevance to the Middle East, see Mohammed Ayoob, "The Security Problematic of the Third World," *World Politics*, Vol.43, No.2 (January 1991), especially pp.265–66.

2. On the relationship between domestic instability and interstate war, see Jack S. Levy, "Domestic Politics and War," in Robert I. Rotberg and Theodore K. Rabb (eds.), *The Origin and Prevention of Major Wars* (Cambridge: Cambridge University Press, 1988), especially pp.94, 98–9; Richard Ned Lebow, *Between Peace and War: The Nature of International Crisis* (Baltimore: Johns Hopkins University Press, 1981), especially pp.66–71; and Jonathan Wilkenfeld, "Domestic and Foreign Conflict Behavior of Nations," *Journal of Peace Research*, 5 (1968), pp.55–69.

3. One of the best arguments for why democracy helps produce peace is by Michael Doyle, "Kant, Liberal Legacies, and Foreign Affairs," parts 1 and 2, *Philosophy and Public Affairs*, 12, 3-4 (Summer and Fall 1983), pp.205–35, 325–53.

4. Stephen Van Evera, "Primed for Peace: Europe After the Cold War," *International Security*, Vol.15, No.3 (Winter 1990/91).

5. John Mueller, *Retreat From Doomsday: The Obsolescence of Major War* (New York: Basic Books, 1989), especially Introduction.

6. For a general study of Islamic (and Western) attitudes toward war, see James Turner Johnson and John Kelsay (eds.), *Cross Crescent and Sword: The Justification and Limitation of War in Western and Islamic Traditons* (NY: Greenwood Press, 1990).

7. On how concerns for his political survival helped lead Saddam Hussein to invade Kuwait, see Efraim Karsh and Inari Rautsi, *Saddam Hussein: A Political Biography* (NY: Free Press, 1991), Ch.9.

8. On the importance of focusing on leaders to understand Third World (including Middle Eastern) foreign policy, see Steven R. David, *Choosing Sides: Alignment and Realignment in the Third World* (Baltimore: Johns Hopkins University Press, 1991), especially Ch.1.

9. Eliahu Kanovsky, *Assessing the Mideast Peace Economic Dividend* (Ramat Gan: Besa Center for Strategic Studies, 1994), p.10.

10. John K. Cooley, "The War Over Water," *Foreign Policy*, Vol.54 (Spring 1984).

11. Not everyone agress that Islamid radicals present a major threat to Western interests. A good overview of the challenge presented by Islamic radicals that argues against exaggerating its negative impact is presented by Graham Fuller, "Islamic Fundamentalism in the Northern Tier Countries: An Integrative View," R-3966-USDP (Santa Monica, Calif.: RAND Corporation, 1991).

12. For an optimistic view of the development of a Palestinian state, see William B. Quandt, "The Urge for Democracy," *Foreign Affairs* Vol.73, No.4 (July/August 1994) pp.2–7; for a pessimistic view, see Amos Perlmutter, "Arafat's Police State," *Foreign Affairs* Vol.73, No.4 (July/Aug.) pp.8–11. A concise examination of some of the immediate problems of the peace process is made by Robert O. Freedman, "Israeli Security After the Signing," *Midstream*, June/July 1994, pp.6–8.

13. Anwar Sadat, *In Search of Identity: An Autobiography* (New York: Harper & Row, 1978); George Breslauer, "Soviet Policy in the Middle East, 1967-1972: Unalterable Antagonism or Collaborative Competition," in Alexander L. George (ed.), *Managing US Soviet Rivalry: Problems of Crisis Prevention* (Boulder, Col.: Westview Press, 1983), pp.65–106.

14. Edward Morse, "The Coming Oil Revolution," *Foreign Affairs*, Vol.69, No.5 (Winter 1990/91), pp.39, 43, 44. See also Joseph Stanislaw and Daniel Yergin, "Oil: Reopening the Door," *Foreign Affairs*, Vol.72, No.4 (September/October 1993), pp.81–93.

15. For a succinct expression of this view, see Stephen Van Evera, "The United States and the Third World: When to Intervene?" in Kenneth Oye, Robert Lieber, and Donald Rothchild (eds.), *Eagle in a New World: American Grand Strategy in the Post-Cold War World* (New York: HarperCollins, 1992), p.128.

16. For threats to Saudi security, see Nadav Safran, *Saudi Arabia: The Ceaseless Quest for Security* (Cambridge: Belknap Press and Harvard University Press, 1985), pp.357–64.

17. For a comprehensive assessment of proliferation prospects, see Leonard S. Spector with Jacqueline R. Smith, *Nuclear Ambitions* (Boulder, Col.: Westview Press, 1990).
18. See, for example, Philip J. Hilts, "'Tally of Ex-Soviets' A-Arms Stirs Worry," *New York Times*, 16 March 1992, p.A3, noting unconfirmed reports that two or three tactical nuclear weapons missing from Kazakhstan may have wound up in neighboring Iran.
19. These points are persuasively made in the Middle East context by Shai Feldman, *Israeli Nuclear Deterrence: A Strategy for the 1980s* (New York: Columbia University Press, 1982). For a more general argument that proliferation will be stabilizing, see Kenneth Waltz in "The Spread of Nuclear Weapons: More May Be Better", *Adelphi Papers*, No.171 (London: International Institute of Strategic Studies, 1981).
20. Nadav Safran, *Israel: The Embattled Ally* (Cambridge, Mass.: Belknap Press, 1978).
21. Gerald Steinberg, "Israeli Responses to the Threat of Chemical Warfare," *Armed Forces and Society*, Vol.20, No.1 (Fall 1993), especially p.89.
22. Scott D. Sagan, "The Perils of Proliferation: Organization Theory, Deterrence Theory, and the Spread of Nuclear Weapons," *International Security*, Vol.18, No.4 (Spring 1994), pp.66–107. Sagan asserts that the nature of military organizations makes nuclear deterrence and the prevention of nuclear accidents problematic. If this argument is correct, it does not bode well for the Middle East given the major role the military can be expected to play in the development of nuclear forces and their command and control.
23. Libyan Television, April 19, 1990, address by Mu'amar Gadaffi to the students of the Higher Institute of Applied Social Sciences at the Great Faith University; in Foreign Broadcast Information Service, *Daily Report: Middle East and Africa*, April 23, 1990; cited by Uzi Rubin, "How Much Does Missile Proliferation Matter?", *Orbis*, Vol.35, No.1 (Winter 1991) p.38.
24. For more on the argument that political contributions are not especially important in determining American support for Israel, see A.F.K. Organski, *The $36 Billion Bargain: Strategy and Politics in US Assistance to Israel* (New York: Columbia University Press, 1990). Organski makes the case that strategic interests have been far more important than pro-Israeli lobbying groups in explaining American support. For an overall view of foreign aid to Israel, see Marvin Feuerwerger, *Congress and Israel: Foreign Aid Decisionmaking in the House of Representatives* (Westport, Conn.: Greenwood Press, 1979).

PART II

U.S. Public Attitudes Toward Israel: A Study of the Attentive and Issue Publics

SHIBLEY TELHAMI AND JON KROSNICK

In international relations scholars' study of the factors that shape foreign policy decisions, a great deal of work has been done to U.S. policy toward Israel. Among the many factors apparently influencing decisions in this arena are American national interests in the Middle East, pro-Israeli lobbying efforts in Washington, the opinions of elite foreign policy opinion leaders, and U.S. public opinion. Our focus in this paper is on this latter factor: public opinion.

Political theorists have proposed various models seeking to account for the relation between public preferences and public policy.[1] Yet past studies of U.S. public opinion toward Israel have been driven nearly exclusively by only one of these: the majoritarian view. In this essay, we explore the potential utility of two alternative possibilities: the guardianship and pluralist perspectives. We begin below by outlining these various perspectives and reviewing previous studies' findings regarding U.S. public opinion on the Arab–Israeli conflict. Then, we report the results of two surveys we conducted to see whether adopting the guardianship or pluralist perspectives might yield usefully different empirical findings from those of most relevance to the majoritarian view.

MODELS OF PUBLIC OPINION INFLUENCE

According to the *majoritarian* view of public opinion influence, policymakers may at times identify the policy preference of the majority of their constituents on some issue, and then pursue that policy. If such influence occurred in the case of the Arab–Israeli conflict, we would expect a majority of the American public to hold opinions consistent with U.S. behavior toward Israel. If a majority

Shibley Telhami is Professor of Government at Cornell University. Jon Krosnick is Professor of Political Science at Ohio State University.

was instead opposed to courses of actions typically taken by the U.S., majoritarians would conclude that no correspondence exists between public opinion and U.S. policy toward Israel. Thus, it would seem unlikely that policy was shaped by the public's will.

The *guardianship* view focuses on the stratification of democratic electorates in terms of their knowledge about and involvement in politics.[2] This view was offered particularly clearly by Almond,[3] who argued that only a subset of democratic citizens are likely to be cognitively engaged in the affairs of politics and are therefore likely to exert any influence upon them. Specifically, Almond suggested, "the college-educated group constitutes... the most alert, informed, interested, and discriminating audience for public policy decisions."[4] It is among this *attentive public*, as Almond called it, that the correspondence between public opinion and government action should be the strongest.

Advocates of the third perspective, the *pluralist* view, would argue that one should not expect to observe correspondence between public policy and the preferences of the majority of either the general public or the attentive public.[5] As Dahl outlined,[6] the legitimacy of a democratic government is likely to be significantly eroded over time if it ignores the wills of intense minorities in order to pursue the weak preferences of majorities. Therefore, one should only expect to see correspondence between government policy on an issue and the opinions of those citizens who have strong feelings on that particular issue. With regard to the Arab-Israeli conflict, pluralists would therefore be most interested in the opinions of what Converse called the relevant *issue public*.[7]

These three visions of how public opinion impacts on policy-making could be realized through a variety of different processes.[8] First, policymakers could gauge public sentiment by consulting opinion poll results and then pursue policies that enjoy majority support. Alternatively, citizens could use their policy preferences on an issue to decide which candidates for public office to support, thus enhancing the likelihood that elected officials will share these preferences. Finally, individual citizens can communicate their views on an issue directly to policymakers.

UNDERSTANDING U.S. POLICY IN THE MIDDLE EAST

The viability of the majoritarian, guardianship, and pluralist visions of public influence can presumably be gauged by examining the correspondence between public policy on an issue and the relevant preferences of the general public or portions thereof. Of course, correspondence does not necessarily indicate that influence has occurred.[9] But lack of correspondence would certainly call into question the influence hypothesis.

Fortunately, many studies of American public opinion toward Israel have been reported, but nearly all have focused exclusively on the general public as a whole. Some such studies have identified significant, understandable variations in Americans' support for Israel during the last 40 years. At the same time, however, there appears to have been consistency in opinions over the long haul: at least two to three times as many Americans have typically reported being more sympathetic toward Israel than have reported being more sympathetic toward the Arabs, and this ratio was even greater during some periods, such as the early 1970s. Thus, one can legitimately conclude from this evidence that there has been substantially more public support for Israel than for the Arabs over the years. To the extent that U.S. policy has been consistent with this preference, the former can conceivably be attributed at least partly to the influence of the latter.

However, some evidence questions the viability of the majoritarian perspective in this context. First, large proportions of Americans, sometimes as many as one-third to one-half of the nation, have said they were equally sympathetic toward both sides or had no opinion one way or the other. This could be viewed as representing a challenge to the majoritarian perspective, because it could be argued that the overall majority has taken no clear stand on the issue, thus leaving government free to base its decisions on other considerations. Furthermore, Iyengar and Suleiman's longitudinal analysis showed that changes in U.S. policy toward Israel tended to precede later, consonant changes in general public opinion, rather than shifts in general public opinion on this issue preceding (and therefore perhaps causing) consonant changes in policymaking.[10] Thus, it is unclear whether or not the majoritarian perspective is viable.

Although no detailed studies have yet examined preferences regarding the Arab–Israeli conflict of attentive public or issue public members, psychological studies suggest that these opinions are likely to have just the features necessary for significant impact on government. First, people who are especially interested or involved in an issue tend to hold attitudes that are unusually resistant to change.[11] Thus, government actions are unlikely to shape attentive and/or issue public members' views. This suggests that Iyengar and Suleiman's[12] pattern of causal flow is likely to have been due to opinion dynamics among non-members, not among members.

Because attentive public and issue public members' preferences most likely remain firmly crystallized, they persistently demand a response from government. Furthermore, prolonged interest in and thought about an issue leads people's attitudes to become more polarized.[13] Thus, preferences regarding U.S. action toward Israel may well be decisively one-sided among the attentive and/or issue publics. Such one-sidedness would presumably exert more pressure on government than the largely neutral stance of the general public. For all these reasons, then, there is reason to believe that careful study of the attentive and issue publics may shed new light on the relation between public opinion and public policy in the Arab–Israeli arena.

The investigation described below represents a first step in exploring the potential utility of studying the attentive and issue publics in this domain. Specifically, we conducted two representative sample surveys to examine whether the policy preferences held by attentive public and issue public members were distinct from those of non-members. If these groups indeed adopted distinct profiles of attitudes, then a full account of public pressures on the U.S. government in this arena would seem to necessitate addressing the roles of these subgroups.

RESEARCH METHODS: IDENTIFYING ATTENTIVE PUBLIC AND ISSUE PUBLIC MEMBERS

The first step in designing such an investigation is the selection of methods to identify members of the attentive and issue publics in surveys. Fortunately, distinguishing attentive public members from non-members is relatively straightforward in the light of explications of the guardianship thesis and past empirical explorations of it. Just as Almond asserted,[14] various indicators of general political knowledge and involvement are fairly strongly positively correlated with one another, and all are positively correlated with the amount of formal education citizens have received.[15] Certainly, educational attainment reflects many other attributes of individuals as well, including their cognitive skills,[16] their incomes and occupations,[17] and more. But our goal here is simply to use educational attainment as an empirical handle to identify attentive public members in a descriptive sense, not to identify the particular aspects of them that are *causally* responsible for their attention levels or their attitudes. Therefore, education appears to be an effective tool for this investigation.

Differentiating issue public members from non-members, however, is a more controversial decision, because it can be done in a number of different ways. Perhaps most simply, some analysts have apparently presumed that all people who take sides on an issue feel strongly about it and are therefore issue public members, and all individuals who profess neutrality or no opinion at all are non-members.[18] Of course, taking this approach begs the question we wish to ask, because non-members, by definition, will not lean one way or the other on the issue. But more importantly, stimulated by Converse's "non-attitudes" hypothesis,[19] survey researchers have shown that respondents sometimes offer opinions on issues that do not in fact represent real or strong attitudes.[20] This suggests that all people who offer opinions in surveys should not necessarily be considered members of the issue public.

Another possible approach is to focus on demographically-defined groups that seem especially likely to be concerned about and invested in a particular issue.[21] However, if the Arab–Israeli issue public is at all of a magnitude comparable to that of U.S. issue publics on other issues,[22] then it may be quite a bit larger than the 2.5 per cent of Americans who are Jewish. Indeed, it seems plausible that some members of the American public (for example, Arab-Americans) may be strongly invested in the issue and yet take an anti-Israeli view. One could attempt to use demographics such as religion, ethnicity, and place of residence to identify individuals who are presumably especially concerned about this issue. But such an approach hinges on potentially tenuous assumptions about links between demographics and concern about the issue, and it seems possible that this demographically-driven approach may fail to fully identify all issue public members or may inappropriately include people who have no passionate feelings on the issue.

A third possible approach to identifying issue public members in surveys is to use citizens' reports of how important the issue is to them personally.[23] A great deal of research has shown that people who consider an issue to be personally important do indeed appear to be more cognitively and behaviorally involved in the issue in a variety of ways. Therefore, personal importance seems like an effective indicator with which to distinguish issue public members from non-members. No studies have yet applied this technique in the study of the Arab–Israeli issue, so we set out to do so.

We also considered another possible approach, involving a somewhat different measure: respondents' reports of how important the issue is *for the nation as a whole*. The view of voters as "sociotropic" rather than selfish in their thinking about economics[24] suggests that considering an issue to be nationally important might be more motivating than simply considering it to be personally important. We therefore explored the possibility of using national importance judgments to identify members of the Arab–Israeli issue public. Furthermore, following the example of Young, Borgida, Sullivan, and Aldrich,[25] we considered the possibility that issue public members may be those individuals who consider an issue both highly important to them personally *and* highly important for the country as a whole.

Finally, we took a step further to explore the pluralists' perspective. From their viewpoint, especially passionate issue public members are likely to shape government policy either by communicating their views directly to government officials or by voting for candidates who share their views. Thus, the most influential citizens on this issue might be those who report exerting pressure on government in either of these two ways.[26] Consequently, we assessed whether the policy preferences of these individuals regarding the Arab-Israeli conflict were different from those of the general American public.

NATIONAL SURVEY OF AMERICAN PUBLIC OPINION

Data

Our first study was done by including a series of questions in a national survey conducted by International Communications Research, Inc. (ICR) in late December, 1988 (see the Appendix for exact question wordings).[27] Two questions were intended to gauge each respondent's general loyalties regarding the Arab-Israeli conflict. One asked whether the respondent's general sympathies leaned toward the Arabs, the Israelis, both equally, or neither. The second item gauged attitudes by assessing people's reactions to the Palestinian uprisings that occurred in 1988. Psychological studies have shown that people's attitudes color their perceptions of events in ways that reinforce those attitudes.[28] We therefore asked respondents whether the Palestinian uprisings aroused in them feelings of sympathy for the Israelis, the Palestinians, or neither.

Two other attitude questions tapped respondents' opinions on specific policy issues. One asked whether respondents favored Israeli withdrawal from occupied territories, opposed withdrawal, or neither favored nor opposed it. The other item asked respondents whether they favored Israel initiating a dialogue with the PLO. With these latter two items, we were able to gauge respondent support for the official positions taken by the Israeli government in 1988: opposition to both withdrawal from the occupied territories and dialogue with the PLO.

To gauge issue public membership, respondents were asked about the importance of the Arab/Israeli conflict to them personally, the importance of the Arab/Israeli conflict for the U.S., the impact their views on the Arab/Israeli conflict had on their candidate preferences during the 1988 presidential election campaign, and whether they had ever taken any actions to directly express their views on the Arab/Israeli conflict to a government official. To assess attentive public membership, respondents were asked how many years of formal education they had received.[29]

Results

1. *General public attitudes.* As expected, opinions in the full sample reflected majority neutrality on the general sympathies question (see Table 1). Very few respondents said they were more sympathetic toward the Arabs (7.3 per cent); more respondents expressed greater

sympathy toward Israel (22.6 per cent); and the greatest number (70.1 percent) said they had equal sympathies or had no sympathies one way or the other.[30] The ratio of Israeli supporters to Arab supporters was 3.1; that is, Israeli supporters outnumbered Arab supporters by more than 3 to 1. Similarly, most respondents said they had no sympathies one way or the other regarding the Palestinian uprisings (55.2 per cent). However, the ratio of Israeli to Palestinian sympathizers on that item was only 1.1.

TABLE 1
NATIONAL SURVEY: GENERAL PUBLIC ATTITUDES

Attitude	Proportion of total sample
Sympathy	
Arabs	7.3%
Israelis	22.6
Equal or No Sympathy	70.1
Ratio: Israeli/Arab supporters	3.1
Uprisings	
Palestinians	15.5%
Israelis	17.3
Neither	55.2
Ratio: Israeli/Pal. sympathizers	1.1
Israeli Withdrawal	
Favor	54.5%
Oppose	14.3
Neither	31.3
Ratio: Oppose/Favor	.3
Dialogue	
Yes	72.9%
No	27.1
Ratio: No/Yes	.4
N	512

Majorities of all respondents said that Israel should withdraw from the occupied territories (54.4 percent) and should initiate a dialogue with the PLO (72.9 percent), thus disagreeing with the Israeli government's official positions on these issues. The ratios of respondents endorsing these official positions to those opposing them were .3 and .4 for withdrawal and dialogue, respectively.

2. *Attitudes of the attentive public.* As expected, the general sympathies of attentive public members were different from those of non-members: members were significantly less likely to be neutral than non-members (see the first two columns of Table 2).[31] Interestingly, the ratio of pro-Israeli sympathizers to pro-Arab

TABLE 2. NATIONAL SURVEY: RELATION OF ATTITUDES TO EDUCATION, PERSONAL IMPORTANCE, AND NATIONAL IMPORTANCE

Sample

Attitude	Education — High	Education — Low	Education — Ratio: High/Low	Personal Importance — High	Personal Importance — Low	Personal Importance — Ratio: High/Low	National Importance — High	National Importance — Low	National Importance — Ratio: High/Low	Personal & National Importance — High	Personal & National Importance — Low	Personal & National Importance — Ratio: High/Low
Sympathy												
Arabs	10.4%	6.4%		9.1%	7.1%		6.7%	7.8%		5.9%	7.1%	
Israelis	28.7	20.5		27.3	22.1		32.6	20.3		41.2	20.7	
Equal or No Symp.	60.9	73.1		63.6	70.8		60.6	71.9		52.9	72.2	
	$x^2(2)=6.4$, $p<.05$			$x^2(2)=1.7$, n.s.			$x^2(2)=6.1$, $p<.05$			$x^2(2)=7.2$, $p<.03$		
Ratio: Israelis/Arabs	2.8	3.2	.9	3.0	3.1	1.0	4.9	2.6	1.9	7.0	2.9	2.4
Uprisings												
Palestinians	31.9%	12.5%		22.6%	17.0%		20.2%	17.1%		18.8%	16.0%	
Israelis	15.0	21.4		32.1	16.4		32.1	17.1		50.0	16.0	
Neither	53.1	66.1		45.2	66.7		47.6	65.8		31.3	67.0	
	$x^2(2)=21.9$, $p<.001$			$x^2(2)=14.8$, n.s.			$x^2(2)=11.7$, $p<.003$			$x^2(2)=23.3$, $p<.001$		
Ratio: Israelis/Pal.	.5	1.7	.3	1.4	1.0	1.4	1.6	1.0	1.6	2.7	1.0	2.7
Israeli Withdrawal												
Favor	64.1%	50.6%		55.8%	54.4%		61.9%	52.8%		58.1%	53.2%	
Oppose	16.2	13.8		19.8	13.5		22.6	12.7		19.4	11.6	
Neither	19.7	35.6		24.4	32.1		15.5	34.5		22.6	35.2	
	$x^2(2)=10.3$, $p<.01$			$x^2(2)=3.2$, n.s.			$x^2(2)=14.5$, $p<.001$			$x^2(2)=2.8$, n.s.		
Ratio: Oppose/Favor	.3	.3	.9	.4	.3	1.4	.4	.2	1.5	.3	.2	1.5
Dialogue												
Yes	76.1%	71.3%		70.5%	73.0%		73.1%	72.3%		69.0%	72.2%	
No	23.9	28.7		29.5	27.0		26.9	27.7		31.0	27.8	
	$x^2(1)=1.0$, n.s.			$x^2(1)=0.1$, n.s.			$x^2(1)=0.2$, n.s.			$x^2(1)=0.1$, n.s.		
Ratio: No/Yes	.3	.4	.8	.4	.4	1.1	.4	.4	1.0	.5	.4	1.2
N	120	381		95	367		91	382		34	294	
Average Ratio: High/Low			.7			1.2			1.5			2.0

sympathizers was 2.8 among attentive public members, whereas it was 3.2 among non-members.

The same pattern appeared for the uprisings item. Attentive public members were less likely to have been unaffected than non-members. And among those who were affected, a majority of attentive public members were more sympathetic toward the Palestinians than the Israelis (the ratio of Israeli to Palestinian sympathizers was .5). This pattern was reversed among non-members, where the majority of those taking sides were more sympathetic toward the Israelis (the ratio of Israeli to Palestinian sympathizers was 1.7).

The same pattern of decreased neutrality among members was apparent in the policy item on withdrawal (which was the only one to measure neutrality). And the slight leaning against official Israeli policy was apparent in the dialogue item. In fact, across all four attitude indicators, attentive public members were less supportive of Israel and its government's positions than were non-members. The ratios in the third column of Table 2 are all less than one, averaging .7 (shown in the bottom row).

3. *Attitudes of the issue public.* Issue public membership was also associated with reduced neutrality on the general sympathies, uprisings, and withdrawal questions, regardless of how issue public membership was operationalized (see columns 4 through 12 of Table 2).[32] Furthermore, in contrast to the attentive public, issue public members were generally more supportive of Israel and its government's positions than were non-members. Consistent with Young, Borgida, Sullivan, and Aldrich's approach,[33] this pattern was most apparent when issue public membership was operationalized via the conjunction of personal and national importance (see columns 10 through 12 of Table 2), where the average ratio of members to non-members in terms of pro-Israeli leaning was 2.0.

The same general pattern is apparent in comparisons of people separated according to attitude expression (see Table 3). Again, neutrality was less common among individuals who expressed their attitudes either directly or indirectly than among those who did not. Furthermore, the average ratios at the bottoms of columns 3 and 6 of Table 3 are again positive (1.1 and 1.8, respectively), indicating that attitude expressers were more supportive of Israel and its government's positions than were non-expressers.

4. *Independence of the attentive public and the issue public.* Membership in the attentive public was generally independent of membership in the issue public. In fact, education was uncorrelated with personal importance ($r = -.05$, n.s.), national importance ($r = -.05$, n.s.), and the conjunction of the two ($r = -.04$, n.s.). Although education was negatively correlated with indirect attitude expression via voting ($r = -.13$, $p < .01$) and positively correlated with direct attitude expression ($r = .18$, $p < .001$), both of these relations are relatively weak. Therefore, the

relation between attentive public membership and attitudes was apparently independent of the relation of issue public membership to attitudes.[34]

TABLE 3
NATIONAL SURVEY: RELATION ATTITUDES TO ATTITUDE EXPRESSION

	Sample					
	Direct Expression			Indirect Expression		
Attitude	Yes	No	Ratio: Yes/No	Yes	No	Ratio Yes/No
Sympathy						
Arabs	25.0%	6.2%		7.4%	7.5%	
Israelis	42.9	21.2		27.9	21.8	
Equal or No Symp.	32.2	72.5		64.7	70.7	
	$x^2(2)=24.1$, p<.001			$x^2(2)=1.2$, n.s.		
Ratio: Israelis/Arabs	1.7	3.4	.5	3.8	2.9	1.3
Uprisings						
Palestinians	35.7%	16.4%		15.9%	18.2%	
Israelis	21.4	19.5		31.9	16.8	
Neither	42.9	64.1		52.2	65.0	
	$x^2(2)=7.5$, p<.03			$x^2(2)=8.5$, p<.02		
Ratio: Israelis/Pals.	.6	.2	.5	2.0	.9	2.2
Israeli Withdrawal						
Favor	66.7%	53.6%		50.7%	55.8%	
Oppose	25.9	13.6		20.3	13.5	
Neither	7.4	32.8		29.0	30.7	
	$x^2(2)=10.4$, p<.01			$x^2(2)=2.0$, n.s.		
Ratio: Israelis/Arabs	.4	.3	1.6	.4	.2	1.7
Dialogue						
Yes	64.0%	73.5%		62.5%	75.2%	
No	36.0	26.5		37.5	24.8	
	$x^2(1)=1.0$, n.s.			$x^2(1)=4.1$, p<.05		
Ratio: Israelis/Arabs	.6	.4	1.6	.6	.3	1.8
N	28	433		69	358	
Average Ratio: High/Low			1.2			1.8

SURVEY OF OHIO RESIDENTS

Data

Our second study was designed to assess whether these same patterns could be replicated in an independent survey. For this study, the Polimetrics Laboratory at the Ohio State University interviewed a representative sample of 403 adults living in the state of Ohio by telephone during January and February, 1990. Respondents were telephone during January and February, 1990. Respondents were asked the sympathies, uprisings, withdrawal, dialogue, personal importance, and educational attainment questions used in the national survey (see the Appendix for details).[35]

TABLE 4

OHIO SURVEY: RELATION OF ATTITUDES TO EDUCATION AND PERSONAL IMPORTANCE

Attitude	Total Sample	Education			Personal Importance		
		High	Low	Ratio: High/Low	High	Low	Ratio: High/Low
Sympathy							
Arabs	4.0%	6.3%	3.2%		9.7%	3.5%	
Israelis	19.5	33.3	14.8		41.9	17.4	
Equal or No Sympathy	76.5	60.4	82.0		48.4	79.1	
		$x^2(2)=18.6$, p<.001			$x^2(2)=15.0$, p<.001		
Ratio: Israelis/Arabs	4.9	5.2	4.6	1.1	4.4	5.0	.9
Uprisings							
Palestinians	8.8%	16.3%	6.3%		6.9%	9.1%	
Israelis	11.8	17.4	10.0		24.1	10.7	
Neither	79.4	66.3	83.7		69.0	80.2	
		$x^2(2)=13.6$, p<.002			$x^2(2)=4.7$, p<.10		
Ratio: Israelis/Pals.	1.3	1.1	1.6	.7	3.5	1.2	2.9
Israeli Withdrawal							
Favor	41.6%	49.5%	38.9%		41.9%	41.2%	
Oppose	15.5	19.4	14.3		29.0	14.3	
Neither	42.9	31.2	46.8		29.0	44.5	
		$x^2(2)=7.0$, p<.04			$x^2(2)=5.5$, p<.07		
Ratio: Israelis/Arabs	.4	.4	.4	1.1	.7	.3	2.0
Dialogue							
Yes	66.6%	69.7%	65.2%		53.6%	67.5%	
No	33.4%	30.3	34.8		46.4	32.5	
		$x^2(1)=0.6$, n.s.			$x^2(1)=2.2$, n.s.		
Ratio: Israelis/Arabs	.5	.4	.5	.8	.9	.5	1.8
N	401	98	303		32	356	
Average Ratio: High/Low				.9			1.9

Results

The Ohio sample closely resembled the national sample in terms of the overall distributions of opinions (see the first column of Table 4). Three-quarters of Ohioans (76.5 per cent) expressed equal sympathies or no sympathies. And about five times as many people expressed more sympathy toward the Israelis (19.5 per cent) than expressed more sympathy toward the Arabs (4.0 per cent). Likewise, the majority of the Ohio sample had no sympathies spurred by the uprisings, and more of those who did take sides felt more sympathies toward the Israelis (11.8 per cent) than felt sympathy toward the Palestinians (8.8 per cent). And as in the national sample, minorities of Ohioans expressed views agreeing with the Israeli government's official positions on the withdrawal issue (15.5 per cent) and the dialogue issue (33.4 per cent). Thus, the ratios of pro-Israeli positions to pro-Arab positions were 4.9, 1.3, .4, and .5, respectively, for the four attitude measures.

As in the national survey, neutrality was less common among attentive public members than non-members on the first three attitude items. And pro-Israeli sentiment was no more prevalent among attentive public members than among non-members: the average ratio in the fourth column of Table 4 was .9. However, issue public membership was again associated with increased support for Israel and its government's positions: the average ratio in column 7 of Table 4 was 1.9.

Finally, the relation of membership in the attentive public to membership in the issue public was comparable to that observed in the national sample. The Pearson product-moment correlation between education and personal importance here was .09 ($p < .05$, $N = 386$). Although statistically significant, this very weak association suggests that attentive public membership was essentially orthogonal to issue public membership.

DISCUSSION

The Issue Public

In sum, we found two sizable and robust differences between the opinions of issue public members and non-members. First, members were less often neutral on the Arab–Israeli conflict than were non-members, a finding consistent with demonstrations on other issues that people who consider an issue to be more important tend to express more extreme preferences.[36] And second, among people who did take sides, issue public members were more supportive of Israel generally and of two of its government's official policy positions than were non-members. This suggests that future investigations of the role of American public opinion in shaping U.S. policy toward Israel may benefit from careful attention to the issue public. That is, because the intense minority on this issue seems to take a stand distinct from that of the general public, the pluralist approach to public influence seems to merit specific study in this case.

Among individuals who expressed general sympathies one way or the other, the majority of the general public supported Israel, and this was even more true in the issue public. Interestingly, this leaning seems to be consistent with that of U.S. foreign policy during the late 1980s, when our surveys were done. U.S. foreign aid to Israel was greater than that given to any other nation and was quite a bit greater than that given to opposing Arab nations. U.S. political support for Israel was quite strong, especially clearly so in the United Nations, where the U.S. was willing to oppose both Arab positions and the positions of a majority of states in the UN in order to pursue Israel's goals. Thus, the general leaning of U.S. policy in the Middle East was apparently closer to the general leaning of issue public members than those of non-members.

This same finding has been obtained in previous studies that examined issue publics concerned about other policy issues as well. And in a combined analysis of numerous public policy issues, Monroe found greater correspondence between general public opinion and government policy on issues that larger proportions of Americans considered to be the most important facing the country.[37] Taken together with the present evidence, these prior studies reinforce the recommendation that future studies exploring public opinion impact on U.S. Arab–Israeli policy should pay special attention to the role of the issue public, because it seems to be more in line with government policy and perhaps more responsible for it.

On the two specific policy issues we examined, the majority of the general public expressed opposition to the Israeli government's official positions in the late 1980s. That is, most of the people who took sides favored withdrawal from the occupied territories and favored dialogue with the PLO. Although the issue public was relatively more opposed to these initiatives and therefore was more in line with official Israeli policies at that time, a majority of those taking sides within the issue public opposed these policies.

This may account in part for developments in U.S. policy in the Middle East that occurred in the early 1990s. At that time, the Bush Administration placed the issue of Israeli territorial compromise high on its list of priorities and took actions accordingly. These various efforts on the part of the U.S. may have occurred at that time partly because U.S. public preferences, and especially those of issue public members, were supportive of these lines of action.

The Attentive Public

As expected, attentive public members expressed neutral stands less often than non-members. However, we found no robust difference between members and non-members in terms of the leaning of individuals who did take sides. If anything, attentive public members appeared to be slightly less pro-Israel than non-members. Interestingly, this finding parallels a pattern that we uncovered through close inspection of Singer and Cohen's tables of the results of an April, 1988 national survey:[38] levels of sympathy toward Israel and the Arab nations was essentially equivalent among both highly-educated Americans and less educated Americans in that survey, with a trend suggesting slightly more sympathy toward Israel among the latter.

This result does not, of course, suggest that no attention should be paid to the guardianship perspective in future studies of the Arab–Israeli conflict. Indeed, this perspective may well prove to be a useful handle for gaining insight into some aspects of U.S. action relating to the Middle East. But our finding does imply that such analysis may be less fruitful than a focus on the issue public. It is certainly possible that a measure of attentive public membership more precise than education would yield different findings than those reported here. So before the guardianship perspective is abandoned completely, it may be worthwhile to consider alternative operationalizations. But for the moment, our results suggest that such efforts may not be especially fruitful. And it may turn out that in this domain, issue public pressure on government ran in the opposite direction to whatever pressure was brought to bear by the attentive public.

Gauging Causality

Although our data reveal unusual correspondence between U.S. foreign policy and general sympathies in the issue public, we certainly cannot conclude that this group influenced policy-making. As Russett has pointed out,[39] such consistency can occur because (1) public opinion shaped public policy, (2) public policy shaped public opinion, (3) each shaped the other, or (4) neither influenced the other, but both were independently shaped by the same national and international events.[40] Thus, evidence of greater opinion-policy consistency in the issue public does not unambiguously support the pluralist view of public influence on government.

However, as we mentioned above, it seems particularly unlikely that such correspondence emerges because public policy shapes the opinions of issue public members. It is true that issue public members are especially likely to be attentive to issue-related events that occur and are therefore likely to be well-informed about government policy.[41] However, issue public members have firmly crystallized attitudes that are highly stable over time[42] and quite resistant to change.[43] Therefore, the correspondence we saw between public policy and the opinions of issue public members is unlikely to represent greater impact of the former on the latter. Furthermore, people who consider an issue to be personally and nationally important are especially likely to express their opinions either directly to government officials or indirectly via voting.[44] Thus, they are exerting pressure on government and are clearly players in this arena with the potential for influence.

One approach to generating more definitive evidence of causal impact of public opinion on policy has been to interview policy-makers themselves and gauge their perceptions of the processes by which decisions were made.[45] However, a vast literature attests to the substantial biases and blind-spots inherent in testimony about the causes of one's own and others' behavior.[46] Fortunately, a clearly preferable method is available: assessing lagged effects of opinion on policy in longitudinal studies. For example, Page and Shapiro examined whether shifts in government policy paralleled shifts in public opinion across a wide range of domestic and international issues and found a great deal of such correspondence.[47] Furthermore, a large fraction of the shifts in public opinion preceded the analogous shifts in policy, thus suggesting a causal impact of the former on the latter.[48] However, as we mentioned above, Iyengar and Suleiman[49] found precisely the opposite results in their study of opinions on the Arab–Israeli conflict, which raises questions about whether Page and Shapiro's[50] general conclusion applies to this particular case. Nonetheless, this sort of approach clearly generates compelling data regarding the causal processes at work.

CONCLUSION

We hope to have illustrated how the majoritarian, guardianship, and pluralist perspectives can be compared and contrasted more precisely when appropriate longitudinal data become available. In particular, to permit evaluation of the pluralist vision, issue public members must be identified in new investigations. Unfortunately, however, issue public membership has been gauged only rarely in public opinion surveys, despite a strong theoretical rationale for doing so.[51] If and when enough surveys have been conducted that include such measures, longitudinal analytic approaches such as Page and Shapiro's[52] can be applied to issue public members in isolation. This method may reveal particularly strong correspondence between opinions and policies and may perhaps thereby locate the sources of greatest influence within electorates. In the meantime, our results justify the collection of the necessary data regarding the Arab–Israeli conflict and should also encourage analysts to consider the potential for issue public opinion influence in this arena more than has been done to date.

The relevance of the issue public is not likely to be substantially affected by changed international circumstances. However, the assumption that the issue-public will remain relatively stable (that is, that relatively stable groups will continue to rank the issue of the

Arab–Israeli conflcit high in their priorities) may be subject to dispute if peace prevails between Israel and the Arab states. If, as one suspects, American Jews and evangelican Christians constitute significant segments of the issue-public, how the priorities of these communities will change will be significant for the issue at hand. This important subject is addressed by others in this volume.

ACKNOWLEDGMENTS

Research for this essay was supported by grants from the Ohio State University Office of Research and Graduate Studies, The Mershon Center, The Ohio State University Department of Political Science, The Ohio State University College of Social and Behavioral Sciences, and the National Science Foundation (Grant BNS-8920430 to the first author). The authors wish to thank Wendy Rahn, Matthew Berent, Shanto Iyengar, Bruce Russett, and Robert Shapiro for especially helpful comments and suggestions. A version of this article appeared in International Studies Quarterly.

NOTES

1. Robert A. Dahl, *A Preface to Democratic Theory* (Chicago: University of Chicago Press, 1956); Robert A. Dahl, *Democracy and Its Critics* (New Haven: Yale University Press, 1989).
2. See, for example, Dahl, *Democracy*; Donald J. Devine, *The Attentive Public* (Chicago: Rand-McNally, 1970); Lester W. Milbrath, *Political Participation* (Chicago: Rand-McNally, 1965); Russell W. Neuman, *The Paradox of Mass Politics* (Cambridge: Harvard University Press, 1986).
3. Gabriel A. Almond, *The American People and Foreign Policy* (New York: Praeger, 1950).
4. Ibid., p. 127.
5. See, for example, Dahl, *Preface*, pp. 90–123.
6. Ibid.
7. Philip E. Converse, "The Nature of Belief Systems in Mass Publics," in David E. Apter (ed.), *Ideology and Discontent* (New York: Free Press, 1964).
8. Anthony Downs, *An Economic Theory of Democracy* (New York: Harper & Row, 1957); E. E. Schattschneider, *Party Government* (New York: Holt, Rinehart & Winston, 1942); Joseph A. Schumpeter, *Capitalism, Socialism, and Democracy* (New York Harper & Row, 1950).
9. Bruce Russett, *Controlling the Sword: The Democratic Governance of National Security* (Cambridge: Harvard University Press, 1990).
10. Shanto Iyengar and Michael Suleiman, "Trends in Public Support for Egypt and Israel, 1956-1978," *American Politics Quarterly*, Vol.8(1980), pp.34–60.
11. T.N. Ewing, "A Study of Certain Factors Involved in Changes of Opinion," *Journal of Social Psychology*, Vol.16 (1942), pp.63–88; H. Hahn, "The Political Impact of Shifting Attitudes," Social Sciences Quarterly, 51 (1970), pp.730–42; Patricia Kendall, *Conflict and Mood: Factors Affecting Stability of Response* (Glencoe, Ill.: Free Press, 1954); Jon A. Krosnick, "Attitude Importance and Attitude Change," *Journal of Experimental Social Psychology*, 24 (1988), pp.240–55.
12. Iyengar and Suleiman, "Trends in Public Support."
13. Abraham Tesser, "Self-Generated Attitude Change," in *Advances in Experimental Social Psychology*, Vol.11, ed. Leonard Berkowitz (San Diego, Calif.: Academic Press, 1978), pp.289–338.
14. Almond, *American People and Foreign Policy.*
15. Jon A. Krosnick and Michael A. Milburn, "Psychological Determinants of Political Opinionation," *Social Cognition*, Vol.8 (1990), pp.49–72; Vincent Price and John Zoller, "Who Gets the News? Alternative Measures of News Reception and their Implications for Research," *Public Opinion Quarterly*, Vol.57 (1993), pp.133–64.
16. Steven J. Ceci, "How Much Does Schooling Influence General Intelligence and Its Cognitive Components? A Reassessment of the Evidence," *Developmental Psychology*, Vol.27 (1991), pp.703–22.
17. Melvin M. Tumin, *Social Stratification* (Englewood Cliffs, N.J.: Prentice-Hall, 1967).

18. See, for example, Joel E. Brooks, "The Opinion-Policy Nexus in Germany," *Public Opinion Quarterly*, Vol.54 (1990), pp.508–29; Benjamin I. Page and Robert Y. Shapiro, "Effects of Public Opinion on Policy," *American Political Science Review*, Vol.77 (1983), pp.175–90.

19. Converse, "Nature of Belief Systems."

20. Hedrick Smith, *The Power Game: How Washington Works* (New York: Ballantine Books, 1988); Jon A. Krosnick and Robert P. Abelson, "The Case for Measuring Attitude Strength in Surveys," in Judith Tanur (ed.), *Questions About Questions: Inquiries Into the Cognitive Bases of Surveys* (New York: Russell Sage, 1992); Howard Schuman and Stanley Pressler, *Questions and Answers in Attitude Surveys: Experiments on Question Form*, (Wording and Context (New York: Academic Press, 1981).

21. Eytan Gilboa, "Attitudes of American Jews Toward Israel: Trends Over Time," *American Jewish Year Book*, Vol.86 (1986), pp.110–25; A.F.K. Organski, *The $36 Billion Bargain: Strategy and Politics in U.S. Assistance to Israel* (New York: Columbia University Press, 1990); Benjamin I. Page and Robert Y. Shapiro, *The Rational Public: Fifty Years of Trends in America's Policy Preferences* (Chicago: University of Chicago Press, 1992).

22. See Jon A. Krosnick, "Government Policy and Citizen Passion: A Study of Issue Publics in Contemporary America," *Political Behavior*, Vol.12 (1990), pp.59–92.

23. David J. Elkins, *Manipulation and Consent: How Voters and Leaders Manage Complexity* (Vancouver: University of British Columbia Press, 1993); Jon A. Krosnick, "The Role of Attitude Importance in Social Evaluation: A Study of Policy Preferences, Presidential Candidate Evaluations, and Voting Behavior," *Journal of Personality and Social Psychology*, 55 (1988), pp.196–210; Krosnick, "Attitude Importance and Attitude Change"; Krosnick, "Government Policy"; Jon D. Miller, *The American People and Science Policy* (New York: Pergamon Press, 1983).

24. Donald R. Kinder, Gordon S. Adams, and Paul W. Gronke, "Economics and Politics in the 1984 American Presidential Election," *American Journal of Political Science*, Vol.33 (1989), pp.491–515; Donald R. Kinder and D. Roderick Kiewiet, "Economic Discontent and Political Behavior: The Role of Personal Grievances and Collective Economic Judgments in Congressional Voting," *American Journal of Political Science*, Vol.23 (1979), pp.495–517; Donald R. Kinder and Walter R. Mebane, Jr., "Politics and Economics in Everyday Life," in Kristen R. Monroe (ed.), *The Political Process and Economic Change* (New York: Agathon, 1983).

25. Jason Young, Eugene Borgida, John Sullivan, and John Aldrich, "Personal Agendas and the Relationship Between Self-Interest and Voting Behavior," Social Psychology Quarterly, 50 (1987), pp.64–71.

26. Schuman and Presser, *Questions and Answers*; S.K. Henshaw and G. Martire, "Morality and Legality," *Family Planning Perspectives*, Vol.14 (1982), pp.53–60; Pamela J. Conover, Virginia Gray, and S. Coombs, "Single-Issue Voting: Elite-Mass Linkages," *Political Behavior*, 4 (1982), pp.309–31.

27. The total sample for the survey was 1018 American adults, half of whom (randomly selected) were asked our questions. Due to interview non-completion and quota restraints, the sample on which our analyses are based is 512 American adults. The sample was a fully-replicated stratified single-stage random-digit-dial design (see Howard Schuman and Graham Kalton, "Survey Methods," in Gardner Lindsey and Eliott Aronson (eds.), *Handbook of Social Psychology* (New York: Random House, 1984); J. Waksberg, "Sample Methods for Random Digit Dialing," *Journal of the American Statistical Association*, Vol.50 (1978), pp.64–71.

28. For example, R.P. Vallone, Lee Ross, and Mark R. Lepper, "The Hostile Media Phenomenon: Biased Perception and Perceptions of Media Bias in Coverage of the Beirut Massacre," *Journal of Personality and Social Psychology*, Vol.49 (1985), pp.577–585.

29. Unfortunately, the survey included no measurement of religion or ethnicity or other demographics that ought to be related to issue public membership.

30. "Don't know" responses to this and all other questions were treated as missing data and dropped from all analyses reported here.

However, there is a crucial and significant difference between the question wordings used in those surveys and that used in ours that is undoubtedly responsible for this discrepancy. Whereas we explicitly offered the "neither" and "equal" alternatives *separately* to our respondents, Roper and Penn and Schoen (*Roper Reports*, 91–3, New York: Roper Organization, 1991), did not. They simply asked their respondents whether their sympathies were more with Israel or more with the Arabs, so people who offered the "neither" or "equal" responses in their surveys were volunteering those answers on their own. Schuman and Presser (Howard Schuman and Stanley Presser, *Questions and Answers in Attitude Surveys: Experiments on Question Form, Wording and Content*, New York: Academic Press, 1981) have shown that omitting response alternative in this way suppresses the number of people who offer those responses, as compared to when they are offered explicitly. Therefore, our results undoubtedly obtained more "neither" and "equal" responses than the other surveys for this reason.

31. Consistent with Almond's (*American People and Foreign Policy*) perspective, respondents who graduated from college were treated as members of the attentive public, and individuals who had attained less formal education were treated as non-members.

32. Individuals who said the issue was the single most important to them personally or one of the two or three most important were assigned to the high personal importance group. Those who said the issue was less important to them personally were placed in the low personal importance group. Respondents who said the issue was extremely important for the U.S. as a whole were placed in the high national importance group, and those who said the issue was less important for the country were placed in the low national importance group. Individuals who said the issue was the single most important or one of the two or three most important were assigned to the indirect expression group. Those who said the issue was less important were considered non-members of this group.

33. Young, Borgida, Sullivan, and Aldrich, "Personal Agendas."

34. We also explored the relations of issue public membership (as measured in the various different ways) to the demographic variables we had available in the survey (race, age, and income). Although some correlations suggested more issue public members among older adults, the result did not replicate across all measures. Furthermore, there was no relation between issue public membership and either race or income. Therefore, issue public membership does not seem to be linked to such variables for this issue.

35. Again, this survey did not include measures of religion, ethnicity, or other such demographic variables that might be related to issue public membership.

36. Edward Brent and Donald Granberg, "Subjective Agreement and the Presidential Candidates of 1976 and 1980," *Journal of Personality and Social Psychology*, Vol.42 (1982), pp.393–403.

37. Alan D. Monroe, "Consistency Between Public Preferences and National Policy Decision," *American Politics Quarterly*, Vol.7 (1979), pp.3–19.

38. D. Singer and Renae Cohen, *In the Wake of the Palestinian Uprisings: Findings of the April 1988 Roper Poll* (New York: American Jewish Committee, 1988).

39. Bruce Russett, *Controlling the Sword: The Democratic Governance of National Security* (Cambridge: Harvard University Press, 1990).

40. See also James L. Gibson, "Political Intolerance and Political Repression During the McCarthy Red Scare," *American Political Science Review*, Vol.82 (1988), pp.511–29.

41. Matthew K. Berent and Jon A. Krosnick, "Attitude Importance and Memory for Attitude-Relevant Information," unpublished manuscript, Ohio State University, 1993; Matthew K. Berent and Jon A. Krosnick, "Attitude Importance and Selective Exposure to Attitude-Relevant Information," unpublished manuscript, Ohio State University, 1993.

42. Krosnick, "Attitude Importance and Attitude Change"; Schuman and Presser, *Questions and Answers.*

43. B.J. Fine, "Conclusion-Drawing, Communicator Credibility, and Anxiety as Factors in Opinion Change," *Journal of Abnormal and Social Psychology*, Vol.54 (1957), pp.369–74; G.J. Gorn, "The Effects of Personal Involvement, Communication Discrepancy, and Source Prestige on Reactions to Communications on Separatism," *Canadian Journal of Behavioral Science*, Vol.7 (1975), pp.369–86.

44. Leandre R. Fabrigar, Jon A. Krosnick, and Joanne M. Miller, "What Motivates Issue Public Membership? Distinguishing Between Personal Importance and National Importance," unpublished manuscript, Ohio State University, 1994.

45. For example, Bernard C. Cohen, *The Public's Impact on Foreign Policy* (Boston: Little, Brown, 1973).

46. Richard E. Nisbett and Timothy Wilson, "Telling More than We Know: Verbal Reports on Mental Processes," *Psychological Review*, Vol.84 (1977), pp.231–59.

47. Benjamin I. Page and Robert Y. Shapiro, "Effects of Public Opinion on Policy," *American Political Science Review*, Vol.77 (1983), pp.175–90.

48. Thomas Hartley and Bruce Russett, "Public Opinion and the Common Defense: Who Governs Military Spending in the United States?" *American Political Science Review*, 86 (1992), pp.905–15; William Mishler and Reginald S. Sheehan, "The Supreme Court as a Countermajoritarian Institution? The Impact of Public Opinion on Supreme Court Decisions," *American Political Science Review*, Vol.87 (1993), pp.87–101.
49. Iyengar and Suleiman, "Trends in Public Support."
50. Page and Shapiro, "Effects of Public Opinion."
51. See Krosnick and Abelson, "Case for Measuring Attitude Strength."
52. Page and Shapiro, "Effects of Public Opinion."

APPENDIX: QUESTION WORDINGS

NATIONAL SURVEY

Our section of the interview began with the following introduction: "During the last few years, there has been a major dispute between Arabs and Israelis in the Middle East over what should become of the occupied territories on the West Bank and Gaza. The next few questions are about your opinions on this topic."

Respondents were then asked ten questions, eight of which are used here. There were actually two different sets of these questions, each of which was asked of a randomly selected half of our sample. The wordings of these questions were varied slightly across the two forms. Specifically, the orders of the response alternatives were varied in order to minimize the impact of response order effects on the marginal distributions of responses (Krosnick and Alwin 1987). The wordings of the Form A questions and the variations for Form B are indicated below:

Sympathy. First of all, in thinking about the Arab/Israeli conflict generally, are you more sympathetic toward the Israelis, more sympathetic toward the Arabs, are you equally sympathetic to both sides, or do you have no sympathies one way or the other? (In Form B, the order of the first two response choices was reversed.)

Israeli Withdrawal. One proposed solution to the Arab/Israeli conflict would be for Israel to withdraw from the occupied territories in exchange for peace. Are you inclined to favor this approach, inclined to oppose this approach, or do you neither favor nor oppose it? (In Form B, the order of the first two response choices was reversed.)

Uprisings. Did the recent Palestinian uprising make you more sympathetic toward the Palestinians, more sympathetic toward the Israelis, or did it have no effect on your sympathies? (In Form B, the order of the first two response choices was reversed.)

Dialogue. Given recent events, do you feel that Israel should initiate a dialogue with the PLO or Palestine Liberation Organization?

National Importance. How important would you say the Arab/Israeli conflict is for the security and welfare of the United States as a whole? Is it extremely important, very important, somewhat important, or not too important? (The order of the response choices was reversed in Form B.)

Personal Importance. As compared to your feelings on other political issues, how important is the Arab/Israeli conflict to you personally? Is it the single most important political issue to you, one of the two or three most important issues, one of the five most important issues, or is it not among the five issues you personally consider most important? (The order of the response choices was reversed in Form B.)

Impact on Candidate Preference. How important was your view on the Arab/Israeli conflict in determining which of these candidates was your favorite? Was it the single most important issue, one of the two or three most important issues, one of the five most important issues, or was it not among the five most important issues? (The order of the response choices was reversed in Form B.)

Direct Attitude Expression. Have you ever written a letter, made a telephone call, or done anything else to express your views on the Arab/Israeli conflict directly to a government official, newspaper, or magazine?

OHIO SURVEY

In the Ohio survey, our section of the interview was introduced with a simple preamble: "Now I would like to ask you some questions on the Arab/Israeli conflict." Respondents were then asked the sympathies, withdrawal, uprisings, dialogue, and personal importance questions used in the national survey. Because we found no effects of the response order variations in that survey, no such variations were included in this questionnaire.

American Support for Israel: History, Sources, Limits

CHARLES LIPSON

The United States and Israel have a strong, durable relationship. But it is not an immutable one. It has varied quite dramatically during Israel's brief history, from America's ambivalence about the formation of a Jewish State to its strong support for Israel's right to exist, from America's embargo on arms to Israel during the late 1940s and the 1950s (while Israel repeatedly fought for its existence) to very high levels of military cooperation and economic aid beginning in the 1970s. From rocky beginnings and grudging support, this *de facto* alliance has matured and strengthened. It is likely to continue, but also to evolve and change. For the United States, it will remain a valued, stable relationship in a turbulent region. At the same time, America's active diplomacy and military involvement in the Middle East are likely to diminish over time now that its bipolar rival has vanished. Over the long term, these shifts are likely to mean a less intense – and more ordinary – U.S. relationship with Israel. From Israel's viewpoint, the stakes are much higher. Its ties with the U.S. will remain its most important relationship by far. Still, there are reasons for Israel to be concerned about the future level of American commitment and about the undertow of divergent interests now that the Soviet Union has disappeared as a common antagonist.

The relationship between Israel and the United States, like all alliances, is subject to a shifting calculus of grand strategy and domestic interests. As the smaller and more dependent partner, Israel is considerably more vulnerable to these shifts. The fundamental sources of U.S. support for Israel suggest why *broad continuity is likely but at lower levels of direct aid and support*. America's support for Israel is deeply grounded in (1) Israel's military strength and its dependability as a regional partner; (2) Israel's firm opposition to radical Arab states, who were longtime Soviet allies and who still pose a threat to oil supplies and to the political stability of some Arab

Charles Lipson is Professor of Political Science and Director of the Program on International Politics, Economics and Security at the University of Chicago.

governments; and, to a lesser extent, (3) Israel's success as a stable democracy, which makes it a desirable American partner in an unstable region.

All three foundational supports are likely to remain intact and significant. They are the basic geopolitical framework that shapes the U.S.–Israeli alliance. This point is fundamental. American policy toward Israel is *not* governed primarily by electoral politics or bureaucratic interests. Rather, it is governed by the calculus of geopolitics and grand strategy, as understood by senior U.S. policymakers.

DOMESTIC ARGUMENTS ABOUT U.S. POLICY TOWARD ISRAEL: THE JEWISH LOBBY

Most studies of U.S.-Israeli relations stress – or rather, they overstress – the role of American domestic politics. They highlight the effectiveness of pro-Israeli lobbying groups and imply that such lobbying accounts for U.S. policy. They rarely mention broader national security considerations: the strategic logic of U.S. policy in the Middle East. It is this strategic logic, not particularistic interests, that has dominated U.S. policy.

In fact, Jewish voters and other pro-Israeli groups play only a supporting role in policymaking, not a controlling one. True, Israel's supporters in the United States are unusually well organized, cohesive, and well financed. They are knowledgeable, experienced, and well connected, both in Washington and in the American Jewish community. Their policy priorities generally track the preferences of the Israeli government, although not always. Their influence is doubtless magnified by nearly universal Jewish support for Israel, by high voter turnout, and by the concentration of Jews in large states like New York, Florida, Illinois, and California, which are critical in Presidential elections. Likewise, financial support from pro-Israeli political action committees (PACs) is important because they are prodigious fundraisers, because they can channel these funds effectively to key races, and because congressional elections are expensive and must be financed privately. These sources of support for Israel are effective mainly because they build on widespread and quite consistent approval for Israel within the U.S. electorate.[1] In effect, these organized groups, notably the American-Israel Public Affairs Committee (AIPAC) but others as well, work to translate broad but inchoate popular support into effective backing for specific policies, such as U.S. aid or the sale of advanced military technology.

The efforts of pro-Israeli PACs do not go uncontested. Major U.S.-based oil companies are also well financed and well organized and for decades opposed closer American ties with Israel, as have other multinational firms with close economic ties to Arab states. From the

1940s onward, they found institutional support within the State Department's Mideast bureaucracy and its Arabist experts, who have consistently favored closer ties with conservative, oil-producing Arab states and opposed them with Israel since the days of Loy Henderson.[2] For many years, both the State Department and the Pentagon were habitually cautious about closer relations with Israel.[3] Finally, on the domestic political scene, there are growing numbers of Arab-Americans, who are becoming increasingly active and well organized politically, although they are still well behind their Jewish counterparts.

This tale of mobilized constituencies, congressional lobbying, campaign finance, and bureaucratic in-fighting is obviously important. Yet, although it may clarify the policymaking process for specific deals, it cannot illuminate the broader pattern of U.S.–Israeli relations. In fact, it is likely to obscure any deeper causal pattern or long-term evolution. *The long-term pattern of policy outcomes in U.S.–Israeli relations does show change and discontinuity. It is this evolving pattern that requires explanation.* Accounts that concentrate on pro-Israeli lobbying cannot explain this pattern. They cannot account for the long-term shift in U.S. support for Israel. Nor can they explain why that change took place when it did, during a Republican presidency with thin Jewish support and few ties to organized pro-Israeli interests. A.F.K. Organski, in particular, is very clear on this explanatory problem, and my own work is indebted to his analysis.[4]

American Jews have *always* strongly backed Israel, they have *always* been highly concentrated in large, electorally important states, and they have *always* been active in backstage lobbying and popular mobilization to help Israel. One could also find relatively consistent lobbying stances among large oil companies, who have opposed closer ties to Israel, and among policy professionals in the State Department. The analytic problem is that these lobbying patterns are *too* consistent. One can find them in the 1950s, when the United States provided Israel with little aid and no arms. And one can find them in the 1970s and later, when the U.S. provided extensive economic aid and military support. With all these *constants*, one simply cannot explain a pattern of sharp *change* in U.S.–Israeli relations. By the same token, the consistent support of the American Jewish community means that methodologically we cannot rule out their backing as a necessary, but not sufficient, condition of U.S. support for Israel.

DOMESTIC ARGUMENTS ABOUT U.S. POLICY TOWARD ISRAEL: IDEAS AND AFFINITIES

A similar critique can be made of the *profound ideological affinities* that link the U.S. and Israel. These affinities are real, and they go well beyond the special ties between American Jews and Israel. They form a supportive backdrop for bilateral relations. But, like American Jewish support, they are relatively constant background conditions that cannot account for significant changes in the bilateral relationship.

Four affinities stand out. First, America's leaders and electorate have long recognized that European Jewry has special moral claims to refuge and support because of the Holocaust. Second, beginning with Woodrow Wilson, the United States has supported the principle that every "nation" (or well-defined ethnic group) deserves its own sovereign state. Third, Israel has always been pro-Western, even in difficult times when the U.S. offered little reciprocal support. The historical details may be forgotten, but Israel is surely understood as a durable and loyal ally of the U.S. and western powers generally. Fourth, Israel has always been a democracy, with many attributes of a liberal state (if not a secular one). These features of Israeli politics are widely recognized in the United States, among policymakers, the attentive public, and the wider electorate. They undoubtedly serve to reinforce the bilateral relationship with Israel. It is difficult, however, to attribute a specific causal role to them.

Interest in the Holocaust has revived in the United States, but unlike in the 1940s it is only loosely connected to support for Israel, at least in the broad American electorate. Some indirect linkages are important, however. First, among Jews, the memory of the Holocaust strengthens ties across national boundaries – in the U.S., Israel, Russia, Ukraine, and Central Europe. It is a powerful reminder of the deadly threat posed by anti-Semitism and xenophobic nationalism, and, as such, it has stimulated considerable financial support for Jewish emigration to Israel. The revival of ethnic hatreds in the Balkans and Central Europe, including virulent anti-Semitism, also underscores one of Zionism's oldest rationales: the need for a permanent safe haven for Jews. The steady exodus of Jews from the Soviet Union during its final years and later from Russia, Ukraine, and other successor states reinforces the point. Although these themes are far more important in Israel than in the United States, they do resonate in America, especially among active Jews.

In seeking safe haven in a specifically *Jewish* State, European Zionists and later Israelis could always draw on a popular (if vague) strand in American thought since the presidency of Woodrow Wilson: a people's right to a national homeland, to an independent, sovereign state. Woodrow Wilson made this ideal central to his proposed settlement to the First World War. It has remained an important American perspective on international politics ever since, even though it has been qualified repeatedly, beginning with Wilson's own compromises at Versailles.

This same democratic ideal was an important consideration in

1947–48, when President Harry Truman reluctantly endorsed a plan for regional partition rather than U.N. trusteeship. Truman made the decision to support an independent Jewish State despite obvious risks to America's growing oil production in the Persian Gulf and despite the genuine possibility that Israel might lose its War of Independence. Since Truman's decision, the recognition of popular national rights to statehood has been a bulwark of American support for Israel against rejectionist Arab states. But it is equally a justification for a *Palestinian* State. Or rather, for many Americans, it is a justification for a West Bank Palestinian state under certain conditions: once they have dropped their anti-American posture, credibly opposed terrorism, and reframed their national aspirations so they are compatible with Israel's security rather than exclusive claims to the entire region.

By engaging in the peace process, Yasser Arafat and the PLO are widely understood to have made an important, if incomplete and erratic, endorsement of these principles. In America, popular memories of Palestinian terrorism are remote and abstract. They are forgotten by many. In any case, the history of terrorism is now widely associated with HAMAS and Islamic fundamentalists. It is no longer so clearly linked to Arafat and the PLO. In fact, Palestinians are now often seen as "underdogs" with legitimate claims to self-rule and eventual statehood. At the same time, Israel's repeated efforts to suppress the *intifada* inevitably raise troubling questions about democratic procedures, as did the Begin government's active settlement policy in the West Bank. This gradual reframing of the Palestinian issue is important because American policies in the Middle East, as elsewhere, are often stated as general principles and moral claims, and are conceived as such by the American electorate.

One of these broad principles surely is the desire for cooperation and alliance with other democratic states. America's history of principled support for such alliances is also an important link between the United States and Israel. It remains an anchor in their diplomatic relations and sharply differentiates Israel from neighboring Arab states and from the Palestinian movement.

Yet one must be quite cautious about attributing causal significance to this shared attribute of democracy. Both the United States and Israel have had close, long-standing relationships with non-democratic and even anti-democratic states. Second, both the U.S. and Israel were democracies when relations were much more difficult during the late 1940s and 1950s . Finally, it is difficult to specify a convincing *causal process or mechanism* through which these democratic links operate. It is quite possible – but hardly certain – that democracies are more willing to make reciprocal commitments to other democratic states even though the payoffs are long-term and even though there are opportunities for betrayal. They can do so because they are more confident about their partner's likely behavior. They know that major policy commitments in a democracy are not easily reversed by the whims of a single leader, by a coup d'etat, or even by the replacement of a governing party. They can also take some confidence in their democratic allies' relatively open, transparent decisionmaking process. This allows them to measure the depth of support for a diplomatic relationship before relying on it, and it lowers the risks of sudden breach.[5]

Sustaining this alliance of two democracies is much easier because of Israel's long and unwavering pro-American record. If this alliance posture seems natural or even inevitable today, it is important to remember that Prime Minister Ben-Gurion forged it while Israel was receiving its vital military supplies not from Washington but from Prague (with Moscow's approval), while Truman and Eisenhower were standing aloof from Israel's fight for survival, and while many Israeli socialists were urging closer ties to East Europe and continued neutrality in the deepening Cold War. Ben-Gurion's policy (adopted in 1950), however, clearly positioned Israel as an integral part of the Western world. It sought, and ultimately gained, a major, long-term strategic advantage: durable and supportive ties with the United States.

America's own unbroken pattern of alliances with democratic states, its ideal that each ethnic group ought to posses its own homeland, the shared memory of the Holocaust, and Israel's consistent pro-Western stance have all influenced U.S. public support for Israel. U.S. public opinion polls have, in fact, shown high and broadbased support for Israel since the 1940s. For years it has ranked just below America's closest allies, Great Britain and Germany, in perceived importance and public approval (although Israel's standing has declined somewhat in recent years).[6] Unlike most opinions about foreign policy, which regularly follow the U.S. government's official stance, American popular support for Israel has remained strong even when diplomatic relationships were strained (as they were during the Eisenhower presidency, for instance). This popular support for Israel, plus the very effective mobilization of Jews into pro-Israel political action committees, has undoubtedly reinforced the U.S.–Israeli alliance, which senior policymakers have supported for their own strategic reasons.

Of course, one could also cite very different national perspectives on security problems, which serve to divide the two countries. The reasons for these differences are all too obvious. America and Israel live in very different neighborhoods and in very different houses. There are vast discrepancies in national size, income, technological self-sufficiency, strategic depth, and threats posed by nearby states. To put it differently, the United States has long viewed the world from a relatively comfortable position of power, wealth, and security, separated by oceans from its major foes. For almost two hundred years, it has not fought an enemy on its own soil. Israel, by contrast, faces existential security threats as a regular fact of life. Just as the ideological affinities make security collaboration easier, these differences make it difficult for the U.S. electorate, and sometimes even sophisticated policymakers, to fully appreciate the dangers, constraints, and policy dilemmas that Israel faces.

In short, there are some significant differences in circumstance and perspective, as well as significant common ideals and ideological affinities linking Israel and the United States. But as important as these are for understanding bilateral communications and perceptions, their very permanence means that they cannot explain basic *changes* in the bilateral relationship.

THE "STRATEGIC LEARNING" ARGUMENT RESTATED

If "domestic determinants" are a weak explanation, how do we explain the sea-change in U.S. policy? The fundamental change, I think, stems from a gradual reconsideration within the White House and National Security Council of how relationships with Israel and key Arab states affect American interests in the Middle East. This was a reassessment of America's *strategic posture*, not its basic regional *goals*. The reassessment took place after the Six Day War and subsequent War of Attrition, after the Soviet Union provocatively chose to enlarge its allies' military capabilities, presumably to produce a better result in the next war. It is important then to underscore the role of superpower antagonism in producing closer relations between the U.S. and Israel. But there was also genuine learning from past policy failures. Taken together, the strategic context and its reevaluation by President Nixon and Henry Kissinger produced a fundamental change in U.S.–Israeli relations that has lasted for more than two decades.

What were the key elements in America's fundamental strategic reassessment of its Middle East diplomacy?

First, a cool, distant policy toward Israel would *not* curb Arab nationalism or radical Arab states, as had been hoped. Appeasement of radical states (such as Nasser's) was bound to fail. This policy echoed America's basic Cold War posture toward the Soviet Union and its client states: containment, not appeasement.

Second, the Soviet Union was seen as increasingly committed to arming Israel's neighbors. It would not agree to mutual restraints, despite repeated requests. A strategy of regional cooperation with the Soviets was not feasible (and was probably not in America's best interest anyway since it would cede a large regional role to the Soviet Union).

Third, the failure to contest this Soviet-led arms buildup might well lead to a war in which Soviet allies prevailed. This would carry a high price for America within the region and would damage its reputation globally.

Fourth, the transfer of weapons and aid to Israel would not entail the direct commitment of American soldiers to defend the country. Financial and military aid would actually reduce the need for American troop commitment in the region. Given the wherewithal, Israel could realistically defend itself, and it actually placed a high value on such self-reliance.

Finally, it was eventually recognized that providing arms and aid to Israel would not rupture relations with conservative Arab governments – a genuine American fear during the Truman and Eisenhower Administrations. These narrowly-based regimes, most of them monarchies, had their own reasons to fear Arab radicalism, their own reasons to maintain close ties with the United States. Even if the U.S. drew closer to Israel, these oil-rich states simply had nowhere else to turn.

In other words, by the late-1960s and early 1970s, in the aftermath of the Six Day War and subsequent War of Attrition in the Sinai, America found that its old policies had largely failed and that the Soviet Union was now making a concerted effort to achieve regional dominance by arming proxy states. The U.S. response was to invoke its conventional Cold War policy: to counter-arm democratic states facing Soviet allies. This fundamental American policy can be traced back to the Truman Doctrine in 1947.

It should be added that the new U.S. policy toward Israel succeeded where the old one had failed. Closer American ties with Israel aid did *not* draw the Soviet Union deeper into the region. Nor did it undermine diplomatic relationships with conservative oil-producing states. Those relations have remained strong, partly because they have nowhere else to turn for external support.[7] Close American ties to Israel have not prevented Saudi Arabia and Kuwait from relying heavily upon the United States for defense of state, crown, and oil.

Throughout this period, the U.S. has tried to encourage a broad regional peace, assuming that only a comprehensive multilateral settlement could stabilize the region. This strategy also failed despite repeated efforts, beginning with Nixon's first Secretary of State, William Rogers. It was Anwar Sadat's recognition of this failure that led him to seek his own separate peace – one without Syria and without the Palestinians. The Camp David Accords were that separate peace. Despite President Carter's hopes, Camp David did not lead to a wider regional settlement. In fact, the accords were built on Sadat's shrewd recognition that a wider settlement might never come. Sadat was right. The wider settlement never came. But the Camp David accords gave both Egypt and Israel unprecedented external security. The effect for Israel was particularly important since it could only be defeated in a two-front war, which was no longer a possibility after Egypt made its separate peace.

The United States, which had acted as mediator, now became the region's guarantor. The U.S. had managed to develop close diplomatic and military relationships simultaneously with Israel and with several major Arab states. These dual relationships were a prerequisite for America's much more prominent role in the region. In the aftermath of Camp David, the United States' most immediate aim was to sustain the peace and to sustain alliance relationships with both Egypt and Israel. A key part of this strategy was a step increase in aid to both countries. The U.S. also worked, as it had since the 1940s, to isolate the Soviet Union and its allies from the key oil-producing regions of the Persian Gulf.

The main lines of this policy were still visible during Desert Storm. By invading Kuwait and threatening the Saudi oilfields, Saddam Hussein showed that radical states were still threats to regional stability – even after the Soviet Union's collapse.[8] This meant that narrowly-based regimes, such as Saudi Arabia, Kuwait, and the Arab Emirates, still had strong reason to lean on the United States for external security. The war sharply illuminated their military dependence. The invasion also showed that the Palestinian problem was not the only important source of regional conflict. The sources of conflict in the Persian Gulf as elsewhere are the usual ones in international politics: fear about what neighbors seek and uncertainty about what they can do. Opposition to Israel, though a unifying ideological force, is hardly central to rivalries among Arab states. American policy had been based on these assumptions for twenty years, and the war did nothing to change them.

Israel also demonstrated its sensitivity to U.S. concerns by refusing to strike back after Iraq's Scud attacks. This restraint overturned two basic tenets of Israeli policy: self-reliance and prompt retaliation. Israel's restraint was thus a costly signal of its deep commitment to the informal U.S. alliance. Precisely because it was so costly, Israel's action (or rather, its inaction) was widely praised in the United States. Much more troublesome for Israel, the war also showed that its value as a "strategic asset" was now in some doubt. Far from serving as a wartime partner or a regional platform for American action, Israel was relegated to a minor role. The Americans feared that any larger role would shatter the carefully constructed alliance against Saddam Hussein. Whether true or not, this perception undermined America's ties to Israel. It underscores a basic problem of U.S.–Israeli relations. The closeness of bilateral ties has always been limited by the Arab–Israeli conflict and by America's security interest in maintaining close ties to Arab regional powers and oil-producing states.

To summarize, America's relationship with Israel has evolved as the U.S. pursued consistent long-term goals in the region under changing strategic conditions. The overriding goals have been to maintain secure access to oil supplies, to contain radical Arab regimes and to limit the influence of other major powers (first Great Britain and then the Soviet Union). As the Soviet Union expanded its ties to Arab nationalists in the 1960s, U.S. policymakers realized that a strong, dynamic Israel would be an effective, low-cost counterweight rather than a burden. This conceptual shift began during the Kennedy and Johnson Administrations, but it was Richard Nixon who dramatically increased the scale of U.S. commitments to Israel.[9] The sharp growth of U.S. economic aid and military sales in the early 1970s, immediately following Soviet efforts to rebuild and expand their allies' armed forces, neatly conforms to this analysis of "strategic learning," not domestic political influence (see Figure 1 for U.S. aid to Israel).

THE TRANSFORMATION OF U.S. POLICY TOWARD ISRAEL

The best way to trace out major changes in U.S. policy is to focus on military sales and economic aid, as well as key moments of diplomatic pressure or support. The record shows a dramatic change in U.S.–Israeli relations during the early 1970s. Both economic aid and military sales reached much higher levels then, following a decade of gradually improving relationships. The basic outlines of this pattern do not require a detailed history of bilateral relations. A brief, highly stylized account is sufficient to clarify the major moments of change and their policy rationale.

FIGURE 1: OFFICIAL U.S. AID TO ISRAEL

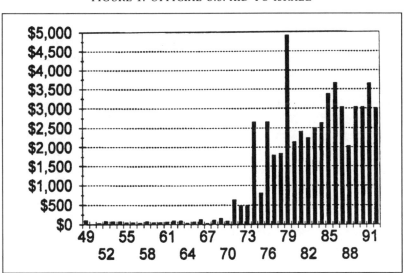

In the 1940s and 1950s, the U.S. was distant and aloof from Israel. Although it did recognize the new Jewish State (after considerable ambivalence about the key UN vote), it also embargoed arms that were desperately needed. The U.S. certainly had no intention of providing American troops if Israel lost its early battles for survival. Secretary of State George Marshall and his department's Middle East experts expected exactly such a crushing military defeat for the new state, as did James Forrestal at the Pentagon. As Forrestal crudely put it to Truman's pro-Israeli political advisor, Clark Clifford, "You just don't understand. There are four hundred thousand Jews and forty million Arabs. Forty million Arabs are going to push four hundred thousand Jews into the sea. And that's all there is to it. Oil – that is the side we ought to be on."[10] Loy Henderson, George Kennan, and others at the State Department came to the same conclusion, mainly because they feared American support for a Jewish State would give the Soviet Union entree to the region as a friend of rejectionist Arab states.

Truman himself was alert to these concerns and was torn over a two-state solution for Palestine. In the end, however, he overrode his military and diplomatic advisors and directed the United States to vote for partition at the United Nations rather than for continued trusteeship.[11] He gave Israel *de facto* recognition as soon as it declared independence and then extended formal recognition the following year. Truman's motives are still not clear, although he was clearly influenced by the Holocaust and by Wilson's idea of a state for each people. The electoral significance of New York Jews may also have played a role, although Truman and his advisors adamantly denied it.[12] Still, urban Jews were an integral part of the New Deal political coalition, and that may have influenced Truman's thinking.

While Truman's recognition was crucial, it hardly represented a solid pattern of U.S. support for the new state. Quite the contrary. The U.S. maintained a tight and effective arms embargo throughout Israel's War of Independence despite sophisticated counter-efforts by the American Jewish community. Israel's friends were able to provide critical financial help and some small arms but no heavy weapons. Israel either captured them in war or bought them in Czechoslovakia and smuggled them in.[13]

Even after the War of Independence, the U.S. would not sell Israel major weapons. It continued to oppose Jewish emigration to the region. It gave little economic aid. To make matters worse, the State Department actually tried to stop American Jews from donating to Israel. In the late 1940s, American Jews were giving about $50 million a year to Israel's Jewish Agency, by way of the United Jewish Appeal. The State Department threatened, unsuccessfully, to eliminate the tax deductibility of these donations.[14]

The Eisenhower Administration continued these cool policies and added sharper pressures during the Suez crisis, including another threat to remove tax deductibility on private contributions to Israel. Throughout the Eisenhower presidency, official U.S. aid to Israel remained well below $100 million annually. The U.S. also refused to become a source of Israeli military supplies. In sharp contrast to later U.S. policy, the Eisenhower administration gave Israel no arms to counterbalance a major Soviet-Egyptian arms deal in 1955.[15] Secretary of State John Foster Dulles opposed any Israeli participation in the Baghdad Pact, the short-lived regional alliance against the Soviet Union.[16] Basic U.S. policy, in other words, assumed that closer ties to Israel would weaken America's growing power in the region and, most importantly, would jeopardize its close ties to major oil producers.

Bilateral relations warmed considerably during the Kennedy and Johnson presidencies, although America's regional strategy did not fundamentally change. In real terms, aid to Israel was little changed from the Truman and Eisenhower periods. What did change was a growing recognition that the Soviet Union had made inroads in the region, that it was developing long-term ties to radical Arab nationalists despite U.S. policy. The U.S., in turn, began to consider a more forthcoming policy on military sales to Israel.

Israel pushed hard for the change. France had replaced Czechoslovakia as a major arms supplier in the 1950s and early 1960s, but that ended after France's loss in Algeria and Charles De Gaulle's decision to jettison Israel in favor of warmer relationships with North African and Middle Eastern states.[17] America was Israel's obvious choice as an arms supplier – they had tried unsuccessfully to develop these ties since the 1950s – but the door was opened only slightly in the early 1960s.

In September 1962, President Kennedy finally decided to sell Israel an older version of the Hawk missile. Though the sale was a relatively small one, the decision represented a major policy shift. As recently as 1957, Eisenhower had refused to sell Israel the basic tanks it supplied to Jordan. To sell Israel the Hawk missile was an important step. Philip Klutznick, a leading figure in the American Jewish community who was then serving in the U.S. delegation to the United Nations, called it a "great reversal" in U.S. policy. As important as the sale itself, President Kennedy expressed an interest in the regional arms *balance*, the first American president to do so.[18]

Lyndon Johnson's policy followed much the same lines: closer relationships, a major arms deal (the Skyhawk jet), but still relatively low levels of aid and military sales. Johnson was also reluctant to give Israel open diplomatic support in the days leading up to the 1967 War, even after Nasser had blockaded the Straits of Tiran and won public backing from the Soviet Union. The U.S. was simply unwilling to give Israel the kind of support the Soviet Union gave Egypt.

Even after the 1967 War, the U.S. did not want to become Israel's principal arms supplier. It was becoming clear, however, that America's restraint was not being matched by the Soviet Union. Given the bipolar rivalry, that put significant pressure on the U.S. to match Soviet efforts. During the Six Day War, for instance, the U.S. and France said they would stop all arms deliveries to the Middle East, but the Soviet Union declined to reciprocate.[19] The problem became more nettlesome after the war as Soviet arms deliveries continued to grow and their political-diplomatic links to Egypt and Syria deepened.

The Soviet posture on aid and arms sales raised fundamental strategic questions for the United States. What were the implications of an arms imbalance in this war-prone region? What benefits would the Soviet Union reap as the major Arab arms supplier? What if Soviet aid and advisors allowed their clients to roll back Israeli gains by military means rather than by a peace accord?

Deteriorating conditions in the Middle East forced the Nixon administration to confront these issues squarely. Israel's sweeping 1967 victory did not convince the losers to sue for peace. There were no post-war negotiations, no peace treaties. Instead, the defeated armies began to rebuild aggressively with Soviet aid and advisors. For the Soviets, the circumstances were especially inviting. Arab armies desperately needed their equipment, and the Americans were pinned down in Vietnam. The War of Attrition, fought along the Suez Canal with Soviet arms and encouragement, made it clear that Israel faced serious, on-going security problems despite its territorial gains. The Soviet presence posed obvious problems for the United States, too, given America's economic interests in the region and its Cold War policy of containment.

Another important consequence of the Six Day War was emerging in Jordan, which had lost control of the West Bank and Jerusalem and gained a fractious Palestinian political movement. By 1970, King Hussein was struggling to control a large, well-organized Palestinian population. His problems were mounting. The PLO, anxious to keep its cause on the international agenda, was using Jordan as a base for major terrorist operations, including aircraft hijacking. A political crisis in Jordan finally erupted in 1970 when Hussein cracked down on the PLO, which he considered a threat to Hashemite rule. The guerrillas fought back tenaciously, aided by Syrian troops and tanks, which crossed into Jordan. The Soviets openly backed Syria. In fact, Soviet advisors accompanied the Syrian tanks up to the border. To complicate matters further, Iraq already had some 18,000 troops stationed in Jordan. There was a real risk that Jordan's civil war might escalate into a full-scale regional battle. In the end, the fighting was contained and the PLO expelled. The Israel Defense Forces (IDF) quietly played a deterrent role in keeping Syrian forces from overrunning Jordan, leading to a reevaluation of Israel's importance as a regional ally.

The conflicts in Jordan and the Sinai underscored the failure of long-standing U.S. policies. The Arab–Israeli conflict was continuing unabated and perhaps worsening. It was drawing the Soviet Union ever deeper into this vital region. And, as the fighting in Jordan also showed, all this turmoil could pose a direct threat to pro-Western regimes.

As a result, the United States faced hard policy choices. Nixon's memoirs show that he made these choices by focusing on fundamental geopolitical issues and on the need to adapt to a changing strategic environment. He emphasizes (1) America's broad strategic goals in the region, particularly the limitation of Soviet influence; (2) the need to learn from old policy failures; and (3) the basic aim of developing strong diplomatic ties to both Israel and conservative Arab states.[20] In other words, a policy of accommodating radical Arab nationalists was bound to fail. Nixon also argues – against conventional wisdom – that U.S. electoral pressures may have worked against Israel rather than for it, at least in the 1950s. "I have often felt that if the Suez crisis had not arisen during the heat of a presidential election campaign a different decision would have been made."[21]

Later, when Nixon speaks of his presidential decision to strengthen ties with Israel, he accurately notes that he "was in the unique position of being politically unbeholden to the major pressure group involved."[22] Since it was Nixon who transformed U.S. economic and military ties to Israel, his comment is particularly instructive. He stresses geopolitical issues, particularly the need to counter Soviet arms sales after the 1967 War. In this case at least, there is every reason to believe him.[23] Nixon ultimately made a decision that has remained a fundamental American policy. "We should give Israel a technological military margin," he said, "to more than offset her hostile neighbors' numerical superiority."[24] And, of course, America would provide the external funding needed for that policy.

The new policy was backed by large increases in American aid. During the Johnson presidency, aid to Israel had averaged under $100 million annually. Under Nixon, it was immediately increased to the $500-$600 million range. The United States was now providing Israel more aid in one year than during the entire Kennedy and Johnson administrations. After the 1973 Yom Kippur War, aid jumped to $2.6 billion for fiscal 1974 and a similar level in fiscal 1976. The increase in aid, though important, did not represent a major American policy shift. It represented an effort to maintain a regional military balance under rapidly shifting conditions. Crude oil prices had increased four-fold in 1973–74, creating a windfall for

Persian Gulf producers and increasing their financial support to other Arab states. The new oil revenues opened the door to major weapons purchases and could have threatened the regional military balance unless the U.S. acted to offset it. Higher aid flows to Israel did exactly that.

Aid has remained at these high levels ever since. In recent years it has been about $3 billion. In 1979, the year of Camp David, the U.S. supplied Israel with some $4.9 billion in aid, almost $4.0 billion of it in military loans and grants. By the late 1980s, the U.S. was supplying Israel with approximately $1.8 billion in military grants and another $1.2 billion in economic grants.

High aid levels and strong military cooperation certainly do not mean the end of serious political disputes. Over the past fifteen years, there have been important bilateral policy conflicts: over AWACs sales to Saudi Arabia, over the 1982 War in Lebanon, especially the fighting in Beirut itself, and over Begin and Shamir's encouragement of West Bank settlements, among others. Nixon, who did so much to engineer the new relationship, himself used direct sanctions on bilateral aid at least four times to try and shape Israeli policy.[25] Likewise, President Reagan's strong support for Israel did not prevent significant disagreements.

Indeed, America's high levels of aid to Israel are an inviting target for policymakers' manipulation. That is why the U.S. has blocked or delayed aid more than a dozen times. It is a simple, direct way to oppose Israeli policies. Such disputes inevitably highlight deeper tensions and asymmetries. Israel understandably resents its financial dependence. Above all, it wants to ensure its autonomy in key security issues. The United States is frustrated that its massive aid flows bring such weak influence over Israeli policy. These frustrations lie just beneath the surface – and sometimes just above it – but they have not prevented high levels of bilateral cooperation since the early 1970s. Aid remains high, and it still commands broad support in the White House and Congress. These levels are likely to face downward pressure, due to lower overall levels of aid and rising demands from other regions, especially in central and eastern Europe.

If, as I have argued, these aid flows, military sales, and diplomatic relationships were forged by strategic learning and geopolitical context, particularly the need to cope with growing Soviet pressure in the Middle East, then we must ask if this relationship will long survive the death of the Soviet Union?

U.S. POLICY TOWARD ISRAEL AFTER THE COLD WAR

The changing strategic context is likely to affect U.S.–Israel relations at every level. As I have argued, there is likely to be significant continuity, based on Israel's own strength and regional military role, its democratic traditions, and the recognition that close American ties to Israel do not prevent close ties to other key states in the region. In fact, they give America a special diplomatic importance, beyond its superpower status, since the U.S. is the only state that can influence both Israel *and* its Arab neighbors.

Even without the Soviet threat, the United States clearly has major stakes in the Middle East: protecting oil flows from the Persian Gulf, slowing nuclear proliferation, and helping to stabilize friendly states in the face of fundamentalist movements. The peace process, too, is likely to entail a continuing American role, as the Camp David accords did. There is the very real possibility that a stable peace in the Golan Heights will require some American forces. The Palestinian territories will undoubtedly require long-term economic aid and technical assistance.

At the same time, the withdrawal of the Soviet Union may encourage a somewhat lower American profile, not only in the Middle East but globally. Former Soviet allies are naturally weakened by the loss of their patron. That clearly strengthens both the United States and Israel, but it also means that a strong U.S. balancing role is no longer necessary. The death of the Soviet Union also weakens the domestic rationale within the United States for an active and expensive global role in all regions. That has already meant a steady, cumulative reduction in the U.S. defense budget. It is likely to be felt in aid flows to Israel and Egypt. They are unlikely to continue at present levels. Why? Because the diminution of strategic concerns, combined with tight budget constraints, are likely to reduce America's regional role to some extent. That will put downward pressure on foreign aid to Israel. There is one important countervailing trend. These same pressures will encourage the U.S. to rely on strong regional partners, such as Israel, to supplement America's own direct presence.

Important changes in the Israeli economy may also affect the bilateral relationship with the U.S. Israel's new economic growth means importers, exporters, financiers, and shippers are developing stronger ties to their American counterparts. Potential foreign investors are encouraged by the peace process and by privatization, as well as a highly skilled and educated workforce. These investors have opportunities to use Israel as an export base, thanks to long-term trade agreements with the United States and European Union. These economic changes, plus Israel's already high levels of income (approximately equal to the Mediterranean region of the EU), will produce a new kind of relationship between Israel and developed countries. This relationship will be one of greater interdependence in trade and investment and less dependence on foreign aid. All this implies greater equality and symmetry in bilateral diplomatic relations as Israel adjusts to lower levels of direct aid and higher levels of international exchange.

Finally, changes within American Jewish life, together with Israel's inexorable development as an independent nation-state, are transforming the close ties between these two Jewish communities. America's Jews are turning inward, concerned about their collective future. They still feel deep links to Israel – rather like cousins – but they are not fearful for its survival or much concerned about its internal policy choices. What does worry them is the future of *American* Jewish life, which is no longer held together by common immigrant experience or by others' hatred. Intermarriage rates are high and climbing, and the children of these marriages frequently do not consider themselves Jewish. In a pluralist society, there are low barriers to "exit" from religion, and many are choosing that route. Except for certain orthodox communities, birth rates are low. The American Jewish community is prosperous but aging and uncertain about its continuity. This inward-looking concern and outward-looking confidence in Israel's future are reflected in charitable giving.[26] Absolute support for Israel is still high, but it has slowly declined from one-half of U.J.A.'s donations to around one-third.[27]

Will weaker links between these two Jewish communities affect ties between their respective governments? Those who stress the critical lobbying role of AIPAC and other Jewish organizations are worried, and understandably so. My own argument, by contrast, says that other influences are more important. U.S. policy is based mainly on policymakers' strategic calculations, not on direct Zionist pressures. What cannot be ruled out, however, is the possibility that some level of domestic American support for Israel is a *necessary* (but not sufficient) cause of high levels of U.S. economic and military aid. That possibility cannot be ruled out because such political support has always been present during periods of high U.S. aid to Israel. On the other hand, it cannot be a *sufficient cause* since strong lobbying and public endorsement were also present when U.S. ties to Israel were weak.

To summarize, we are now entering an era without superpower conflict. This change is echoing through the Middle East, forcing old Soviet clients to realign. In the short run, the demise of the Soviet Union makes both Israel and the United States more secure. In the long run, however, it may diminish America's interest in the region (although oil remains critically important) and weaken the national-security rationale for large aid allocations. In other words, the disappearance of the Soviet Union dramatically alters the strategic landscape and America's role within it. It has powerful effects at both the international and regional levels. Looking forward, it is these strategic changes, much more than congressional lobbying or the changing demographics of American Jewry, that will shape the future of U.S.–Israeli relations.

ACKNOWLEDGMENT

The author thanks Uri Bialer, Benjamin Frankel, Ido Oren, Arnold Jacob Wolf, and Gabriel Sheffer for their helpful comments.

NOTES

1. See, for example, Eytan Gilboa's "Trends in American Attitudes Toward Israel," in Gabriel Sheffer (ed.), *Dynamics of Dependence: U.S.–Israeli Relations* (Boulder, CO: Westview Press, 1987) and Gilboa's *American Public Opinion toward Israel and the Arab–Israeli Conflict* (Lexington, MA: Lexington Books, 1987).
2. See Robert D. Kaplan, *The Arabists: The Romance of an American Elite* (New York: Free Press, 1993).
3. U.S. intelligence agencies have usually been Israel's strongest proponents within the Executive Branch, perhaps because of their long record of cooperation with the Mossad. Over the past two decades, as U.S. military aid and collaboration have risen, the Pentagon too has moved away from its traditional opposition and aloofness.
4. A.F.K. Organski, *The $36 Billion Bargain: Strategy and Politics in U.S. Assistance to Israel* (New York: Columbia University Press, 1990).
5. These issues are discussed in Charles Lipson, "Why are Some International Agreements Informal?" *International Organization*, Vol.45 (Autumn 1991), pp.495–538.
6. See John E. Rielly (ed.), *American Public Opinion and U.S. Foreign Policy, 1991* (Chicago, IL: Chicago Council on Foreign Relations, 1991), pp.21, 23, 24. I am indebted to Arthur Cyr of the Chicago Council for providing me with this data.
7. There was tension with oil-producing states, however, when their cartel raised prices four-fold during the winter of 1973–74. In spite of this economic conflict, their geopolitical alignment did not shift. Virtually all the major producers remained closely tied to the United States.
8. While some radical Arab states remained obstinate even without Soviet backing, others showed a new flexibility – in other words, a recognition of the United States' increased regional power. President Asad's decision that Syria should join the U.S.-led coalition against Saddam Hussein was particularly important and opened the door to possible U.S. mediation or guarantees over the occupied Golan Heights.
9. Especially see Richard Nixon, *The Memoirs of Richard Nixon* (New York: Grosset & Dunlap, 1978) and Henry Kissinger's two volume memoirs, *The White House Years* (Boston, MA: Little, Brown, 1979), and *Years of Upheaval* (Boston, MA: Little, Brown, 1982) for their repeated discussions of the strategic issues in Middle East diplomacy in the years between the Six Day War and the Yom Kippur War.
10. Walter Isaacson and Evan Thomas, *The Wise Men: Six Friends and the World They Made* (New York: Touchstone [Simon and Schuster], 1986), p.452.
11. The story is vividly told in Peter Grose, *Israel in the Mind of America* (New York: Knopf, 1983), Ch.10.
12. John Snetsinger, *Truman, the Jewish Vote, and the Creation of Israel* (Stanford, CA: Hoover Institution Press, 1974).
13. See Mordechai Gazit, "Israeli Military Procurement from the United States," in Sheffer (ed.), *Dynamics of Dependence*, p.87.
14. See Grose, *Israel*, pp.211, 303.
15. Nadav Safran, *Israel, the Embattled Ally* (Cambridge, MA: Harvard University Press, 1978), p.579.
16. Yaacov Bar-Siman-Tov, *Israel, the Superpowers, and the War in the Middle East* (New York: Praeger, 1987), p.14; David Schoenbaum, *The United States and the State of Israel* (New York: Oxford University Press, 1993), p.84.
17. Bar-Siman-Tov, *Israel, the Superpowers*, pp.107, 130.
18. Gazit, "Israeli Military Procurement", pp.95, 99.
19. Ibid., p.102.
20. Nixon, *The Memoirs*, p.179.
21. Ibid.

22. Ibid, p.435.
23. Ibid., p.343.
24. Quoted in Gazit, "Israeli Military Procurement", p.105.
25. Leopold Yehuda Laufer, "U.S. Aid to Israel: Problems and Perspectives," in Sheffer (ed.), *Dynamics of Dependence*, pp.155–6.
26. Gabriel Sheffer, "The End of Dual Loyalty?" manuscript, Hebrew University, 1994, and Sheffer (ed.), *Modern Diasporas in International Politics* (New York: St. Martin's Press, 1986).
27. See the article by Arthur Hertzberg in this volume.

Reclaiming Zion:
How American Religious
Groups View the Middle East

KENNETH D. WALD, JAMES L. GUTH,
CLEVELAND R. FRASER, JOHN C. GREEN,
CORWIN E. SMIDT, LYMAN A. KELLSTEDT

In the eyes of "realist" critics, American foreign policy is marred by a penchant for moralism.[1] Testifying to the persistence of this foreign policy style, recall Ronald Reagan's "Evil Empire" rhetoric and George Bush's claim of religious sanction for the Gulf War.[2] Considering the salience of moralism in American foreign policy, how odd that scholars have paid so little attention to the religious foundations of American foreign policy. Historians may acknowledge the contribution of religion to the distinctive American "style" in world affairs but few scholars have explored how individuals link religious values with their understanding of the international realm or how religious differences translate into contending foreign policy perspectives.[3] The failure to consider religion as a foreign policy influence is particularly striking in the context of America's Middle Eastern policy. If there is one area where we might expect religious perspectives to affect foreign policy preferences, it would be the part of the world that has such compelling religious significance for Americans. Yet aside from sustained work on the role of American Jews in the formation of policy toward Israel, there is remarkably little research on the contribution of religious forces to the Mideast beliefs of ordinary Americans.

The analysis will focus on Protestants and Catholics, the two largest religious groups in the United States. Though America has never been monolithically Christian and maintains a resolutely secular governmental system, Christians constitute the over-whelmingly majority of the population and dominate national

Kenneth D. Wald is Professor in the Department of Political Science at the University of Florida; James L. Guth and Cleveland R. Fraser teach at Furman University, John C. Green at the University of Akron, Corwin E. Smidt at Calvin College, and Lyman A. Kellstedt at Wheaton College.

political life. As we will see, the "Christian" label encompasses a variety of traditions that differ from each other in major respects. Yet in whatever guise, Christians have been the major force in American life, and their considerable impact upon foreign policy attitudes warrants careful analysis.

RELIGION AS A SOURCE OF AMERICAN PUBLIC OPINION ON FOREIGN POLICY

Unlike Israelis, for whom "politics" necessarily means foreign policy, Americans have usually had the luxury of distinguishing sharply between domestic and international affairs. To the extent it monitors public life, the American public usually cares much more deeply about home affairs than the domain of international relations. Despite the clamor of elites and interest groups who portray world politics as vital to the nation, 75–90 percent of ordinary Americans remain cognitively disengaged from the international arena.[4]

This public indifference to global issues may give opinion leaders an advantage in influencing mass attitudes. When they are unable to draw on experience to form their own judgments, Americans are likely to rely for guidance on those whose opinions they respect and value. In the United States, churches and religious leaders play such a leading role in opinion formation by virtue of the high public regard in which Americans hold religion. By the tangible indicators of religious commitment commonly utilized in cross-national research – church attendance, religious group membership, contributions to religious agencies, and maintenance of orthodox religious beliefs – Americans exhibit strikingly high levels of religious attachment.[5] By these measures, the United States remains much as Chesterton described it in the 1930s, "a nation with the soul of a church."[6] It is also a nation where religious factors and cultural variables continue to play a strong role in political life, contributing significantly to vote choice and attitudes on many aspects of public policy.[7]

These conditions provide a basis for anticipating religious influence on policy attitudes. We believe that each of the three faces of religion – creed, organization, and community – makes that prospect likely in *foreign* policy as well.[8] Religious values seem relevant to many international issues and world conflicts. More than disembodied faith, religions are also networks of institutions with organizational links that may draw them into international political disputes. The global presence of Roman Catholicism generates a persistent concern for the interests and influence of the church. Similar dynamics have drawn other religious communities into an active engagement with global politics.

In view of these linkages, we should not be surprised to learn that previous research has identified religion, along with age, education, socioeconomic status, ethnicity, gender, region and race, as an influence on American foreign policy attitudes.[9] Most empirical research on American foreign policy opinion has compared the Cold War attitudes of Catholics and Protestants, finding the former more disposed to favor active resistance to Communist states and to support specific military engagements. These differences, observed from the onset of the Cold War until the late 1960s, appear to have eroded in the aftermath of Vietnam. By the time the nuclear freeze movement gained momentum in the early 1980s, the Catholic Church had emerged as a leading voice of anti-nuclear sentiment and individual parishes spearheaded resistance to the Reagan policy in Central America. Ordinary Catholics appear to have followed these cues, becoming no more hawkish or less dovish than their Protestant counterparts.[10]

Some scholars contend that Catholic–Protestant differences were long ago supplanted by a more fundamental type of religious conflict. They point to evidence that certain forms of religious commitment were linked to particular international outlooks. Irrespective of denomination, the degree to which individuals subscribed to religion – a condition variously described as intensity, salience, orthodoxy or religiosity – appeared to predict the content of Cold War attitudes. The more ardent the level of religious commitment – usually in the direction of religious orthodoxy and traditionalism – the firmer the belief in military resistance to the Soviet Union. Rosenberg attributed the "hard-line" stance of churchgoers and orthodox believers to Cold War propaganda that put God on the side of America against its atheistic communist opposition.[11] Milton Rokeach had a more sophisticated explanation for this pattern. He argued that religious traditions embraced particularistic visions rooted in the group's sense of itself as a community of the elect. The resulting ethnocentrism easily overwhelmed the universalistic motif in most religious visions.[12] Along similar lines, Alfred Hero emphasized the logical fit between the Manichean worldview of religious enthusiasts and the tendency to perceive the Cold War as a clash of moral absolutes.[13]

Some analysts have further refined the categories, postulating that apparent differences in religious intensity are better understood as contending religious worldviews anchored in distinctive theological systems.[14] One vision adopts a God of control and order who mandates obedience and rectitude. It sees the world as a dangerous place where unrestrained impulses will give vent to the worst excesses of human nature. The task of the state is to promote order within and defend boundaries from without. In that vision, the military becomes the chief and indispensable agent of national interest. In contrast, the competing "communitarian" vision presupposes a loving and caring

God who is very much part of the world. To honor God means building a world where humans will be free to develop and thrive without artificial constraint. In the realm of international politics, this style of commitment mandates international cooperation and envisions a world of global harmony. This view is expressed and implemented through efforts to promote economic development and non-military cooperation among nations. Though the staunchest proponents of these disparate views are equally intense in religious commitment, their values lead them in very different political directions.

Whatever the precise aspect of religion that influences foreign policy attitudes, this review gives us reason to anticipate a relationship between the religious factor and Middle Eastern attitudes.

THE AMERICAN RELIGIOUS MOSAIC

If Americans remain deeply religious, they now appear to be religious in a different way. Modern religion is suffused with an individualist motif that undermines the unity and cohesion of religious categories. Will Herberg's influential study of religion in the postwar era encouraged people to think of the United States as a nation with three religious communities, Protestant, Catholic and Jewish.[15] This tripartite scheme overlooks those outside the three major communities, a category that includes non-Western religions, diverse spiritual currents such as nature religion or the New Age movement, and secularists who forsake religion entirely. The three-religions model also overlooks the diversity of the major religious groups which comprise competing and often incompatible factions. Roman Catholics, long known for racial, ethnic and language differences, are now divided as well over questions of liturgy, social action, the authority of Rome, the role of women, priestly celibacy, forms of worship and other matters.[16] The distances between major Jewish denominations in the United States over questions of identity and conduct raise the possibility that American Judaism is becoming a set of different religions.[17]

The impact of diversity is most apparent among Protestants who have a long history of factionalism. In the early years of the nation, the different Protestant denominations competed aggressively for the loyalty of the population. Only when mass immigration of Catholics and Jews threatened Protestant hegemony late in the nineteenth century did a common cultural identity develop to override sectarian concerns.[18] That sense of unity faded, leading to the development of a full-blown "two-party" system that survives to the present day.[19]

It is no simple matter to characterize the principal cleavage within contemporary Protestantism, the "mainline" and "evangelical" styles. The two movements represent dispositions only imperfectly related to denomination. Some Episcopalians, members of the prototypical mainline denomination, clearly adhere to an evangelical style of Christianity, and numerous individuals in "evangelical" churches share the worldview associated with the mainline tradition. Even some Roman Catholics find it possible to profess the evangelical identity once considered quintessentially Protestant. Describing these alternatives as styles or orientations allows us to encompass these complex realities.

In terms of denominations, the mainline label is most clearly applicable to United Methodists, Congregationalists and Episcopalians, and the evangelical label nicely fits Southern Baptists, independent Baptists, and the Assemblies of God. In some traditions, the separate denominations fall on different sides of the divide. The recently formed Evangelical Lutheran Church of America, despite its name, exemplifies the mainline style, while Lutherans affiliated with the Missouri and Wisconsin synods belong in the evangelical camp. Among Presbyterians, members of the Presbyterian Church of the USA are mostly mainline types but the smaller Presbyterian Church in America is part of the evangelical movement. In some of the largest traditions – such as the various Wesleyan Methodist families – the divisions may not be formalized into competing denominations but tend to divide congregations internally. In terms of population share – if not cultural dominance – the evangelical movement has achieved parity with (if not superiority over) the historic mainline denominations.[20]

The two styles of Protestantism are associated with different political styles as well.[21] Among the laity, the major political differences are concentrated on questions of social regulation that enforce traditional morality – prayer, sex roles, abortion, alcohol and drug use.[22] On average, mainline Protestants tend to embrace more liberal social policies, support greater tolerance for civil liberties, approve some redistribution of resources, and assign greater priority to civil rights legislation. The sermons in their churches call on Christians and the state to mobilize against social evils such as homelessness, war, and urban decay. In each of these domains, evangelicals are, as a whole, further to the right on the political spectrum. Accordingly, they favor solutions that emphasize commitment to traditional values. As with every other characterization about mainline–evangelical differences, these generalizations refer to central tendencies and admit numerous exceptions. But despite the existence of left-wing evangelicals who draw progressive political lessons from the Bible, the modal evangelical embraces a more conservative political agenda than the typical mainline Protestant.[23] The differences we have just described are sometimes – wrongly in our view – portrayed as conflict between fundamentalists and other Protestants. We strongly warn against the mistaken assumption that all evangelicals are fundamentalists. Fundamentalism is itself but one variant of evangelicalism,[24] and, like evangelicalism, an imprecise label. In a memorable quip, the Reverend Jerry Falwell once described a fundamentalist as an evangelical who had gotten mad about something. Many evangelicals use "fundamentalist" as an epithet to denote intolerance, anti-intellectualism and low social status. However defined, fundamentalism is a distinctive form of evangelicalism, found widely in some evangelical traditions, occasionally in others, and hardly at all in still others. While fundamentalists are one component of evangelicalism, the whole should not be mistaken for the part.

This lengthy disquisition has been necessary to insure that we look for differences between the correct groups. Simple Protestant/ Catholic comparisons are unlikely to yield significant differences because that distinction lumps together too many incompatible groups under the Protestant label. Yet that has been the scheme used to analyze the Mideast attitudes of American religious groups.

RELIGIOUS GROUP PATTERNS

Given the political differences between Catholics, evangelicals and mainline Protestants, what patterns should we expect to find when we focus on attitudes toward the Middle East? To answer that question, we turn to the framework known as symbolic politics.

According to the symbolic politics perspective, individuals select positions in political debate on the basis of their affective orientation to the groups in conflict.[25] People develop group images and loyalties early in life and typically maintain and strengthen them as they age. When a social conflict pits groups against one another, the individual takes the side of the group that is more positively valued. This framework is particularly appropriate in situations where individuals lack direct experience of the subject matter, the condition facing most Americans regarding the Middle East.

What group loyalties are activated when Christians consider the Middle East? The first possibility is that American Christians think about the Middle East in terms of their attitudes toward Jews. That would be a reasonable way to conceive the issue because American Jews have been vocal in support of Israel and Jewish organizations have spearheaded pro-Israel lobbying in the United States. The identification of Israel as a Jewish state may further activate the salience of Jews as the key factor in forming Mideast allegiances.

If that is so, we expect to find evangelical Protestants least supportive of Israel, Catholics in the middle, and mainline Protestants exhibiting the strongest support for Israel.

This prediction is based on the recurrent finding in previous surveys that members of evangelical churches entertain the most negative and stereotyped opinions about Jews. Roman Catholics have exhibited less anti-Semitism than members of evangelical denominations but more than adherents of churches associated with the mainline tradition.[26] There has been considerable debate about whether these patterns reflect religious values *per se* (the conclusion of the survey authors) or whether they are due to social factors correlated with religion. Whatever the causal ordering, evangelicals have been found to be less positively disposed to Jews than other Christians and that, by the logic of the symbolic politics model, should spill over into their views of the Middle East.

But the symbolic politics model yields a conflicting hypothesis. Suppose Americans assess the Middle East not primarily on the basis of their attitudes toward Jews but rather as an arena for East–West competition? Until quite recently, American presidents and other opinion leaders portrayed Israel as a strategic asset and defended the alliance with Israel as a means to promote American interests in the Middle East. The case for American–Israeli cooperation also cited the common political values of the two Westernized and democratic societies.

If Israel was perceived through the lens of East–West conflict, then its cause would resonate most deeply with the most nationalist of Americans. That assumption leads us to anticipate a very different ordering from the prediction based on attitudes toward Jews. Largely by virtue of the increasing foreign policy moderation of Catholics that we noted earlier, evangelicals have become the most reliable advocates of the use of force to secure American national interests. At the height of the Cold War, they stood out as exceptionally anti-communist.[27] In the Gulf War, where communism was not engaged, evangelicals still proved more willing than other Christians to support military action.[28] If the Middle East is understood primarily as a conflict between the United States and its foreign competitors, then we would expect evangelicals to be the strongest allies of Israel. By contrast, well before the collapse of the Soviet Union, the mainline churches and Roman Catholicism had developed fundamental doubts about the Cold War practice of partitioning the world into free and communist blocs. Searching for a Christian ethic in world affairs, many mainline and Catholic theologians adopted a version of liberation theology, a movement primarily of Catholic origins but with sufficient echoes of the Social Gospel to appeal as well to progressive mainline Protestants. The movement's admonition to put the church on the side of the poor and oppressed translated into sympathy for leftist movements around the globe. Both the National and World Council of Churches, often regarded as unofficial voices of mainline Protestantism, have embraced many movements of national liberation.[29] With that frame of reference, we predict that mainline Protestants and Catholics will be significantly less supportive of Israel than members of the evangelical community.

This second pattern appears most consistent with elite activity since the Six Day War. Before that seminal event, most mainline Protestant elites had supported Israel both as atonement for the Holocaust and as an expression of the western progressive heritage. Though some evangelicals had regarded the establishment of the state of Israel as a herald of the Second Coming, their general indifference to social and international matters inhibited them from connecting this positive attitude with any systematic political program. As Franklin Littell has argued,[30] the two sides drew very different lessons from Israel's stunning victory in 1967. The military success of Israel transformed its image in the eyes of mainline Protestants from a beleaguered nation warranting Christian sympathy to an occupying power, the carrier if not the organizer of Western imperialism. Out of sympathy for the Palestinians, who were portrayed as innocent Third World victims of superpower rivalry, mainline leaders favored a more "balanced" American position. This meant calls for American neutrality during the Yom Kippur War and a willingness to solve the Gulf crisis by linking Iraqi withdrawal from Kuwait with Israeli evacuation of the territories acquired in 1967.[31] On the other hand, Israel's remarkable victory in 1967 dramatically intensified its positive image among many evangelical leaders and they began to argue for the necessity of strong American support. Indeed, for evangelicals who see the world through the lens of dispensationalist theology, Israel's success was proof of God's favor.[32] God's plan for the world, as revealed in Bible prophecy, calls for Israel to be restored on the eve of Jesus' return.[33] The creation of the modern Israeli nation in 1948 seemed like a striking confirmation of that forecast.[34] Each successive Israeli military victory, particularly the miracle of 1967, seemed to mark another step toward the scenario outlined in Revelation. With Israel playing such an integral role in the redemption of humankind, support for Israel became the only "Godly" option in the Middle East. This theme was taken up with great vehemence by politically-active evangelical ministers in the 1980s[35] but was actually a restatement of a position with strong roots in the Christian Zionist tradition.[36]

DATA ANALYSIS

To examine the impact of religious variables on attitudes toward Israel[37], we draw on three specialized surveys of clergy, religious activists, and the mass public. The surveys are unusual precisely because they contain detailed religious queries, items on Middle East policy, and sufficient detail to distinguish among the three major religious traditions of mainline Protestantism, evangelical Protestantism and Roman Catholicism.

We will proceed as follows: First, we investigate the relationships between religious tradition and Middle East attitudes among religious professionals (Protestant clergy). Presumably we should find the strongest relationship here, given the attitude constraint typical of the theological and political views of the clergy.[38] Next, we review the same variables among a large sample of contemporary religious activists. These respondents, drawn from a broad array of religiously-motivated political interest groups, also range across the theological spectrum. Among these politically-conscious believers, we should see the same patterns discerned among the clergy, but perhaps less well-defined. Finally, we undertake the hardest test of all, the mass public, with its notorious lack of attitudinal constraint and prolific "non-attitudes."

To focus our attention on the key variable of religious tradition, we use Multiple Classification Analysis (MCA). In each analysis, the dependent variable is a question tapping attitudes toward the major parties involved in the Middle East conflict and the key predictor is a religious tradition measure that distinguishes between Catholics, evangelical and mainline Protestants. The equations also include a theological measure that taps elements of religious traditionalism and the premillennial "dispensationalist" theology credited with promoting evangelical sympathy for Israel. Though our focus is the difference between the three major religious communities, the theological index provides a useful check to determine when observed differences between the three traditions are solely a function of a particular theological current or whether they might reflect other factors.

The equations also contain a number of controls. The analysis is restricted to whites because religious affiliation and beliefs often have strikingly different political meanings in minority traditions. We also control for the effects of demographic and political variables which predict support for Israel in earlier studies. Gilboa reports that education, age, partisanship, and ideology are important correlates of pro-Israel attitudes.[39] Americans who are young, well-educated and (after the 1970s) Republican and conservative are more supportive of Israel. Of these, Gilboa argues that education (and related status measures) appear most powerful, although he reports no multivariate analyses. In any case, we have included these variables as simultaneous controls (covariates) in each analysis. As we report below, these variables often have little impact when included with precise religious measures in multivariate analyses.

The clergy are important because they help connect the normative ideas of their tradition to assessment of people and events in the political world.[40] Clergy also exhibit highly constrained worldviews, combining theological, social and political perspectives in coherent ideological form. Thus, if religious tradition and theology have clear attitudinal effects, they should be most evident among religious professionals. Here we use surveys of Protestant ministers in five major denominations, coordinated by one of the authors in 1988–89.[41] These surveys included a question on Middle East policy and detailed theological batteries. We have divided the clergy into religious traditions, with the Assemblies of God (AOG) and Southern Baptists (SBC) in the evangelical Protestant tradition, and the United Methodists (UMC), Disciples of Christ (DOC), and Presbyterian Church in the U.S.A. (PCUSA) in the mainline Protestant camp. This assignment is consistent with much recent research.[42]

In Table 1, as in the tables that follow, we provide the grand mean, a term for the average score on the dependent variable among all respondents, as well as the mean scores for each subgroup of respondents. In Table 1, where denomination is used as an indicator of religious tradition, the "unadjusted means" are the averages for members of each of the five specified denominations. The column labelled "adjusted for independent" indicates the mean for each group when the theological variable is included and the final column standardizes the group mean for the effect of theology and the other controls. In effect, the final column indicates what the group mean would be if all groups had similar theological, political and social profiles. Except for differences in religious categories across the three surveys, the reporting of results follows this common format.

Our dependent variable in Table 1 is a question asking about the desirability of Israel accepting a Palestinian state. In the clergy sample as a whole, weighted with a preponderance of ministers from mainline churches, the average response to the question was located between the neutral midpoint and mild agreement. As the mean scores in Table 1 reveal, denominational affiliation has a clear impact. Assemblies pastors are most likely to reject a Palestinian state, followed by Southern Baptists, Methodists, and Disciples of Christ, with Presbyterian ministers most inclined to support the Palestinians. Because attitudes to a Palestinian state are strongly and negatively affected by traditionalist theology, the inclusion of that variable diminishes but does not eliminate the pattern of the unadjusted means. The differences narrow further but still persist when all other factors are included in the equation. The MCA shows that denomination remains powerful when all variables including age, education, ideology and party are taken into account. The covariates are all significant predictors, but in this sample do not always run in the same direction as in recent mass public surveys. Support for Israel is lower among younger and better-educated clergy (especially among those with extended seminary training), although Republicans and conservatives do take the expected pro-Israeli stance. Most covariates have only minor effects, except for ideology, which accounts for somewhat less variance than theology (data not shown).

TABLE 1

1988 PROTESTANT CLERGY STUDIES SUPPORT FOR ISRAEL BY DENOMINATION, WITH DISPENSATIONALISM, PARTY IDENTIFICATION, IDEOLOGY, AGE AND EDUCATION CONTROLLED MULTIPLE CLASSIFICATION ANALYSIS

QUESTION: "A lasting peace in the Middle East will require Israel to recognize some kind of Palestinian State."
[1=Strongly Disagree, 5=Strongly Agree]

Grand Mean = 3.67

	(Weighted N)	UNADJUSTED MEAN SCORES MEAN	Eta	ADJUSTED FOR INDEPENDENT MEAN	Beta	ADJUSTED FOR INDEPEND/COVAR MEAN	Beta
RELIGIOUS TRADITION							
Evangelical:							
Assemblies of God	653	2.80		3.13		3.28	
Southern Baptist	711	3.33		3.50		3.61	
Mainline:							
United Methodist	694	3.89		3.81		3.76	
Disciples of Christ	711	4.06		3.89		3.77	
Presbyterian USA	739	4.19		3.97		3.89	
			.48*		.29*		.20*
MULTIPLE R					.526		.562
MULTIPLE R-SQUARED					.276		.136

*p<.001

Source: 1988 Clergy Surveys, conducted by James L. Guth, Helen Lee Turner, John C. Green, and Margaret M. Poloma (see Guth, et al., 1991).

We next examine respondents in the Wheaton Religious Activist Study, a 1990 survey of religious activists from eight political interest groups.[43] Members of these groups are recruited on the basis of explicit religious appeals and are often contacted, directly or indirectly, through prior membership in a church. Presumably then, having already shown a desire to act publicly on their religious convictions, these church activists should be swayed more by their religious beliefs than the average citizen, should be more likely to pick up political cues provided by local clergy, and finally, may be more attentive to the urgings of prominent national figures from their traditions. Of course, even religious activists might not exhibit the strong attitudinal constraint characteristic of clergy.

The survey asked the 4,000 laity in the sample how close they felt to the state of Israel. Table 2 reports the MCA results. Based on the unadjusted means, evangelical laity are much more pro-Israel than mainline Protestants, but Catholic activists are even less pro-Israel than mainline Protestants. When the equation is expanded to include theology and other social forces, the group differences narrow appreciably. Evangelicals remain slightly more pro-Israel than mainline Protestants and Catholics who are largely indistinguishable from one another. The control variables are all significant in this case, but the direction differs from earlier studies in some instances. Republicans and conservatives are again more pro-Israel, but as with the 1988 clergy studies, younger and better-educated respondents feel further from Israel, not closer. Although all four control variables have significant effects, their impact is modest compared to the religious measures (data not shown).

TABLE 2

1990 WHEATON RELIGIOUS ACTIVIST STUDY SUPPORT FOR ISRAEL BY RELIGIOUS TRADITION, WITH DISPENSATIONALISM, PARTY IDENTIFICATION, IDEOLOGY, AGE AND EDUCATION CONTROLLED MULTIPLE CLASSIFICATION ANALYSIS

(Laity Subsample)

QUESTION: "How close do you feel to the State of Israel."
[1 = Very close, 5 = Very far]

Grand Mean = 2.90

	(N)	UNADJUSTED MEAN SCORES		ADJUSTED FOR INDEPENDENT		ADJUSTED FOR INDEPEND/COVAR	
		MEAN	Eta	MEAN	Beta	MEAN	Beta
RELIGIOUS TRADITION							
Evangelical	2177	2.69		2.85		2.87	
Mainline	647	3.31		3.03		2.99	
Catholic	348	3.48		2.99		2.92	
			.25*		.06*		.04*
MULTIPLE R					.441		.466
MULTIPLE R-SQUARED					.195		.217

*p < .001

Source: 1990 Wheaton Religious Activist Study, conducted by Lyman A. Kellstedt, John C. Green, Corwin E. Smidt, and James L. Guth (see Guth, *et al.*, 1993).

As we conclude our look at religious elites and activists, we should note that in each of the studies we have additional measures of religious orientation that we have not used because they are not available in all the samples. These measures not only reinforce our findings but, if incorporated, add to the predictive power of the models.

Now we approach the most difficult task: determining whether religious factors assist us in understanding the American public's attitudes toward Israel and Middle East policy. This task is difficult because previous literature has found relatively low structure to American foreign policy attitudes in general and the literature on religion and politics has identified few religious effects on policy preferences beyond social-moral issues. Nonetheless, we draw on data from a 1992 survey of 4,001 Americans, conducted by the Survey Research Center of the University of Akron. This survey was designed to chart the links between religious affiliations, beliefs and behaviors and American political life.[44] Unlike the previous data sets, which were restricted to clergy and religious activists, this general population sample did not screen out the irreligious. This permits us to add secular respondents – those who disclaim any religious identity – as a separate category for analysis. Because secular respondents tend to be young, well-educated and affluent, we anticipate that they will resemble mainline Protestants in their Middle East views.

The dependent variable is an item asking respondents whether the U.S. should back Israel rather than the Arabs in the Middle East. This is a relatively "hard" question that asks respondents to balance priorities. According to the group mean, the entire sample was centered slightly on the "disagree" side, close to the neutral midpoint of the response scale. In Table 3, the unadjusted group means reveal the same clear pattern of declining support for Israel when moving from evangelical Protestants, through mainline Protestants and Catholics. The secular citizens prove to be the least pro-Israel of all population groups. The most striking gap separates evangelicals from all the other groups. If we take the neutral midpoint position of "3" as the dividing line, we can say that evangelicals are on the pro-Israel side of the spectrum whereas all other groups fall on the pro-Arab side of the spectrum. The group differences narrow but retain the same general pattern in the full equation. The only major difference introduced by the controls is that seculars become indistinguishable from mainline Protestants as per original expectations. In this mass sample, party identification, ideology, and education fall short of significance, even with the large N, and younger citizens are only marginally more pro-Israel than older voters.

Because of its substantive focus, the Akron study contains many items which tap religious identifications, beliefs, and practices. These

TABLE 3
AMERICAN PUBLIC SUPPORT FOR ISRAEL BY RELIGIOUS TRADITION, WITH
DISPENSATIONALISM, PARTY IDENTIFICATION, IDEOLOGY, AGE AND EDUCATION
CONTROLLED MULTIPLE CLASSIFICATION ANALYSIS

(National sample; whites only)

QUESTION: "The United States should back Israel over the Arabs in the Middle East."
[1=Strongly Agree; 5-Strongly Disagree]

Grand mean = 3.14

				UNADJUSTED MEAN SCORES		ADJUSTED FOR INDEPENDENT		ADJUSTED FOR INDEPEND/COVAR
	(Weighted N)	MEAN	Eta		MEAN	Beta	MEAN	Beta
RELIGIOUS TRADITION								
Evangelica	707	2.77			2.90		2.91	
Mainline	500	3.20			3.22		3.23	
Catholic	629	3.33			3.30		3.30	
Secular	439	3.40			3.21		3.21	
			.21*			.14*		.13*
MULTIPLE R						.261		.268
MULTIPLE R-SQUARED						.068		.073

*$p<.001$

Source: University of Akron Study of Religion and Politics in America, 1992, conducted by
John C. Green, Lyman A. Kellstedt, Corwin E. Smidt, and James L. Guth.

variables offer a rare opportunity to determine which of the many
differences between the major religious traditions most powerfully
affect Middle East attitudes. Considerable experimentation reveals
that incorporation of other beliefs often associated with conservative
Protestant theology increases our predictive ability. The most
powerful is a three-point item asking whether respondents considered
themselves "born-again" Christians and whether that meant having a
specific experience in time or gradual development in faith. Those
with dramatic experiences are considerably more pro-Israel. So are
those respondents who consider themselves "fundamentalists" or
"charismatics," even after other religious variables are taken into
account. Following up an earlier lead from the Wheaton study, we
also broke the evangelical and mainline traditions into their
constituent denominational families. For the larger families, the mean
support for Israel from highest to lowest is as follows: (Evangelicals)
Pentecostal (2.46), Holiness (2.57), Non-Denominational Evangelical
(2.67), Baptist (2.77), (and for the Mainline) Presbyterians (3.12),
Methodists (3.14), Lutherans (3.25), and United Church of Christ
(3.54). Once again, the consistency of results among the various
samples is striking. Finally, those who consider their religious beliefs

important for political decisions are stronger supporters of Israel. Incorporating these additional variables in the MCA substantially raises the explained variance (data not shown).

DISCUSSION

Utilizing three distinct data sets, we have found persistent religious differences in Middle East attitudes. The data converge on one singular conclusion – *evangelical Protestants are more supportive of Israel than mainline Protestants and Roman Catholics*. The latter two groups are close together in their attitudes. The results also suggest that religious traditions may be regarded as the cause of these differences. We know that some of the variation in Mideast beliefs reflects contrasting theological values and sociopolitical differences between the groups. Yet even with these additional controls, the three major traditions diverge on the Middle East.

That pattern was predicted by one version of the symbolic politics model. Greater evangelical sympathy for Israel was anticipated on the assumption that evangelicals were more likely than other Christians to frame the Middle East conflict as a situation involving American national interests and to hear messages from the pulpit and other religious sources that tilted toward the Israeli position. Having documented that evangelical ministers entertain stronger pro-Israeli sympathies than other clergy, it is reasonable to surmise that they transmit these views to congregants. There is also evidence that nationalism does indeed contribute to the pro-Israeli orientations of evangelical laity. Using a proxy measure of nationalism – attitudes toward proposed cuts in the level of American defense spending – we found a strong correlation among evangelicals between opposition to defense cutbacks and support for Israel. Even with the other controls included in Table 3, the addition of this defense spending item contributed modestly to the level of support for Israel. In attributing pro-Israeli sentiment to nationalist attitudes and clergy mobilization, we appear to be on the right track.

These patterns are remarkable because they contradict a widely-held image of evangelicals as more prone than other Christians to anti-Jewish stereotypes. In much the same way that racial attitudes strongly predict American preferences about South Africa,[45] it was thought that the anti-Jewish perspectives attributed to evangelicals would diminish their commitment to Israel. The hypothesis may have failed because the symbolic politics framework does not operate in this manner – perhaps evangelicals simply do not conceptualize the Middle East in terms of how they think about Jews. Alternately, evangelicals may compartmentalize their thinking and invoke other factors – such as American nationalism – when developing their preferences about the region. Then again, it may be that the core assumption behind the falsified hypothesis is itself wrong. Perhaps evangelical Protestants are not more anti-Jewish than other Christians or, even more audaciously in light of conventional wisdom, perhaps they are more sympathetic toward Jews. If evangelicals have developed more positive images of Jews than their Christian counterparts and those views do factor into their Middle East preferences, that would also explain the patterns we have observed.

We can test these various possibilities with the general population survey question about how close the respondent felt toward Jews. In the main, the best predictors of closeness to Jews were age and education (results not shown). Even allowing for such factors and including traditional theology as a contributing factor, religious tradition was a significant influence on closeness toward Jews. However, the pattern contradicted conventional wisdom as evangelical Protestants reported closer identification with Jews than mainline Protestants, Catholics and secular respondents. The inclusion of felt proximity to Jews in the model explaining closeness to Israel produced results virtually identical to those reported in Table 3. Reading down the final column in Table 3, the revised group means for the four groups after including the proximity question are 2.95, 3.21, 3.29 and 3.21. From a statistical perspective, the consistency is not surprising because the equation already included variables that strongly influenced attitudes toward Jews. So attitudes toward Jews do not appear to play a major independent role in explaining the religious differences in Mideast preferences. If they did, the effect would not diminish the differences between evangelicals and other Christians nor alter the finding that evangelicals were the most pro-Israel of the groups. Similar results from another survey[46] suggest that our findings are not anomalous.

Is it possible that previous research was wrong about evangelical anti-Semitism, or have evangelicals changed dramatically since the surveys that identified them as holding anti-Jewish stereotypes? We would like to suggest a third, more complex possibility. It may be that "closeness toward Jews," the attitudinal measure used in the mass survey, is a very different phenomenon from the indices of anti-Semitism commonly utilized in prior research. The former taps theological orientations, the latter, we suspect, reflect cultural norms. This distinction permits so prominent an evangelical leader as Jerry Falwell simultaneously to reiterate the binding quality of the Abrahamic covenant (Genesis 12:3) on Christians and yet to repeat blithely the old canard about the alleged Jewish facility for money-making. As a rule, evangelical Protestants are more likely than other Christians to subscribe to anti-Jewish stereotypes by attributing negative qualities to Jews. Had such items been included in the surveys used in our analysis, we might well have found the same pattern.

It is critical to distinguish this essentially cultural disposition from a theological understanding of Jews. The two are sufficiently independent that it is possible for Christians to feel a sense of kinship or religious affinity with a people they regard as flawed in certain respects. For evangelicals, the disjuncture may have its roots in the worldview of premillenial dispensationalism which promotes a complex disposition toward Jews.[47] On the one hand, like other Christians and evangelicals, premillenialists believe that Jews need to accept Jesus as savior in order to obtain eternal salvation. This belief has prompted some Christians to perceive Jewish "obstinacy" as a barrier to the redemption of the world, a situation that must be put right by aggressive evangelization and conversion. But the premillenial view, which forecasts the return of Jesus before the world is redeemed, does not insist that Jews convert as a precondition of that return. Rather, dispensationalists believe that "the Jews had always remained God's people, despite their rejection of Christ and... would in the End Times be restored to the Land which God had promised them and would acknowledge Christ as Messiah at his Second Coming."[48] Christians who interfered with that process were not fulfilling their religious duty and were, in fact, delaying the onset of redemption. To underline the seriousness of this sin, dispensationalists remind their listeners that people who persecute the Jews during the period preceding the Second Coming will be consigned to death and eternal torment.[49] This scenario, permitting Jews to accept Jesus freely rather than have Christianity imposed upon them, is much more sympathetic toward Judaism than typical expressions of Christian triumphalism. It sees the Jews as errant but nonetheless capable of finding their way back to the truth. This mindset has not insulated evangelicals entirely from "the caricature and stereotypes that their culture attributed to Jewish people"[50] – which is what typical survey measures of anti-Semitism tap – but it promoted a sense of fellowship and common fate. Imbued with this vision, evangelicals would report greater fellow feeling toward Jews and Israel than other Christians. Put simply, stereotyping need not imply hostility.[51] To be sure, much hinges on the way anti-Semitism is conceived. The premillennial view still denies the religious integrity of Judaism, and to the extent that it shares this view with other forms of Christianity, it is hard to contend that evangelicals are any less anti-Semitic. But this is not the only way in which contested terms such as tolerance and anti-Semitism can be defined.

RELIGION AND US–ISRAELI RELATIONS

How do these findings speak to the broad theme of US-Israeli relations in a changing global order? The finding that evangelicals are the most pro-Israel of the Christian religious groups (and more sympathetic to Israel than the non-religious) may appear at first glance to reinforce the historic ties between the United States and Israel. Evangelicals, the fastest growing segment of the American religious community, have acquired renewed political influence and are now key targets of electoral mobilization in Presidential elections. That such a critical political bloc shares a strong commitment to Israel is good news for the bilateral relationship, suggesting that calls for a more "balanced" American approach to the Middle East may not pay political dividends among this constituency. If an American president embarked on a foreign policy that was openly antagonistic to Israel's interests, arousing national controversy, the evangelical community would be expected to enlist on the Israeli side of the debate. The evangelical tilt toward Israel also provides political allies when Jewish groups seek to maintain the pro-Israeli tilt in American foreign policy. We believe, however, that it would be unwise for the pro-Israel movement to put too much stock in the evangelical connection, however deep and sincere its roots. There are reasons to doubt the political efficacy of evangelicals as an ally in promoting American support for Israel.

Religious groups in general seldom exert substantial influence on the formation of international policy. Except in special circumstances, the foreign policy process appears relatively well insulated from mass pressure. The conditions that magnify Jewish influence on American policy toward Israel – experience, single-mindedness, salience – are largely lacking in the case of evangelicals and the Middle East. In the first place, the evangelical lobbying organizations in Washington, D.C., have not exhibited an impressive degree of political skill.[52] As relative newcomers to the world of pressure politics, they have often stumbled and alienated more than they have persuaded. Until they learn to appreciate the realities of political influence in the national arena, embracing the value of compromise, withholding moral judgment, providing information rather than outrage, their influence will be severely restricted or actually counterproductive. Second, even if their lobbying skills improve, it is doubtful that Israel will be at the top of the evangelical political agenda. While support for Israel is widespread among the evangelical laity, it has a relatively weak relationship to the social-moral issues that have been the mobilizing issues for Christian activists.[53] The evangelical lobbying effort has focused on school prayer, restrictive abortion policy, benefits for religious schools, and other such social issues. Because "the putative moral decay of American culture is perceived as a more imminent threat to Christian values and Christian civilization than any looming foreign policy issue,"[54] evangelical lobbyists have given little practical emphasis to the pro-Israeli sentiment of their constituency, effectively dissipating the pro-Israeli fervor that emerges from dispensationalist theology. The foreign policy concerns expressed by evangelical lobbyists, such as opposition to family planning, have more to do with moral traditionalism and social conservatism than the fate of Israel. Third, and most compelling, evangelical legislators have shown a willingness to jettison Israeli concerns when they conflict with other priorities.

This has been apparent in the annual debate over Israel's $3 billion share of the US foreign aid appropriation, the core "bread and butter" issue on Israel's American agenda as defined by Israel itself and its most influential ally, the American–Israel Public Affairs Committee (AIPAC). In voting on both the 1994 and 1995 Fiscal Year appropriations, the congressional representatives in the evangelical camp were, as a group, least supportive of the foreign aid bill. They split against the bill by 48 percent to 52 percent in 1993 and 44 percent vs. 56 percent in 1994. They were noticeably less supportive than fellow House Republicans who voted for the aid bills by margins of greater than 2 to 1. It was also noteworthy that social liberals, often drawn from mainline Protestantism or elected from districts where it predominates, were the most sympathetic of all Congressional blocs to the foreign aid appropriations. The most socially-liberal representatives gave nearly unanimous support to the appropriations, exceeding the high level of support among House Democrats as a whole.[55]

It may be tempting to dismiss these data by noting that roll call votes are blunt instruments that do not reflect the nuances of opinion and to claim that evangelical legislators may take pro-Israeli positions in other ways. Perhaps, but it seems sensible to take Israel and AIPAC at their word that foreign aid is the crucial way to translate pro-Israeli sentiment into pro-Israeli behavior. A more compelling response is to note that the social conservatives did not vote against the bill expressly to torpedo the Israeli allocation but rather to protest the size of the entire appropriation, the generosity to other aid recipients, the sponsorship of a Democratic president, or perhaps the very principle of exporting American tax revenues. Conversely, social liberals may have supported the bill in spite of their doubts about Israeli behavior. In making this argument, the case is effectively conceded to those who warn Israel against making too much of evangelical sympathy. By voting tactically at the expense of the program that Israel defines as its paramount objective, those sympathetic to the social agenda of evangelicals make clear that Israel is secondary and can be sacrificed readily in pursuit of more compelling goals. There is no evidence that evangelical voters punish representatives who vote against Israeli aid and, judging by their record level of support for George Bush's re-election in 1992, absolutely no indication that they judged him harshly for challenging Israeli policy in the Territories.

There are other portents of decay in evangelical commitment to Israel. The decline of Soviet influence in the Middle East may render

Israel a less compelling issue for evangelical supporters concerned with superpower rivalry. For those pro-Israeli evangelicals with a theological foundation in dispensationalist thought, strategic considerations are less compelling. But even they may desert the pro-Israeli camp as illustrated by the case of the Reverend Jerry Falwell, the latter-day paragon of evangelical Christian Zionism.[55] Falwell supported George Bush in 1992, despite the latter's hard line toward Israeli loan guarantees, and subsequently announced his intention to support former White House aide Pat Buchanan in the 1996 primaries. Buchanan has raised charges of "dual loyalty" against American Jews, charged Congress with cowering in the face of Jewish pressure, and pointedly suggested that Israel and the United States no longer share common geopolitical interests. The conservative editor William F. Buckley Jr. has found Buchanan's comments anti-Semitic in nature. That Falwell can so easily shed his Israeli commitment to support Buchanan on domestic grounds does not augur well for the future of the alliance. Of course, Falwell is just one evangelical political activist and his behavior does not itself foretell the actions of his coreligionists. Nonetheless, this development should give further pause to those who regard evangelical Protestants as reliable allies of Israel.

NOTES

1. David L. Larson (ed.), *The Puritan Ethic in United States Foreign Policy* (Princeton, N.J.: Van Nostrand, 1966).
2. Tami R. Davis and Sean M. Lynn Jones, "City Upon a Hill," *Foreign Policy*, Vol.66 (1992), pp.20–38; Kenneth L. Vaux, *Ethics and the Gulf War: Religion, Rhetoric, and Righteousness* (Boulder, Col.: Westview, 1992).
3. Robert Dallek, *The American Style in Foreign Policy* (New York: New American Library, 1983); Michael H. Hunt, *Ideology and U.S. Foreign Policy* (New Haven: Yale University Press, 1987).
4. Barry B. Hughes, *The Domestic Context of American Foreign Policy* (San Francisco: W.H. Freeman, 1978).
5. Kenneth D. Wald, *Religion and Politics in the United States*, 2nd ed. (Washington, D.C.: CQ Press, 1992), Ch.1.
6. At the same time, we recognize that the United States has experienced some types of religious change that do conform to rather more refined notions of secularization.
7. Cf. David C. Leege, Joel A. Lieske, and Kenneth D. Wald, "Toward Cultural Theories of American Political Behavior: Religion, Ethnicity and Race, and Class Outlook," in William Crotty (ed.), *Political Science: Looking to the Future* (Evanston, Ill.: Northwestern University Press, 1991); David C. Leege and Lyman A. Kellstedt (eds.), *Rediscovering the Religious Factor in American Politics* (Armonk, N.Y.: M. E. Sharpe, 1993).
8. Wald, *Religion and Politics*.
9. Hughes, *Domestic Context*; Milton J. Rosenberg, "Attitude Change and Foreign Policy in the Cold War Era," in James N. Rosenau (ed.), *Domestic Sources of Foreign Policy* (New York: Free Press, 1967), pp.111–60.
10. Kenneth D. Wald, "Religious Elites and Public Opinion: The Impact of the Bishops' Peace Pastoral," *Review of Politics*, Vol.54 (1992), pp.112–43.
11. Rosenberg, "Attitude Change," p.157.
12. Milton Rokeach, "Religious Values and Social Compassion," *Review of Religious Research*, Vol.11 (1969), pp.24–39.
13. Alfred O. Hero, Jr., *American Religious Groups View Foreign Policy: Trends in Rank-*

and-File Opinion, 1937–1969 (Durham, N.C.: Duke University Press, 1973).

14. Peter L. Benson and Dorothy L. Williams, *Religion on Capitol Hill: Myths and Realities* (San Francisco: Harper & Row, 1982); Andrew Greeley, "Evidence That a Maternal Image of God Correlates With Liberal Politics," *Sociology and Social Research*, 72 (1988), pp.150–4; David C. Leege, "Toward a Mental Measure of Religiosity in Research on Religion and Politics," in Ted G. Jelen (ed.), *Religion and Political Behavior in the United States* (New York: Praeger, 1989).

15. Will Herberg, *Protestant, Catholic, Jew* (Garden City, N.Y.: Doubleday, 1955).

16. Eugene Kennedy, *Reimagining American Catholicism* (New York: Vintage, 1985).

17. Jack Wertheimer, *A People Divided: Judaism in Contemporary America* (New York: Basic Books, 1993).

18. Robert T. Handy, *A Christian America?*, 2nd ed. (New York: Oxford University Press, 1984).

19. Martin E. Marty, *Righteous Empire: The Protestant Experience in America* (New York: Harper & Row, 1970).

20. Wade Clark Roof and William McKinney, *American Mainline Religion: Its Changing Shape and Future* (New Brunswick, N.J.: Rutgers University Press, 1987).

21. Leege and Kellstedt, *Rediscovering the Religious Factor*; Wald, *Religion and Politics*, Ch.4.

22. Dean R. Hoge and Ernesto Zulueta, "Salience as a Condition for Various Social Consequences of Religious Commitment," *Journal for the Scientific Study of Religion*, Vol.24 (1984), pp.21–38.

23. Robert Booth Fowler, *A New Engagement: Evangelical Political Thought, 1966–1976* (Grand Rapids, Mich.: William B. Eerdmans, 1982).

24. George M. Marsden, *Understanding Fundamentalism and Evangelicalism* (Grand Rapids, Mich.: William B. Eerdmans, 1991).

25. David O. Sears, Richard R. Lau, Tom R. Tyler, and Allen M. Harris, Jr., "Self-Interest vs. Symbolic Politics in Policy Attitudes and Presidential Voting," *American Political Science Review*, Vol.74 (1980), pp.670–84.

26. Charles Y. Glock and Rodney Stark, *Christian Beliefs and Anti-Semitism* (New York: Harper & Row, 1966); Gregory Martire and Ruth Clark, *Anti-Semitism in the United States: A Study of Prejudice in the 1980s* (New York: Praeger, 1982); Harold E. Quinley and Charles Y. Glock, *Anti-Semitism in America* (New York: Free Press, 1979); Gertrude J. Selznick and Stephen Steinberg, *The Tenacity of Prejudice: Anti-Semitism in Contemporary America* (New York: Harper & Row, 1969); Rodney Stark, Bruce D. Foster, Charles Y. Glock, and Harold E. Quinley, *Wayward Shepherds: Prejudice and the Protestant Clergy* (New York: Harper & Row, 1971).

27. Kenneth D. Wald, "The Religious Dimension of American Anti-Communism," *Journal of Church and State*, forthcoming.

28. Ted G. Jelen, "Religion and Foreign Policy Attitudes," paper presented at the Conference on the Political Consequences of War, sponsored by the National Election Studies, the Center for Political Studies, and the Brookings Institution, Washington, D.C., 1992.

29. Allen D. Hertzke, "An Assessment of Mainline Churches Since 1945," in James E. Wood, Jr., and Derek Davis (eds.), *The Role of Religion in the Making of Public Policy* (Waco, Txs.: J. M. Dawson Institute of Church-State Studies, Baylor University, 1992).

30. Franklin H. Littell, *American Protestantism and Antisemitism* (Jerusalem: Study Circle on World Jewry, 1985).

31. Andrew R. Murphy, "The Mainline Churches and Political Activism: The Continuing Impact of the Persian Gulf War," *Soundings*, Vol.76 (1993) pp.525–50.

32. Timothy P. Weber, *Living in the Shadow of the Second Coming: American Premillennialism, 1875–1982* (Chicago: University of Chicago Press, 1987).

33. Hal Lindsey, *The Late Great Planet Earth* (Grand Rapids, Mi.: Zondervan, 1970).

34. Ronald R. Stockton, "Christian Zionism: Prophecy and Public Opinion," *Middle East Journal*, Vol.41 (1987), pp.234–53.

35. Merrill Simon, *Jerry Falwell and the Jews* (Middle Village, N.Y.: Jonathan David, 1984).

36. Yaakov S. Ariel, *On Behalf of Israel: American Fundamentalist Attitudes Toward Jews, Judaism and Zionism, 1865-1945* (Brooklyn, N.Y.: Carlson, 1991); Lawrence J. Epstein, *Zion's Call: Christian Contributions to the Origins and Development of Israel* (Lanham, Md.: University Press of America, 1984).

37. This section draws heavily on Ch.17 in John C. Green, James L. Guth, Corwin E. Smidt and Lyman A. Kellstedt, *Religion and the Culture Wars* (Lanham, MD: Rowman and Littlefield, 1996).
38. Jeffrey K. Hadden, *The Gathering Storm in the Churches* (Garden City, N.Y.: Doubleday, 1969); Harold Quinley, *The Prophetic Clergy* (Berkeley: University of California Press, 1974); James L. Guth, John C. Green, Corwin E. Smidt, and Margaret Poloma, "Pulpits and Politics: The Protestant Clergy in the 1988 Presidential Election," in James L. Guth and John C. Green (eds.), *The Bible and the Ballot Box: Religion and Politics in the 1988 Election* (Boulder, Col.: 1991), pp.73–93.
39. Eitan Gilboa, *American Public Opinion Toward Israel and the Arab–Israeli Conflict* (Lexington, Mass.: Lexington Books, 1987).
40. Hadden, *Gathering Storm*; Quinley, *Prophetic Clergy*; Guth *et al.*, "Pulpits and Politics."
41. For details, see Guth *et al.*, ibid.
42. Lyman A. Kellstedt and John C. Green, "Knowing God's Many People: Denominational Preference and Political Behavior," in Leege and Kellstedt, *Rediscovering the Religious Factor.*
43. For details, see James L. Guth, Corwin E. Smidt, Lyman A. Kellstedt, and John C. Green, "The Sources of Antiabortion Attitudes: The Case of Religious Political Activists," *American Politics Quarterly*, Vol.21 (1993), pp.65–80.
44. See John C. Green, "Survey of Americans' Religious Beliefs and Politics," Ray C. Bliss Institute, University of Akron, 1992.
45. Kevin Hill, "The Domestic Sources of Foreign Policymaking: Congressional Voting and American Mass Attitudes Toward South Africa," *International Studies Quarterly*, Vol.37 (1993), pp.195–214.
46. Ronald L. Stockton, "The Falwell Core: A Public Opinion Analysis," paper presented to the annual meeting of the Society for the Scientific Study of Religion, Chicago, 1984.
47. David A. Rausch, *Fundamentalist Evangelicals and Anti-Semitism* (Valley Forge, Pa.: Trinity Press International, 1993).
48. Guth and Fraser, "Religion and Foreign Policy Attitudes," p.3.
49. John F. Walvoord, *Armageddon, Oil and the Middle East Crisis*, rev. ed. (Grand Rapids, Mi.: Zondervan, 1990).
50. Rausch, *Fundamentalist Evangelicals*, p.63.
51. Patricia G. Devine, "Stereotypes and Prejudice: Their Automatic and Controlled Components," *Journal of Personality and Social Psychology*, Vol.56 (1989), pp.5–18; Patricia G. Devine, Margo J. Montieth, Julia R. Zuwerink, and Andrew J. Elliott, "Prejudice With and Without Compunction," *Journal of Personality and Social Psychology*, Vol.60 (1991), pp.817–30.
52. Matthew C. Moen, *The Christian Right and Congress* (Tuscaloosa, Al.: University of Alabama Press, 1989).
53. Lyman A. Kellstedt and John C. Green, "The Falwell Issue Agenda: Sources of Support Among White Protestant Evangelicals," in Monte L. Lynn and David O. Moberg (eds.), *Research in the Social Scientific Study of Religion*, Vol.1 (Greenwich, Conn.: JAI, 1989), pp.109–32; Stockton, "Falwell Core."
54. Dean C. Curry, "Where Have All the Neibuhrs Gone? Evangelicals and the Marginalization of Religious Influence in American Public Life," *Journal of Church and State*, Vol.36 (1994), pp.97–114, especially p.107.
55. Social conservatives and liberals were identified by votes on key congressional issues in the annual Congressional voting ratings compiled by the *National Journal*. Conservatives were those who ranked in the top 10% and liberals in the bottom 10% on an index of social conservatism that reflects the major issue concerns of Christian conservatives. All of the 46 social conservatives were Republicans and all but two of the 54 social liberals were Democrats. There is no necessary link between personal religious identity and classification as a social liberal or conservative. The 1994 appropriation was Vote#467 in the *Congressional Quarterly* listing for 1993 and the 1995 appropriation was the subject of Vote #208 in 1994.

Israel and the Diaspora: A Relationship Reexamined

ARTHUR HERTZBERG

Historians keep telling each other the same story: near the beginning of creation, Adam fell into a deep sleep and when he awoke, his side was hurting and a human creature like himself, but of different gender, was nearby. He turned to her and said, "We are living in an age of transition." From the moment that Zionism appeared as an organized movement more than a century ago, the Jewish people has been living in an age of transition. In the beginning the Zionists in the Diaspora set out to create a Jewish State in Palestine. When that state arose, it insisted that it ought to dominate the Diaspora.

The most recent turnings in the ever-changing tension between Israel and the Diaspora come on September 13, 1993, when Yitzhak Rabin and Yasir Arafat shook hands at the White House. Yossi Beilin, then Deputy Foreign Minister of Israel, soon suggested that Israel, on the way to peace with the Arab world, is now strong enough to dispense with the financial aid of the Diaspora. He was immediately dressed down by Prime Minister Yitzhak Rabin, but Beilin's notion is not a new heresy. On the contrary, a century ago, Theodor Herzl himself had been far more radical: he had said that when the Jewish State came into being, he would encourage those who chose to remain among the Gentiles to assimilate into the majority. Beilin is right that peace with the Arab World would put the relations between Israel and the Jewish Diaspora into a new historical framework, but one cannot predict this new age. At the very least, before we imagine that a new heaven and a new earth are about to appear, we must take a sober look at what has gone before in the last century.

At its very beginnings, the Zionist movement was split between those who "denied the Diaspora" and those who wanted to find a new way of keeping it alive. There is almost no trace of any loyalty to traditional Jewish culture in Theodore Herzl's writing, or in his

Arthur Hertzberg is Bronfman Visiting Professor of Humanities at New York University. He is President of the American Jewish Policy Foundation and Co-Chair of the Advisory Council of the World Jewish Congress.

personal life. Herzl was no revolutionary. He was too bourgeois, too eager to be accepted as a proper European gentleman, to be much influenced by a contemporary such as Friedrich Nietzsche, but Nietzsche was a profound influence, then, on the younger generation in Europe. Some East European Jewish intellectuals, such as the writers Yosef Hayyim Brenner and Micah Yosef Berdichevski, followed after Herzl because they thought that Zionism offered the chance for a Nietzschean "transvaluation of values" within Jewry; the Zionist settlement in Palestine would create its own world, unencumbered by the culture that had reigned in the Jewish ghetto. Brenner and Berdichevski had not learned their distaste for traditional Jewish culture only from Nietzsche. They were prepared by the writers in Hebrew and in Yiddish in the second half of the nineteenth century who had pleaded the need for "enlightenment." The greatest figures in both literatures, such as Mendele Mocher Sefarim and Yehuda Leib Gordon, were testy and even angry with the Jewish life in the ghetto. They deplored the suffering of the Jews during centuries of persecution, but they insisted that suffering was no excuse; it was within the power of the Jews themselves to broaden their culture and to become modern men. The windows of the ghetto should be opened, to let in the air of the general culture.

Nietzsche, the radical thinker, and Herzl, the political innovator, pointed a path for the handful of young Jewish ideologues who came to Palestine after the turn of the century. They proposed creating a society that would be Jewish, but very new. Many of these pioneers hoped that the Zionist community would achieve a just, socialist life, a model for all the progressive forces in the world – and the antithesis of the ghetto in which they had been born.

Herzl's detachment from Jewish culture evoked the first great battle within the Zionist movement over the issue of values and tradition. The leading traditionalist among the Zionists was Asher Ginzberg, who wrote under the pen-name Ahad Ha-am. He came to the first Zionist congress in Basel in 1897 and described himself as "a mourner at a wedding." Herzl, and especially many of his new followers in Eastern Europe, were dreaming of a modern Jewish state that would transcend the past and make it irrelevant. Ahad Ha-am was a cultural nationalist who regarded all of the Jewish past as precious. He wanted a Hebraic Jewish community in Palestine that would radiate renewed spiritual energies of the tradition to the Diaspora. Ahad Ha-am did not deny the Diaspora or hold it in contempt. On the contrary, he admired and even revered its creativity throughout the centuries. Within a few years, Ahad Ha-am was engaged in a bitter battle with Berdichevski and Brenner over these very issues of continuity. They mounted one powerful argument against Ahad Ha-am: they demanded to know how he defined the Jewish tradition. By what authority did Ahad Ha-am impose any limits on contemporary Jewish life? Having once been rabbinic scholars, both Brenner and Berdichevski understood that an Orthodox believer could and, indeed, had to insist that the meaning of Judaism was clear and essentially unchanging. God had revealed His will to man in the Torah. Those who disregarded His teaching were not creators of new values; they were rebels against the will of God. But Ahad Ha-am was, like them, an ex-believer, an agnostic. Ahad Ha-am invoked "the spirit of the people" as a judge of what had to be preserved and of those new ideas that had to be excluded, but he seemed to be speaking for himself. Brenner and Berdichevski argued against him that the Jewish tradition was not to be found within the constraints proposed by Ahad Ha-am. On the contrary, the true Jewish history had been carved in the revolts throughout the ages against the dominant religious and intellectual establishments. The first Christians, the Cabalists, the repeated messianic movements, and the Hassidim who appeared in the eighteenth century had been spiritual revolutionaries. Why was a contemporary revolt, in the name of physical power and even the worship of the body, entirely out of court?

The few, some thirty thousand, who came to settle in Palestine in the early years of the twentieth century were not clear-cut followers of either of these views, but those who came thought of themselves in heroic terms. These pioneers could suffer hunger and malaria – and attacks by Arabs – only if they could imagine that their life was both new and morally superior to the life in the Diaspora. This was all the more necessary because the overwhelming majority of their contemporaries were on the move westward to the United States. A.D. Gordon, the leading moral figure among the few who chose Palestine, assured his followers that theirs was the greater destiny. They were creating a new Jew, who was rooted in the land. Such healthy, primal Jews last existed in biblical times, when Jews had lived on their own land and worked it. To create these "new Jews" was the central task of the Jewish people in the modern age. All other Jewish purposes were secondary, or really irrelevant. This "new Jew" had the right to the admiration of the Diaspora, which he was engaged in transcending. He could expect support without feeling demeaned as a suppliant. David Ben-Gurion often summarized this attitude by saying that Jewish history ended in the second century and began again in the middle of the nineteenth when the first modern agricultural settlement was founded in Palestine.

Even the conservative Ahad Ha-am's thinking downgraded the contemporary Diaspora. He believed it would continue to exist and he wanted to help it, but his basic metaphor was that the new Zionist center in Palestine would be a sun, which would give light and warmth to its periphery, the Diaspora communities, which would be passive moons. He did not believe that the Diaspora could continue to create substantial culture from its own energies. Ahad Ha-am was well-read in a half dozen languages. He certainly knew that in his time, at the turn of the century, Jews were significant figures in all fields of European culture, but this was not what Ahad Ha-am meant by Jewish cultural creativity. Jewish culture was Hebraic literature. Ahad Ha-am's most famous disciple, the Hebrew poet Chaim Nachman Bialik, held this view even more clearly. Bialik maintained that the great spiritual creations during the centuries since the end of the Talmud, that is, from the sixth to the nineteenth centuries, needed to be collected. The best of these works should be edited into a new canon, to stand beside the Bible and the Talmud. This survey of the culture of the past was to be studied and remembered. It would be the springboard for the new, Zionist stage of Jewish creativity. When Bialik spoke in 1925 at the dedication of the Hebrew University in Jerusalem, he proclaimed that its lecture hall and laboratories would be the crucibles in which the national spirit would fashion itself in this age, as it once had defined itself in the academies for the study of Talmud. Bialik more than implied that those who chose not to participate in this enterprise were serving their own careers, or they were contributing, often mightily, to other national cultures, but what they were doing was not an expression of the Jewish national spirit.

This conviction that the Zionist settlement, and the state that grew from it, were superior to the Diaspora became, very early, central to the Zionist narrative of Jewish history. Ben-Zion Dinur, who was professor of Jewish history at the Hebrew University and the minister of culture in Israel's first cabinet, constructed a Zionist explanation of the whole of Jewish history in nationalist terms. The Jewish people had gone through three great stages. The first was the creation of their national existence in their own land in biblical times; the second was their survival in the Diaspora, not primarily because of their religion but because they always thought of themselves as a people in exile; the third and final stage was the present, the return of this exiled people to its own land. This account was contested even in Israel, but it dominated the teaching of history in the schools. The Dinur thesis clearly implied that those who chose not to come to the land of Israel, now that Jewish history had reached its climactic stage, were shirking their duty. David Ben-Gurion spoke in this rhetoric immediately after the State of Israel was declared; he insisted that the term Zionist could apply only to those Jews who were already in Israel or on their way. All others, no matter how deeply concerned and helpful they might be to the Jewish State, were "friends of Israel"; they were of lower status in the hierarchy of Jewish values.

This negative view of the Diaspora was the doctrine of the elite that created the Jewish State. It was necessary doctrine. It made removing rocks by hand from bad soil, or draining marshes while suffering malaria, into mythic tasks. The battles with the Arabs and with the British were the birth pangs of a new age for the new Jew. That is the central story of contemporary Jewish history, and all the rest is off-stage noise. When the Diaspora has helped Israel in crucial ways, that effort is largely ignored. So the Israeli historians who have written about its War of Independence in 1948 all tell of the ways by which arms were procured by agents of the new government, but they hardly mention that American Jews paid for the purchases. If the creation of the Zionist state is the central mandate of Jewish history, only those who fought the battle on the ground are the noble essence of the drama, and all the rest is of little consequence.

These attitudes have, inevitably, been qualified over the past forty years. Those who founded the Zionist settlement in the early decades of the century have died off, and many of their children are in their seventies. This sabra generation is socialist in name only, for Israel has now become a bourgeois society that measures itself against contemporary Western standards of consumerism. Nevertheless, enough remains of the old idealism, and even more of its rhetoric, to help sustain Israel's sense of superiority over the Diaspora. The overwhelming bulk of Israelis, men and women alike, serve in the army. There is hardly a family in Israel that has not lost someone in its wars, or in the continuing attacks by terrorists. Precisely because Israel's army is based on national service, the losses of war are felt by every social class. During a term that I spent at the Hebrew University in 1982, I attended the memorial meeting that is given each year on campus in honor of students and professors who fell in Israel's wars. The number in 1982 was already nearly six hundred. I stood there in tears, holding onto friends who were there mourning some of their children. From right to left, and throughout the social structure, Israelis feel that they are paying with their safety and their lives for the future of the Jewish people.

This feeling has been reinforced by two recent phenomena. One is the number of *yordim*, the hundreds of thousands of Israelis who have left the country, mostly for the United States, to live permanently abroad. This immigration is often cited in the Diaspora as a kind of proof that the demand on Jews in New York and Los Angeles to move to Israel is misplaced; aren't many Israelis opting for the better life in America? This is not the perception of the yordim that is generally held in Israel. To be sure, those who have become very successful are called upon to be helpful to Israel. Essentially, however, the yordim are deplored, in the near certainty that their children or grandchildren will disappear by intermarriage into American society. This conviction has been reinforced by repeated, and ever more worried, accounts from the United States and other Diaspora communities that intermarriage and assimilation are eroding the numbers of committed Jews. Israeli demographers are predicting, with a mixture of concern and "I told you so," that by the year 2025 the majority of the identifying Jews of the world will live in Israel, because the numbers in the Diaspora will have shrunk to less than four million. Zionist theory a century ago suggested, in the words of Theodore Herzl, that a Jewish State was necessary in order to provide a refuge for those who would ultimately everywhere be endangered by anti-Semitism. Ahad Ha-am argued that the real problem was not anti-Semitism, but the danger of assimilation. It is that second danger that now provides Israel with much of its sense that it is the last chance of the Jews.

It must be noted that the Zionist conceptions of the meaning of Jewish existence are challenged by two other accounts of Jewish existence. The religious believers, liberal as well as Orthodox, continue to insist that the Jewish people survives because it bears Divine teaching, and that teaching is valid everywhere. The many secular movements among Jews, in the modern era, repeat such names as Spinoza, Marx, and Freud – separately or together – as a kind of incantation, to suggest that the true destiny of Jews is to be in the vanguard of universal human culture. But even these two camps are touched by Zionism. Among the Orthodox believers, there are many who think that we are living in the days of the Messiah and that all Jews must strive toward being ingathered in the Holy Land. Many secularists in Israel, and even some in the Diaspora, prefer Spinoza, Marx, and Freud to the Gaon Elijah of Vilna and Rabbi Abraham Isaac Kook, but they insist that a secular life that is lasting and Jewish can only be lived in Hebrew in the land of Israel. It is, thus, the dominant belief in most of Israel, and much of the Diaspora, that the future of Jewish life, whatever form it might ultimately take, is best secured in Israel. This estimate is not held by those Jews who care little or nothing about the discrete survival of the Jews as a people, but a majority of those who do care believe that a Jewish life in Israel is superior to the life of the Diaspora.

One other element must be added to this consideration of the deepest sources of the relationship between Israel and the Diaspora. It is the matter of charitable giving. We know that in ancient times, during the last two centuries of the existence of the Second Temple in Jerusalem, there were many more Jews in the Diaspora than in the Holy Land. These communities, with some sectarian exceptions, accepted the responsibility to transmit large donations for the upkeep of the Temple – and to leave it to the discretion of the priests to use the money without accounting to the donors. Throughout the centuries, many, and in some generations, most of the Jews who lived in the Holy Land were supported by money transmitted by the pious abroad. In recent centuries, especially from the seventeenth to the nineteenth, fights broke out repeatedly between the donors and the recipients. Often the donors suspected that much of the money was not even reaching the causes for which it was being collected, or that it was being spent in the Holy Land on the friends of those who distributed these alms. Indeed, to be in charge of money from abroad was a post most sought after; those who attained such power were usually feared, and often reviled. Those functionaries who died with clean hands were remembered, and their saintliness became the stuff of legend.

The receivers of alms had power not only over their clients but even over the donors. Usually in any relationship between donors and recipients, it is presumed that the dominant power is in the hands of the donors, but this was almost never true among Jews. The ancient Diaspora that contributed to the upkeep of the Second Temple had been taught in the Bible itself that the priests were in charge of spending the money and that nobody was ordained to check on them. In the Middle Ages, few Jews managed to survive the wars between the Crusaders and the Muslims. Those who remained in the Holy Land were regarded as representing the whole of the Jewish people, all of which remained in mourning for Zion. How could one really question these candidates for martyrdom? In more recent centuries, the justification for Jewish presence in the Holy Land was often overtly messianic. In every version of Jewish theology some foothold in the Holy Land was required, so that the Jews there would act as the vanguard in receiving the Messiah whenever he would appear. Even amid repeated unhappiness with how some Jews in the Holy Land were behaving, how could one treat people who were, by definition, a consecrated elite, as if they were poor country cousins living off alms?

Modern Zionism inherited this definition of the Israel–Diaspora relationship with great eagerness. The founders of the Yishuv, or the Jewish community in Palestine, were depicted, and they proposed themselves, as the priesthood of the new Jew. In 1921, a bitter and complicated battle erupted between Chaim Weizmann and Lewis D. Brandeis over leadership and policy of the World Zionist Organization. The most tangible issue was control of money. Brandeis, the American, insisted on absolute accountability; Weizmann, the European, who was a principal architect of the Yishuv, fought for the right of the Zionist organization to spend its funds as it wished, and to move funds among its various purposes without public explanation. Weizmann's rationale was that a movement engaged in acquiring land for settlement amid unrelenting battles with the British and the Arabs needed both secrecy and flexibility, but this rationale was not the essence of the matter. A larger issue was at stake: who would decide Zionist policy? Weizmann came to America and won a bitter campaign against Brandeis. The majority of the American Zionists accepted the idea that those on the scene in Palestine, or most closely linked to that scene, had the superior right to decide what to do with Jewish charity funds. To be sure, in the 1930s and 1940s, important forces among the Zionists in the Diaspora – and even more among the non-Zionists – refused to accept the dominance of the leaders of the Yishuv, but it was a losing battle. By the time the state was declared, and immediately thereafter, David Ben-Gurion was the undisputed leader of world Jewry. He played without hesitancy on the ancient guilt of Jews over not living in the land of Israel. This total secularist wrapped himself in the mantle of an ancient high priest who decided what was pure and what was impure among Jews.

In the Western Diaspora, and especially in the United States, the Zionists produced their contrary version of the relationship between the Jews in their own land and those who persist in living on foreign shores. The overwhelming majority of Zionists in America have always refused to accept the notion that America is exile or that American Jews too are candidates for expulsion by anti-Semites. The American Zionists wanted to help the millions of Jews in Europe who were the targets of attack. But what was the difference between Zionists in America and other American Jews who simply wanted to rescue their endangered brethren abroad? An answer was usually given in the middle years of the century, when the issue of "dual loyalty" was often raised, with much bitterness. The Zionists insisted that they were not merely saving refugees; they were helping the creation of a Jewish National State, and they did not regard their efforts for this cause as traducing their Americanism. The deeper truth was that Zionist endeavors became the tool that many American Jews used to preserve their Jewish identity. This notion was first defined in the 1930s by Mordecai M. Kaplan. It did not look very likely, then, that the British government, which ruled in Palestine, would permit the Yishuv to create a Jewish State. In these discouraging years, Kaplan argued that it did not matter whether the Zionists' purpose would ever be achieved; the task of working for this ideal would bind American Jews together and preserve their Jewish loyalties. This elegant formulation by an intellectual is really not far removed from a remark I heard many years later, from an avowed anti-intellectual among the leading fundraisers. He said that he did not want to know what Israel was doing with his money; he gave his substantial check every year to assuage his guilt at not being a better Jew in his personal life and in the hope that his giving would be a model for his children of some Jewish commitment.

Israel and the Diaspora are actually divided – and not united – by the central formula of poststate Zionism, which is enshrined in the platform of the World Zionist Organization. Both Israel and the Diaspora assent to the proposition of "the centrality of Israel to Jewish life." Israel interprets this formula to mean that its purposes and needs must predominate in all Jewish agendas, everywhere. The

Diaspora explains the Zionist formula to mean that the effort for Israel is the prime tool for preserving the Diaspora. For Israel, to assert its centrality in Jewish life is a way of reminding the Diaspora that it is less than legitimate. In the American Diaspora, the effort on behalf of Israel makes one a leader of the organized Jewish community; it is the surest ticket to receptions and dinners at the State Department and the White House. Pro-Israel endeavor, as seen through Diaspora lenses, seemed to be the way to preserve Jewishness, and to increase the dignity of Jews in American life. The cozy marriage between the two communities was, thus, based on illusions that each had about the other. Israel believed that American Jews would always accept its authority and follow its lead. American Jews believed that Israel would solve their deepest problem, their fear of evaporation. Both these illusions have become harder to believe in recent years. Israel has been finding out that it no longer commands the Jewish world, as it did in the first twenty-five years of its existence. The Diaspora knows that Israel is not the magic pill that it can use to solve its own internal problems.

Israel's disillusionment with the leaders of the Diaspora, and especially with the Americans, began in the early 1970s. The two parts of the Jewish World came into conflict over Russian Jewry. The exodus had begun, and the Israeli representatives in all international Jewish forums insisted, with considerable vehemence, that Jewish support should be given only to those Russian Jews who were on their way to Israel. The Israelis argued further that the efforts inside the Soviet Union should be directed toward preparation for *aliya* and that any attempts to help to create Jewish institutions for a continuing life in the Soviet Union were futile. In this battle, the Israelis lost. The proportion of immigrants from the Soviet Union who wanted to go to the United States kept increasing, and the American Jewish fundraising establishment insisted on helping these Soviet Jews find their way in America. The arguments by the leaders of the Diaspora ranged from the assertion that Jews who had chosen to live in America had no right to tell other Jews that they must go to Israel to a flat admission that American Jewish organizations that had long been dealing with refugees would not now go out of business at the behest of the Israelis.

The next open battle took place in the mid-1980s over the issue of "Who is a Jew?" – and the fight still continues. Israel's religious establishment wanted to amend the law of personal status and to define a Jew as someone who was born of a Jewish mother or is "converted according to the Halachah." In the Israeli context, this would have meant that the only acceptable conversions would be those performed by Orthodox rabbinic authorities. If this amendment had passed, tens of thousands of converts in the Diaspora, who had been admitted to Judaism by Conservative and

Reform rabbis, would have been declared to be still Gentile by the law of Israel's parliament. This proposal aroused open rebellion in American Jewry. More than four-fifths of American Jews are not Orthodox, and the representatives of the Orthodox minority are dominant only in their own national organizations. The mass of the non-Orthodox, and especially their leaders, were not moved by pleas from Israel that the religious parties needed to be indulged in order to keep the governing coalition intact. When this battle was joined in the mid-1980s, the rate of intermarriage was sufficiently high – already more than one in three – that most families in American Jewry included a close relative who was married to a convert. The leaders of the fundraising organizations, of the political bodies, and even of the synagogue bodies had such converts among the spouses of their children, or of their nephews and nieces. They could not allow Israel to delegitimize their Conservative and Reform rabbis. The outcry in America, including the overt threat to withhold contributions, was sufficiently loud that the amendment did not pass.

During the 1980s, a quiet process that came to little public notice was at least as important as the two overt battles over Russian Jews and "Who is a Jew?" The percentage of money that was going to Israel from central Jewish fundraising kept dropping. In 1970, at the high point of Israel's reputation in America, soon after the Six Day War, nearly two-thirds of these dollars were allocated to Israel; by 1990, the proportion had fallen by degrees to not much more than one-third. This change did not represent a conscious decision, countrywide in the United States, that Israel was less important to American Jews. In each community, there were other considerations. The local organizations were pushing for more budget; local institutions wanted new and, of course, more elaborate and elegant buildings; Israel was getting more and more direct support from Washington, so that those who decide on dispensing charity funds felt freer to use more of the money at home. Occasionally, Israeli representatives would explode, usually in private meetings, that the people who gave to combined fundraising appeals were moved by concern for Israel, and not by local causes, but they were soon proved wrong. In every Jewish community in America, people felt that they needed a retirement home for some of their aging parents, or a Jewish community center for themselves and their children, and they were not ashamed to use substantial proportions of charity funds to help support such institutions.

The most important force for changing the attitude of the Diaspora toward Israel was almost never discussed. After 1948, the Diaspora had imagined that the State of Israel had promised it that the children and grandchildren of the activists in its cause would remain Jewish in Topeka, Los Angeles, or Seattle. By the 1980s, this was clearly not true. The raw data on the intermarriage rate was that in 1948, it was less than one in ten; by 1990, it was approaching six out of ten. This happened during four decades when the American Jewish community performed heroic tasks, in politics and in fundraising, in support of Israel. Israel was also increasingly problematic to the Diaspora in politics. The Likud Party was voted into office in 1977 and it dominated Israel's politics for the next fifteen years. American Jews, and especially their organizations, tried hard to support Israel's government, but the heart of the majority was not in it. In every poll that was taken in those years, the majority of the American Jewish community opposed the permanent control of the West Bank by Israel and favored some version of "territorial compromise." This rift was largely kept quiet, but it did come to the surface on occasion, especially when American presidents were putting pressure on Israel to be more moderate. In 1982, when Ronald Reagan briefly proposed territorial concessions, and again in 1991, when George Bush called the conference between Israel and the Arabs in Madrid, some American Jewish leaders and organizations went public on the side of Washington against the footdragging in Jerusalem.

The deepest of all the issues between Israel and the Diaspora is generational. In 1948, when the state was declared, the language of international Jewish gatherings was still essentially Yiddish. The leaders of the state and the leaders of the Diaspora had all, almost without exception, been born in East Central or Eastern Europe, and they shared a common culture of their youth. Ben-Gurion insisted on speaking Hebrew everywhere, and Abba Hillel Silver, the reform rabbi in Cleveland, was a peerless orator in English, but both had spoken Yiddish into their teens, and they had each received an early education in the classic religious texts. Now, nearly a half-century later, there is no common language and very little shared Jewish culture. Very few American Jews speak and read enough Hebrew to have any insight into the culture of contemporary Israel. It is not true, as many have argued, that the lack of Hebrew is unimportant because even semi-educated Israelis speak English. I am not the only one who has taken part in conversations at Israeli homes when, after the last American who speaks only English has gone to his hotel, the very same Israelis speaking about the very same subjects are a totally different milieu. Whatever might be the meaning of the slogan, so much favored by Diaspora activists, that "we are one," this heartfelt outcry certainly does not include culture.

The dominant cliche, since the famous handshake on the White House lawn on September 13, 1993, is that the making of peace between Israel and the Arabs will create a new relationship between Israel and the Diaspora. What this "new relationship" will be no one seems to know, even though some American Jews have already cast themselves for the role of being the catalyst of Arab–Israeli economic connections and of helping to transform Jews and Arabs into friendly neighbors. Such endeavors will continue and increase, but the basic efforts, even the economic ones, will have to be made by people on the ground in the Middle East. American Jewish participation in joint Arab–Israeli investments in Gaza is not going to give the Diaspora transforming new content. What will remain in the next decade or so, as Israel is working out its new relationship to the Arab World, is the usual business of marshaling political support in the United States, and of raising money. Israeli leaders of several political persuasions, including both Menachem Begin and Yitzhak Rabin, have wanted to believe that Israel's strength in America is based on its importance to American policy and strategic interests, that is, that the Jewish lobby is not important. The truth that even these leaders have known, at least when they are alone, is that Israel is a special case in American public life because the American Jewish community has made it so. The political connection between Israel and the Diaspora will continue, because it will be particularly necessary to Israel in difficult and changing times.

It is equally beyond doubt that charity dollars will continue to be raised by Jews in America for various causes in Israel. In his angry putdown of Yossi Beilin, Prime Minister Rabin insisted that absorbing Russian and Ethiopian Jews, and all the other humanitarian tasks that Israel has accepted upon itself, are not its responsibility alone. He could have added that the Diaspora shares with Israel the concern that its universities, research institutions, and hospitals – and its museums and symphony orchestras – belong to the front rank of contemporary culture, thus doing some honor to the Jews, in the biblical phrase, as a "wise and perceptive people." But one of the deepest reasons for the need to continue American Jewish fundraising for Israel has not been stated publicly: if Jews of America stopped giving money to Israel, Congress might have second thoughts about the much larger sums that it is appropriating. So long as Jewish fundraising is perceived to be centered on Israel, and to be strikingly successful, American Jews will be seen to care. That caring will have power in Washington.

Politics and fundraising will thus continue, but the relationship has changed at its very roots. Israel and the Diaspora imagined, in the first generation after the state was born, that each was the solution to the problems of the other. Israel expected that the support and the manpower that it might need would come from the Diaspora; the Diaspora imagined that the labors for Israel would sustain Jewish life in all countries of its dispersion. In the last ten years, both hopes have been disappointed. The Diaspora knows that Israel cannot solve its problems of Jewish survival. Jews all over the world, and especially in America, are no longer united in uncritical admiration of Israel. Opinions are divided over the difficult political decisions that Israel will have to make about the future nature of the state. For many Jews these embittered quarrels are an embarrassment. The clustering of the Diaspora around Israel no longer resembles the bustle of the heady years after the Six Day War in 1967. Then it seemed like a family gathering to admire a close cousin who has just received a Nobel Prize. Now Israel has become a problem that all the relatives must help solve.

On the Israeli side, there is now little illusion that the Western Diaspora, the richest and best educated, will ever come en masse to Israel. At the very height of its prestige, in the late 1960s and early 1970s, between the Six Day War in 1967 and the Yom Kippur War of 1973, a few thousand, but no more, came annually to Israel from America. A large proportion of those who did come were from that small minority of American Jews who were zealots in the cause of the "undivided land of Israel." Regrets were being expressed more than twenty years ago, when Rabbi Meir Kahana first moved to Israel, that this immigration was not the one for which the country longed. The most striking turning point for Israel was not, however, its disappointment with American Jews, who had always been regarded as deficient in their attachment to true Zionist ideology. Rather, it was South Africa that was the unmistakable sign that well-off and well-educated Western Jews, on the run from social disturbance and some fear of anti-Semitism, were not coming to Israel. As the racial turmoil increased in the 1980s, and the end of white rule became more certain, South African Jews began to leave the country. This community had always been very Zionist, with a pronounced tendency toward the right-wing ideology of the Likud. Nevertheless, few of the South Africans on the move went to Israel; the large majority preferred the United States, Canada, and Australia. Anger has been rising in Israel in recent years that the hard cases will come, those most difficult to absorb, like Kahana followers from Brooklyn or premodern Ethiopian Jews, but many – even most – of those who can navigate in the twentieth century go elsewhere. Israel feels let down by the Diaspora.

These problems of Israel are not the central concerns of the American Diaspora. Its internal agenda is headed by a new buzzword, "Jewish continuity." Some observers knew many years ago that the tide of assimilation was rising. In an essay published in 1963, when the rate of intermarriage was less than one in ten, I predicted, on the basis of evidence that was already available, that it would rise to at least one in three within the next twenty years. Sociologist and historian Charles Liebman soon came to the same conclusion. Nevertheless, the American Jewish community persisted in ignoring such Cassandras. It preferred to believe the sociologist Charles Goldscheider and the writer Charles Silverman that a stable, unprecedented American Judaism had been evolved. This American

Judaism had a secure future, and thus "all was for the best in the best of all possible worlds." The earthquake came with the publication of the results of a major population study that was done in 1990 on behalf of the Conference of Jewish Welfare Funds. The greatest single shock occasioned by its findings was the proof that intermarriage had risen to one in two. It was almost equally upsetting to learn that there were only four and a half million fully identified Jews in America, and that there was a large penumbra of at least three and a half million who had some Jewish memories or biological connections but who were in various stages of leaving the community.

Since this study had been commissioned by the most central agency of the Jewish community, it could not be ignored. Every national convention that has been held in the last several years has put the question of "Jewish continuity" in a prominent place in its deliberations. Many suggestions have been debated. The consensus seems to be that more Jewish education, and more exposure of the young to Israel through a year abroad during high school or college, will raise the level of Jewish commitment. Others are talking of an expanded network of Jewish day schools or, more nebulously, of national effort to "strengthen the Jewishness of the Jewish family." No one has suggested the one answer that Israel continues to give, unhesitatingly: if American Jews want to save their Jewishness, let them move to Israel.

The attention of American Jews is shifting toward themselves in the political realm as well. They are thinking, more anxiously than in the last generation, of their future in the United States. American society has passed a watershed. Early in the next century, white Europeans will cease to be the majority and will become one of many minorities in the most multi-ethnic of all countries. Jews will have to work out their relationship not, as before, to a majority consisting of white Christians and a deprived minority of African-Americans, but to Hispanics and a number of Asiatic communities. This will not be an easy process, because Jews have no important ancient connections with any of these newer immigrant groups. The American Jewish community of the next century will constitute an ever smaller percentage of the population of the whole – it is now a bit more than two percent – and it will have to come to terms with the new arrivals, and especially their children, who will demand roles in the economy and the society as a whole. The immediate battles today with a few white and black anti-Semites are much less important than the deeper problems of living with all the many minorities that have now appeared. But no one seems to be suggesting that American Jews ought to prefer to put their future troubles in one basket and join the Israelis, who have only the Arabs as their problem.

Both Israel and the American Jewish Diaspora will be turning in on themselves in the years ahead, but the drifting apart will be checked, at least to some degree, by some countertendencies. The dreams of vast new cooperative economic enterprises after peace comes are too rosy, but American Jewish investment will increase. A larger economic involvement will require frequent visits to Israel by investors. American executives and experts, who are most likely to be Jews, will be stationed in the offices in Israel of the new enterprises. Another increased connection will come from the new concern for the Jewishness of the Diaspora. These discussions are evoking the obvious thought that Jewish culture, in any formulation, is inconceivable without the knowledge of Hebrew and classic Jewish texts. Such awareness will persuade some people in the Diaspora that the way to learn Hebrew, and texts in that language, is to spend some time in Israel, for it is the only country in the world in which Hebrew is the language of everyday life.

Cultural and religious connections between Israel and the American Diaspora will undoubtedly increase, precisely because these will be the main elements of their shared Jewishness. But the deepest political and societal tides will be pushing the two communities apart. The generational clock keeps ticking, and Israelis and American Jews become ever more distant cousins. In the years ahead Israel will be integrating itself in the Middle East; American Jews will be finding ways to live in the new America. Jewish unity has been sustained in the past by religion and culture, but that happened in believing times. We do not know if it can be made to work in a secular age. More tangibly, Jews of all persuasions, and of none, have joined in the last two centuries in the fight for equal rights and in defense against anti-Semitism. This shared battle may seem, at the moment, more necessary than it was ten years ago, but the defense against anti-Semitism is, nonetheless, weakening as a factor of Jewish unity. For the last half-century the world Jewish community has been united in the fight against its enemies, and yet these endeavors have not stemmed the tide of assimilation. The future of the Diaspora cannot be guaranteed by lobbying for Israel or building more Holocaust museums. These are necessary and important endeavors, but they are not a permanent substitute for Jewish faith. But we do know that Israel and the Diaspora will not willingly let go of each other, and that most Jews everywhere want to continue, somehow, to be Jewish.

U.S. Nuclear Non-Proliferation Policy: Implications for U.S.-Israeli Relations

SHAI FELDMAN

INTRODUCTION[1]

For decades, Israel has been regarded by Washington as having developed and manufactured nuclear weapons.[2] Yet both the legislative and executive branches of the U.S. government have shown great reluctance to apply their nuclear non-proliferation policy and legislation in the case of Israel. Washington has long tended to regard the Jewish State as a "special case," that is, Israel is a friendly and democratic strategic ally of the United States and, therefore, can be trusted to handle nuclear weapons safely and responsibly.

Indeed, U.S. willingness to ignore Israel's nuclear option, while simultaneously making efforts to halt proliferation to other countries in the region – notably Iraq and Iran – has attracted much Arab criticism that Washington was pursuing a highly discriminatory policy. In fact, a senior Egyptian commentator has referred to this approach as manifesting a "nuclear Apartheid."[3] Such criticisms were voiced with increasing vigor during the year that preparations were made for the 1995 NPT review conference. Similar Arab sentiments are also expressed in the multilateral talks on Regional Security and Arms Control (ACRS), launched in the framework of the Madrid-Moscow Arab–Israeli peace process. The Clinton administration is likely to refrain from exerting such pressures. It will continue to express its desire that Israel sign the NPT – and might ask Israel to pledge its eventual participation once the Arab–Israeli conflict is settled – but it is not likely to press Israel to sign the Treaty. It is also likely to urge Israel to join the proposed Comprehensive Test Ban Treaty but is also unlikely to press it to accept the suggested – but yet-

Shai Feldman is Senior Research Associate at Tel-Aviv University's Jaffee Center for Strategic Studies and is Director of the Center's Project on Security and Arms Control in the Middle East.

to-be-formulated – international convention to "cap" the production of fissile material. Instead, the U.S. may encourage Israel to undertake a unilateral commitment to "freeze" its nuclear option at its present dimensions.

U.S. NUCLEAR NONPROLIFERATION POLICY

The end of the Cold War, the breakup of the Soviet Union, and the 1990–91 Gulf War have affected Washington's nuclear nonproliferation agenda considerably. On the one hand, the odds of a U.S.-Russian nuclear exchange have – at least temporarily – diminished to nearly zero, thus eliminating the danger that nuclear proliferation might catalyze a superpower nuclear exchange. On the other hand, the breakup of the Soviet Union created an entirely new and complex set of proliferation concerns: it resulted in three additional and newly independent states possessing considerable nuclear arsenals. Among other issues, the emergence of these states presented a serious challenge to the viability of the NPT, which recognizes only five nuclear powers. This remains the case with respect to the Ukraine, which views itself threatened by Russia, and therefore seems reluctant to divest itself of its nuclear assets.

The 1990–91 Gulf Crisis and Gulf War crystallized America's concerns about the implications – for regional stability and the security of U.S. forces overseas – of the possible acquisition of nuclear weapons by a country like Iraq. Thus the focus of U.S. nuclear nonproliferation policy has shifted to specific cases where U.S. interests are directly involved: Iraq and Iran because of their effect on Gulf stability, and North Korea in light of its immediate impact on the security of South Korea and U.S. forces in the Korean Penninsula, and its long-term effect on the future of Japan's nuclear posture.

Increasingly, U.S. policy also emphasizes the nature of the regimes involved as the key determinant of its proliferation concerns. Here, the Clinton administration approach is based on a clear distinction between democratic and non-democratic governments. This also explains the more relaxed view with which Washington regards the nuclear capabilities of India – and, to a lesser degree, of Pakistan – in contast to its approach to the nuclear efforts of the dictatorial regimes of Iraq and North Korea.

At the same time, U.S. nuclear nonproliferation policy increasingly recognizes that while in recent years some nuclear programs – notably in Brazil, Argentina, and South Africa – have been rolled-back successfully, such reversal will continue to ellude other regions where countries perceive more enduring security threats. Thus, the global dimension of U.S. nuclear non-proliferation policy has shifted from an "absolute" approach – requiring universal adherence to the NPT and the application of IAEA safeguards to all nuclear facilities – to a "phased" approach adopted by the Bush and Clinton administrations. This more gradual approach centers on the proposals to "freeze" or "cap" the production of weapons-grade materials.[4]

In July 1992, the Bush administration announced a global arms control initiative that included a call for the application of the ban on the production of fissile material to other regions as well. The initiative noted the Middle East as one of the areas where special efforts must be made to apply the ban. Indeed, the two Bush proposals also marked a shift in U.S. non-proliferation policy from a largely global approach to a greater emphasis on the particular circumstances of specific regions. As a result, while still committed to the NPT as the backbone of the nuclear nonproliferation regime, the U.S. has demonstrated increasing interest in the application of Nuclear-Weapon-Free Zones in various regions.

CLINTON ADMINISTRATION POLICY

On September 27, 1993, President Bill Clinton took the Bush "freeze" proposals a step further. In a statement defining his administration's approach to arms control, Clinton called for a global treaty banning nuclear weapons-grade material production. The initiative contained a separate promise that the U.S. would "encourage more restrictive regional arrangements to constrain fissile material production in regions of instability and high proliferation risks."[5]

The principle strength of the Bush-Clinton "capping" proposals is their realistic approach. Recognizing that under prevailing political and strategic circumstances some states will continue to refrain from rolling-back their nuclear capabilities, the proposed bans will at least freeze such capacities at their present levels. Thus they constitute a "next best" alternative to unrestrained nuclear arms-racing.

Clearly, the assumption driving these initiatives was that some states, whose strategic circumstances propelled them to develop a nuclear capability clandestinely, might be content with the quantities of fissile material which they had already acquired, and that consequently, these states might accept a ban on any further production of such material. It was also hoped that these states – having refused to join the NPT and the application of full-scope safeguards to all their nuclear facilities – might more readily accept a convention banning the further production of weapons-usable material. Thus, the proposed ban might be acceptable to nuclear weapon states, non-nuclear weapon states and undeclared nuclear weapon states alike. The resulting potential universal participation constitutes another attractive feature of the proposed treaty.

Yet the Clinton initiative contains a number of somewhat

complicating qualifications. First, the formulation describing the suggested convention implies that the production of plutonium or highly enriched uranium would be permitted if such production is subject to international safeguards or is unrelated to nuclear explosive purposes. As such, the convention will suffer the same weaknesses as the 1968 Nuclear Non-Proliferation Treaty: under its framework a country would be able to produce such weapons-grade material under international safeguards, and would be able to escape such safeguards once it would deem it necessary or advantageous to develop a military nuclear capability. By that time it may be in possession of a large quantity of plutonium or highly enriched uranium with which nuclear warheads could be produced.

Second, the formulation describing the suggested convention also implies that for a state to be found in non-compliance with the convention, it would be necessary to demonstrate not only that it produced plutonium or enriched uranium, but also that the production of these materials was intended "for nuclear explosive purposes." Yet conclusive evidence regarding such intentions will not be found easily. Hence, verifying non-compliance with the suggested convention will not be easy.

In any case, the September White House "Fact Sheet" provided only one facet of the Clinton administration's stated policy with respect to the challenges posed by weapons proliferation. In an address delivered on December 7, 1993, then U.S. Secretary of Defense Les Aspin announced that the administration would supplement its nonproliferation efforts by a "Defense Counter-proliferation Initiative."[6] It emphasized that in the aftermath of the Cold War, U.S. defense policy is propelled to accord nonproliferation a much higher priority, and that this would be reflected in its armed forces' missions, force structure, doctrine, and modes of intelligence gathering.

The Aspen speech seemed to reflect two conclusions reached by U.S. policymakers in the aftermath of Iraq's nuclear efforts: first, it has been increasingly recognized that it may be easier to deal with clandestine nuclear programs at their infancy, rather than at their later stages of development. At the same time, and in contrast to the strong exception that the U.S. took at the time to Israel's 1981 bombing of Iraq's OSIRAQ nuclear reactor, Washington recently adopted the position that in some cases the use of force might be required to combat the spread of nuclear weapons. While Aspen's speech did not mention "preemptive" and "preventive" missions for U.S. armed forces, an examination of U.S. policy statements with respect to North Korea's nuclear program makes clear that such missions may indeed be incorporated within the new "counter-proliferation" approach.

In addition, the incoming Clinton administration proved as

determined as President Bush to compel Iraqi compliance with UN Security Council resolutions 687 and 715, particularly with respect to Saddam Hussein's nuclear program. During this period, Iraq tested America's determination to enforce the UN monitoring regime on more than one occasion. All such efforts have been met with forceful American responses, leading to Iraqi acquiescence.

Defending the Aspen initiative, Department of Defense officials argue that it provides a comprehensive response to the threat posed by the proliferation of ballistic missiles and unconventional weapons. Thus, in addition to a greater willingness to consider more assertive preventive measures, it incorporates traditional non-proliferation efforts with active and passive defense measures – for U.S. forces and America's regional allies. Yet the efficacy and standing of Aspen's initiative are far from clear. Finally, the only truly novel dimension of the Aspen approach – the increased willingness to consider forceful prevention – continues to be surrounded by ambiguity. Most important, it is not clear to what extent this dimension will enjoy the required degree of determination: namely, a willingness on the part of the administration, the U.S. Congress, and the American public to assume risks and costs in the pursuit of arresting proliferation. By early 1994, this uncertainty was further increased by the apparent inconsistencies in U.S. nonproliferation policies. Thus, indications of an assertive approach toward the nuclear programs of Iraq and North Korea were mixed with numerous indications to the contrary – illustrating a willingness to engage the latter in endless negotiations.

In addition, there were growing signs that the Clinton administration intended to waive the Pressler amendment banning military and economic assistance to Pakistan in a belated response to the latter's acquisition of nuclear weapons. The U.S. policy signalled a willingness to regard Pakistan's production of such material to date as a *fait accompli*. Such willingness undermined the logic of applying the Pressler amendment in the first place and seemed also to contradict the rationale of the U.S. sanctions applied earlier to China.[7] These sanctions were applied following the latter's alleged transfer of M-11 missiles to Pakistan – in violation of the MTCR guidelines – but it was now difficult to argue that F-16s comprise a less efficient means of delivering nuclear weapons than M-11 missiles. While U.S. efforts to arrest proliferation have always been selective, recent manifestations of this approach are likely to present serious obstacles to mobilizing congressional and public support for the employment of forceful preventive measures.

U.S. NONPROLIFERATION POLICY AND ISRAEL'S NUCLEAR OPTION

Throughout the past four decades, the equivocal nature of U.S. nuclear nonproliferation policy was reflected in the Middle East as well. During most of this period, U.S. dilemmas have resulted primarily from the fact that the clearest case of proliferation in the region, namely Israel, also constitutes America's closest ally in the Middle East.

In addition to America's general fears regarding the ramifications of nuclear proliferation, there have been a number of reasons why Washington was particularly concerned about Israel's nuclear capability. First, there was fear that Israel's capability would propel the Arab states to emulation, thus exposing the region and the world to the dangers of a multi-nuclear Middle East. Within this context, there was particular concern that if Israel made its nuclear capability explicit, many other states – within and outside the Middle East – would follow, resulting in a collapse of the entire NPT regime.

Second, the intense involvement of both superpowers in the region during the Cold War led to a U.S. estimate that there was a higher danger in the Middle East than elsewhere that a local nuclear confrontation might escalate to a superpower nuclear exchange. In addition, there was considerable anxiety that Israeli nuclearization would undermine America's ability to influence her allies in the region, since the Arabs were likely to regard Washington as Israel's accomplice. Yet throughout most of the same period, there was also a strong tendency in Washington to regard Israel's nuclear option as a "special case" and to exempt Israel from the letter if not spirit of U.S. nuclear nonproliferation policy.

The most conclusive evidence regarding Washington's equivocal approach to Israeli nuclearization is to be found in its lack of forceful reaction despite mounting official assessments, leaks of these assessments, and other media revelations regarding Israel's nuclear activities. Over the years, neither the executive nor the legislative branch of the U.S. government has shown a propensity to take significant measures to halt this program.[8] U.S.–Israeli relations have not been affected negatively by these leaks, and U.S. economic and military assistance to Israel has not been reduced.

The Clinton administration merely continued past U.S. predisposition to avoid pressuring Israel to sign the NPT.[9] Indeed, in only a small number of occasions during this period have U.S. officials called upon Israel to sign these conventions.[10] Two such occasions were a press briefing given by U.S. Assistant Secretary of State Robert Galluci in July 1993 and a statement made in Jerusalem by Assistant Secretary of Defense Frank Wisner in December 1993.[11] On the contrary, a study released in October 1993 by the U.S. Congress Office of Technology Assessment cautioned against pressing Israel "to give up its nuclear weapons," arguing that such pressure might "endanger Israel's survival."[12]

More important, on January 16, 1994, in a joint press conference with Syria's President Hafiz Asad, U.S. President Bill Clinton was asked whether Israel's refusal to sign the NPT did not contradict the concept of peace toward which Clinton was striving. The President responded that "the best way to arrest the proliferation of mass destruction weapons – which includes not only nuclear weapons but chemical and biological weapons as well – and to slow the conventional arms race in the Middle East is the successful conclusion of the [peace] process."[13]

The approach expressed by President Clinton was also reflected in the attitude to this issue adopted by the Bush and Clinton administrations in the framework of the multilateral negotiations on Arms Control and Regional Security (ACRS) launched in the aftermath of the Madrid and Moscow conferences. The initial rounds of talks held within this framework in Washington and Moscow were plagued by fundamental disagreements on priorities, primarily between Israel and Egypt. The latter attributed the highest priority to arresting the proliferation of nuclear weapons in the Middle East and, within this context, to focusing on Israel's nuclear weapons first.

Accordingly, Egypt called for an early consensus regarding the end-products of a Middle East arms control process, and pressed Israel, directly as well as indirectly, to commit itself to de-nuclearization.[14] Within this context, Foreign Minister Amre Mousa and his senior advisor, Dr. Nabil Fahmy, urged that Israel adopt a long list of declaratory, political, and legally-binding measures, expressing Israeli willingness to transform the Middle East into a nuclear-weapons-free-zone and to sign the 1968 Nuclear Non-Proliferation Treaty.[15] Repeatedly, these spokesmen emphasized that Egypt would not be able to accept Israeli possession of nuclear weapons as an indefinite proposition.

Conversely, Israel stressed the profound mistrust prevailing in the region and the impact of conventional weapons with which all Middle East wars have been waged and which have taxed the region's nations heavily in human lives and financial resources. Hence, it emphasized the importance of addressing the asymmetries of the conventional forces in the region. Israel's approach also implied that sensitive issues involving the various parties' central strategic systems should be implemented only after these parties develop a minimum measure of self-confidence and mutual trust.[16] Accordingly, Israel proposed the application of a wide range of regional confidence-building measures designed to prevent misperceptions, misassessments, and unintended escalation, and to reduce mutual fears of surprise attack. Behind this approach lay Israel's conviction that during the long and uncertain transition to reconciliation in the Middle East, and until the stability of peace was assured, Israel should continue to maintain a credible deterrent.

The compromise negotiated by the U.S. during the ACRS working group's September 1992 meeting held in Moscow incorporated both

Israeli and Egyptian priorities.[17] In effect, the U.S. urged a joint effort to define long-term objectives ("a vision") for the process, but argued that progress toward the realization of these goals must be built "brick by brick," through the gradual growth of mutual confidence.[18] Thus, the early implementation of regional confidence-building measures was stressed.[19] In effect, the United States agreed that while the ACRS process should ultimately lead to the de-nuclearization of the Middle East, Israel could not be expected to disarm its strategic deterrent until peace and mutual confidence in the region were established.

The tendency to regard Israel as a "special case" and to exempt it from the thrust of U.S. nonproliferation policy seems to have been propelled by a number of considerations. The first and most important was a latent predisposition to regard Israel's quest of an "existential" deterrent as justified. Israel was seen as a small country surrounded by numerous and more populous nations, all unwilling to accept its existence and all-too-ready to bring about its destruction. Thus, if ever there was a justification for "the few" to enjoy an "ultimate deterrent" against "the many," Israel was such a case. Indeed such justification was totally consistent with the "New Look" – the Eisenhower administration's nuclear doctrine: the deterrence of the quantitatively superior Warsaw Pact conventional forces.

Within this context, the Holocast may have played a particularly important emotional role. Indeed, for some Americans in key positions, regret that their government failed to help Jews escape the European hell before the Second World War errupted, and to act effectively to demolish the Nazi death machine during the later stages of the war, may have led them to conclude that the U.S. owed Israel the right to possess an ultimate deterrent.

Related to this was the feeling that, given America's moral commitment to Israel's security and survival, the U.S. would have to intervene if a threat to Israel's existence ever developed. In this context, it may be that successive U.S. administrations and key members of Congress found it convenient that Israel's "existential deterrent" exempts America from ever having to exercise such intervention. Thus, in a book published in 1992, McGeorge Bundy, National Security Advisor to Presidents Kennedy and Johnson, explained why he was no longer so opposed to Israeli nuclearization. He explained that Israel's governments have demonstrated "nuclear restraint," and that if the U.S. were to force Israel to abandon its nuclear arsenal, it would have to provide it with an alternative guarrantee.[20]

Similarly, in early 1992 Lise Hartman – then-legislative assistant to Representative Howard Berman – noted that Israeli possession of nuclear weapons enjoys wide support in the U.S. Congress. Hartman, an active participant in drafting nonproliferation legislation in the

U.S. House of Representatives during the late 1980s, argued that most members of the House were content that Israel's existential deterrence releases the U.S. from responsibility for Israel's security and survival.[21] Such sentiments were also echoed in a 1993 report of the Office of Technology Assessments (OTA). An arm of the U.S. Congress, OTA warned that U.S. pressure on Israel to disarm its nuclear arsenal may threaten Israel's survival and would damage U.S.–Israeli relations significantly. The report asked: "Would the U.S. be ready to sacrifice its relations with Israel and even to endanger Israel's survival by pressing it to forgo its nuclear arsenal which it believes is essential to its security?"[22]

Likewise, in a seminar held at MIT in February 1993, Brad Gordon, a former Deputy Director of Arms Control and Disarmament Agency and former staff director of the Senate Foreign Relations Subcommittee on the Middle East, said it was inconceivable that the U.S. would press Israel to disarm its strategic assets. He added that any mention of the term "disarmament" ignores the depth of the tacit U.S. understanding of Israel's need to maintain strategic deterrence, regarding which there would be no difference between the Bush and Clinton administrations. He said the U.S. would not press Israel on such a politically – and, even more so, psychologically – sensitive issue.[23]

Finally, the combination of the basic values common to the U.S. and Israel,; America's perception of Israel as an advanced industrialized country, the Israelis' expressed affection for Americans and their culture, and Israel's commitment to pluralistic democracy, have combined to form a tendency among Americans to regard Israelis as "just like us." In the nuclear realm, this translated to a willingness to consider Israel and Israeli governments as "responsible" and, hence, as capable of handling the "ultimate weapon."

To date, this sympathy remains the only valid explanation for Washington's tolerance of Israel's nuclear program since the Kennedy and Johnson administrations. This tacit understanding between the two governments seems to have further evolved during the Kissinger-Nixon era and survived even the most anti-proliferation administration of President Jimmy Carter. So long as Israel refrained from making its nuclear option explicit by declaration or testing, and avoided contributing to further nuclear proliferation by the transfer of sensitive technologies, Washington would exempt Israel from the trials and tribulations of its nuclear nonproliferation policy.

FUTURE U.S.–ISRAELI NUCLEAR RELATIONS

In the immediate future, U.S.–Israeli relations are unlikely to be affected significantly by the nuclear issue. Thus, the tacit understanding between the two countries – namely, that Israel's undeclared nuclear posture will not be altered and that it will not contribute to further proliferation – is likely to endure. Moreover, the Clinton administration seems to have accepted the proposition that Israel cannot be expected to undertake any measures that might erode its existential deterrence at the same time that it is asked to make significant territorial concessions – particularly in the Israeli–Syrian context – in the framework of the efforts to resolve the Arab–Israeli dispute. Given the priority attached by Washington to these efforts – and the magnitude of the concessions to which Israel is being asked to commit itself during 1994–95 – the U.S. is unlikely to confront Israel's nuclear option during this period.

Indeed, the Clinton administration's top priority nuclear nonproliferation initiative – the proposed Comprehensive Test Ban Treaty – is unlikely to become a source of tension in U.S.–Israeli relations. A central pillar of the continued ambiguity surrounding Israel's nuclear option is the fact that it has never detonated a nuclear device. Since Israel is ulikely to seek a change to its nuclear status, it is unlikely to regard an international ban on nuclear testing as compromising its national interests. Hence, Israel is likely to sign and ratify the CTBT.

By contrast, greater U.S. and Israeli dilemmas were associated with the preparations for the convening of the 1995 NPT Review Conference. The conference was intended to decide whether the Treaty would be extended indefinitely or for a fixed period or periods of time. The U.S. has made its interest in the indefinite extension of the NPT crystal clear. Hence, Arab intimations that they might refuse to vote for the NPT's indefinite extension so long as Israel did not sign the Treaty became a source of concern in Washington.

At yet another level, preparations for the NPT's extension presented other US–Israeli dillemmas, particularly concerning the future of Israel's "undeclared" nuclear status. Some distinguished U.S. scholars and former statesmen have called for the incorporation of Israel, India, and Pakistan within the NPT framework in order to constrain them from contributing to further proliferation.[24] Yet granting these parties NPT membership as "nuclear states" requires that the Treaty's definition of such states be altered – since the Treaty recognizes as nuclear states only those who were known to possess nuclear weapons in 1969. Led by the U.S., supporters of the NPT might be reluctant to alter the Treaty's definitions, fearing that once a single facet of the treaty is amended – its entire structure and rationale would become open to an endless re-negotiation process.

From Israel's perspective, the main question is whether obtaining an official "nuclear" status would serve its interests. In this context, one Israeli concern will be that such a change might accelerate the proliferation of nuclear weapons in the Middle East by placing Arab governments under new domestic pressures to produce a response to Israel's now explicit nuclear capacity. Israel might also fear that its adoption of an overt nuclear posture would grant legitimacy to Arab efforts to acquire nuclear weapons, thus making it more difficult to dissuade suppliers of nuclear technology – European and others – from transferring such technology to Arab states. And, Israel will be concerned that an "official" nuclear status might trigger the application of some U.S. nonproliferation legislation nearly automatically, thus threatening important facets of U.S. military, economic, and technological assistance to Israel.

From the Arab states' perspective, the possible ramifications of the proposed change are equally monumental. Most important, the suggested amendment to the NPT would make Israel's perceived nuclear capability unambiguous and legitimate. Granting such recognition to Israel's advanced nuclear capability while continuing to apply the NPT's nonproliferation clauses to all Arab countries would require that the latter accept that the present disparities in nuclear capabilities in the Middle East would remain indefinitely. The Arab states are most likely to view such a change as unacceptable from a strategic, political, and technological-cultural standpoint.

In turn, these expected Arab objections are likely to make Israel all the more wary of any changes that might affect its nuclear status. This is particularly the case given the evolution of the ACRS process. Since Israel has attempted to reach some measure of strategic understanding with its neighbors in the framework of these talks, and since it has made every effort to obtain agreement that the most sensitive issues – primarily nuclear weapons – should be dealt with only after considerable mutual trust has been built, Israel is unlikely to embrace an initiative which would bring Israel's nuclear status to the forefront of the international nuclear debate.

Given its own reluctance to tamper with the NPT for fear that its entire structure would collapse, and faced with both Israeli and Arab skepticism regarding the possible utility of such a change, Washington did not initiate any change in Israel's ambiguous nuclear posture; hence the 1995 NPT Review Conference did not become a source of tension in U.S.–Israeli relations.

Paradoxically, however, these very same issues may come to haunt the U.S.–Israeli discourse with respect to a different focus of the Clinton administration nuclear nonproliferation efforts: the suggested global convention to ban the production of nuclear fissile material. Here the main dilemma involves the tension between the proposed treaty and U.S.–Israeli interest in maintaining Israel's nuclear ambiguity. The tension results from the fact that it would be nearly impossible to verify that a state is not engaged in the production of nuclear weapons-grade material without fully exposing its past activities in the nuclear realm. But if the state's past activities are exposed, its nuclear status will not remain ambiguous.

Yet it is far from clear whether the proposed "capping" convention would indeed become a source of tension in U.S.–Israeli relations. So far, signs of the Clinton administration's determination to negotiate the treaty are inconclusive. Six months after it was incorporated in the President's arms control initiative of September 17, 1993, the administration has yet to engage other governments in negotiating its stipulations. Clearly, much higher priority has been given to negotiating the less problematic CTBT.

On the other hand, Washington has signaled its continued interest in nuclear "capping" by engaging India and Pakistan in discussions of the possible application of this concept in their arena. Indeed, in exchange for Pakistan's acceptance of such a freeze, Washington was willing to grant Islamabaad a one-time waiver from the stipulations of the Pressler amendment, thus allowing the aforementioned delivery of 70 bought-and-paid-for F-16 combat aircraft.

But it is far from clear whether the discussions of the possible application of nuclear "capping" in South Asia are conducted in the suggested convention. Clearly, unilateral commitments to implement a nuclear "freeze" – as envisaged by the earlier initiatives of President George Bush in May 1991 and July 1992 – are less effective than a verifiable treaty. By contrast, the unilateral-voluntary route avoids the inherent contradictions between the requirements of effective treaty verification and the interest in preventing ambiguous nuclear postures from becoming overt.

Hence, at this writing it remains unclear whether Washington will indeed pursue the suggested plan to formalize a global nuclear "freeze" within an international convention. Should it abandon the proposed treaty, a potential source of U.S.–Israeli tension will have been lifted. Instead, Washington may engage Israel in discussions regarding the conditions for its implementation of a unilateral "freeze" – similar to its evolving dialogue in South Asia. While such discussions may not result in immediate agreement, they are also unlikely to become a source of serious tension between the two countries. While U.S. and Israeli interests in the nuclear realm are not identical, they are also not entirely in contradiction.

CONCLUSIONS

Over the past three decades, Israel has been largely exempted from the spirit if not the letter of U.S. nuclear nonproliferation policy. Thus, the Jewish State has been considered a "special case," notwithstanding America's global efforts to stem the spread of nuclear weapons. Thus, a tacit understanding between the two countries has evolved to the effect that as long as Israel's nuclear option would remain within its present parameters, the U.S. would refrain from eroding Israel's existential deterrence.

Within this framework, Washington refrained from exerting pressure on Israel to sign the NPT. Similarly, it did not support Egypt's efforts to make Israeli denuclearization a first priority of the ACRS talks.

In the foreseeable future as well, the U.S. and Israel are unlikely to permit the nuclear issue to become a source of serious tension between them. This is particularly the case given the magnitude of the security risks that Israel will be asked to undertake for some years in the framework of the efforts to resolve the Arab–Israeli dispute. Given the priority attached by the U.S. to these efforts, Washington is unlikely to take measures that might result in an erosion of Israel's existential deterrence.

NOTES

1. This essay comprises an update of the author's previous work on the subject. See particularly Chapter 4 in Shai Feldman, *Israeli Nuclear Deterrence* (New York: Columbia University Press, 1982), pp.192–236, and Shai Feldman, "Superpower Nonproliferation Policies: The Case of the Middle East," in Steven L. Spiegel *et al.* (eds.), *The Soviet-American Competition in the Middle East* (Lexington, Massachusetts: Lexington Books, 1988). Parts of this essay also appeared in Shai Feldman, "Progress Toward Middle East Arms Control: 1992–1993," in Shlomo Gazit (ed.), *The Middle East Military Balance: 1993–1994* (Tel Aviv: The Jaffee Center for Strategic Studies, 1994).

2. Avinoam Bar-Yosef, "Head of American Intelligence: Israel Has Nuclear Capability," *Ma'ariv*, December 1993.

3. For a recent illustration of this perception, see Muhammad Sayyid Ahmad, "Clinton Supports `Nuclear Apartheid," *al-Ahali* (Egypt), November 17, 1993. In FBIS-NES-93-225, November 24, 1993, p.12.

4. "Fact Sheet on Middle East Arms Control Initiative." Release from the White House Office of the Press Secretary, Kennebunkport, Maine, May 29, 1991.

5. "UN Nonproliferation and Export Control Policy." White House Fact Sheet issued on September 27, 1993, on President Clinton's address to the UN General Assembly.

6. Remarks by Honorable Les Aspen, Secretary of Defense, National Academy of Sciences, Committee on International Security and Arms Control, December 7, 1993.

7. William Clark Jr., "A Few Are O.K.': America's Nonproliferation Policy Takes a Turn," *International Herald Tribune*, April 27, 1994.

8. This is the central point made in Seymour M. Hersh *The Samson Option: Israel's Nuclear Arsenal and American Foreign Policy* (New York: Random House, 1991).

9. Aluf Ben, "The Understanding with the U.S. is a Central Pillar of Israel's Nuclear Policy," *Ha-aretz*, September 29, 1993.

10. Aluf Ben, "U.S. Urging Israel to Join the Biological Weapons Convention," *Ha-aretz*, August 4, 1993.

11. Aluf Ben , "Christopher's Assistant: Israel Must Join the Nuclear Nonproliferation Treaty," *Ha-aretz*, July 25, 1993; Amir Oren, "Bamba in the Sense of Bomba," *Davar*, December 3, 1993.

12. Aluf Ben, "American Pressure on Israel to Give Up Its Nuclear Weapons May Endanger Its Survival," *Ha-aretz*, October 17, 1993.

13. See transcript of the Clinton-Assad joint press conference held following their meeting in Geneva on January 16, 1994, translated and printed in *Yediot Aharonot*, January 17, 1994, p.5.

14. Egypt's Foreign Minister Amre Mousa quoted by MENA from Cairo January 28, 1993. See FBIS, ME/1600 January 30, 1993, p.A/7.

15. "One On One," interview with Amre Mousa, Egyptian Foreign Minister, *Defense News* February 1–7, 1993. See also Aluf Ben, "Egypt Demanding that Israel Declare Its Willingness to Place its Nuclear Facilities under International Safeguards," *Ha-aretz*, February 5, 1993.
16. Aluf Ben "Jerusalem's Priorities in Demilitarizing the Middle East: Nuclear Weapons – Last," *Ha-aretz*, November 29, 1993.
17. "Multi-lateral Arms Control Committee Talks in Moscow Ended," *Ha-aretz*, September 18, 1992; Aluf Ben, "Summary of Arms Control Talks: Compromise between Israel and Egypt," *Ha-aretz*, September 20, 1992.
18. Aluf Ben, "Arms Control Talks: Discussion of Operating Joint Communication Center in Gulf of Eilat," *Ha-aretz*, September 14, 1992.
19. Aluf Ben, "Cornerstone for Building Trust," *Ha-aretz* January 26, 1993.
20. Amir Oren "Sweet Heavy Water," *Dvar Hashavua* (Friday supplement to *Davar*), November 17, 1989.
21. Proceedings of the First Ginosar Conference on Security and Arms Control in the Middle East held by the Jaffee Center for Strategic Studies, Ginosar, Israel, January 1992.
22. Aluf Ben, "U.S. Pressure on Israel to Disarm its Nuclear Arsenal May Endanger its Survival," *Ha-aretz* October 17, 1993.
23. Avner Cohen, "Hawks, Doves, and Ostriches," *Davar*, February 26, 1993.
24. McGeorge Bundy, William J. Crowe, Jr., and Sidney Drell, *Reducing Nuclear Danger: The Road Away from the Brink* (New York: Council on Foreign Relations, 1993) pp.67–72.

Strategic Aspects of U.S.–Israeli Relations

EDWARD N. LUTTWAK

LESSONS FROM THE PAST

Clio is the Ironical Muse

From 1967 by the very latest reckoning, Israel was thoroughly enmeshed in the Cold War. Directly confronting at least two of the Soviet Union's clients in the Middle East, including Egypt the most important by far, Israel was ipso facto a component of the U.S. structure of anti-Soviet containment. In practice, it manned a fallback front in the wake of the successful Soviet leap over the Turkey–Iran segment of the global perimeter of containment. It was of course as a Cold War ally of the United States that Israel received increasing quantities of increasingly sophisticated U.S. weapons on increasingly concessionary terms.

Yet by the time Israeli leaders began to seriously argue that Israel was deserving of U.S. support as a valuable Cold-War ally (arund 1981), the Cold War was only a few years away from its rather sudden end.

Institutional Perspectives

With neither a muse nor irony, bureaucracy is far more predictable. Whenever claims were made for Israel as a producer rather than a consumer of security, the reaction of the domestic producers of the same substance in the United States was firmly protectionist. With rare unanimity, military, intelligence and diplomatic assessments of Israel's *positive* value as an ally were equally dismissive. But predictably, it was the Joint Staff (the multi-service staff which serves the Chairman of the Joint Chiefs and which thus thinks or at any rate

Edward N. Luttwak is Senior Fellow at the Center for Strategic and International Studies of Washington, D.C., International Associate of the Institute of Fiscal and Monetary Policy of Japan's Ministry of Finance, Adviser to U.S. and European corporations, Consultant to the U.S. National Security Council, the White House Chief of Staff, the State Department, and the Department of Defense, and research contractor for U.S. and allied armed forces.

speaks for the armed forces as a whole) that was most categorical. Whenever the question came up, it offered the following theorem:

Axiom 1: The United States would only be engaged in combat in the Middle East as a consequence of an Arab–Israeli war;

Axiom 2: Such a war would fully engage the Israeli armed forces;

Conclusion: Israeli military power could not add anything to military strength in the Middle East. Q.E.D.

(When, as it happened, the armed forces did finally engage in large-scale combat in the Middle East on the occasion of the 1991 Gulf War, neither axiom applied inasmuch as there was no prior Arab–Israeli combat nor therefore any engagement of Israeli military power, yet the theorem was forced to yield the same result as before by introducing the ad hoc presumption that any Israeli combat intervention would promptly induce the collapse of the anti-Iraqi coalition. Remarkably, the unquestioning faith of military leaders and defense chiefs in that presumption was undiminished by the sundry Egyptian and Saudi declarations that an Israeli military response to Iraqi missile attacks would not, repeat not, induce any change in their own decision to confront Iraq. Granted that Israel had excellent reasons not to attack Iraq even as it was itself attacked, and granted also that the likes of Bangladesh might have withdrawn their air wings and armored divisions in the event of an Israeli raid or two, it does seem that this was a case of being more Islamic than the Mufti).

As for the intelligence appraisals of the worth of Israeli intelligence, they were not quite so categorical. But given the dominant importance accorded to overhead imagery, Israel's lack of the same circumscribed the value of its intelligence capabilities to the murky realm of espionage, and to the swamps of analysis. As far as the latter was concerned, it was commonly said in U.S. intelligence circles that Israeli assessments were "tendentious." As for the undoubted Israeli ability to execute forcible secret operations in a covert (civilian) mode, that evoked far more admiration among civilians at large than respect from the handful of professionals that remained in the trade. As for clandestine commando-type operations (a military, not an intelligence function), it was revealing that the various service components of the U.S. Special Operations "community" had little contact with their Israeli counterparts (chez Delta, spectacularly unsuccessful though it was till 1991, the Israelis were mostly dismissed as trigger-happy amateurs with nothing whatever to teach, unlike the much-admired British SAS, whose repertoire was of course far more narrow). Certainly there were no institutional demands to partake of the great wealth of practical experience that the various Israeli commando-type forces had accumulated over the years in every known type of operation. That stood in clear contrast to the regular exchanges and joint training with British, Dutch and German special operations units.

Finally, U.S. diplomats considered the very question of Israel's contribution to be an absurdity. For them, America's Israel connection was only a constant irritant – except on those occasions (1967, 1973, 1982...) when it was outright disastrous, the direct cause of mob attacks, perilous evacuations, and terrorist outrages.

Diplomatic Convivialities Versus Diplomatic Leverage

Needless to say, there was much less than met the eye in these bureaucratic certitudes, which reflected a sort of reverse fallacy of composition. If 1967 was the year in which the U.S. military performance in Indochina was exposed to invidious comparisons, and U.S. diplomats were subjected to mob attacks in Arab lands, it was also the year in which the Soviet Union's promise of making its allies strong in war was clamorously invalidated. Because so much of the Soviet Union's influence in the Middle East, and indeed in the Third World at large, derived from that very promise, the crushing defeat of Soviet arms and Soviet military doctrine in the fighting of June 1967 was a disaster of great proportions for Moscow, and a commensurate gain for the United States in those zero-sum Cold War days.

True, after the briefest interval for mutual recriminations, the defeated Arab states in its camp turned to the Soviet Union once again, for arms in still greater quantities and many more advisors than before. Hence the Soviet presence in the Middle East was even enhanced. At the same time, the United States was so vehemently blamed for the Arab defeat (albeit inflicted very largely by French arms) that diplomatic relations were actually broken off. Needless to say, it could then be argued – and was so argued, most notably by oil company executives and diplomats chased out of their posts – that the United States was "losing the Middle East" because of its Israel connection.

But the apparent strengthening of Soviet influence in the Middle East apparently achieved at U.S. expense was a deceptive, short-lived phenomenon. The damage inflicted on Soviet prestige by the Israeli victory of 1967 turned out to be irreparable after all, in spite of the fact that some Soviet weapons and several forms of Soviet training performed very well in the subsequent October 1973 war. That became quite clear in the immediate aftermath. Exhibiting a cold-blooded realism that surprised their denigrators, the Arab protagonists first recognized that even with the fullest Soviet military, diplomatic and intelligence support, even in something very close to a best-case scenario, Israel could not be defeated in war; next they made the obvious choice between their two remaining options: a Soviet alignment plus a military stalemate, or an American alignment plus an active diplomatic search for a settlement.

What followed was the decisive Arab turn away from the Soviet Union in favor of the United States, whose influence thus became dominant in the region as never before, not in spite of its support for Israel, but because of its support for Israel. That turned out to be the lasting post-1973 reality that still obtains, not the emotional outbursts or the painful episode of the oil embargo.

Thus the Israeli connection caused both the loss of congenial postings and assorted convivialities for U.S. diplomats in the Arab World, and also a far more consequential gain in effective diplomatic influence for the United States. In practice, U.S. military aid, very efficiently converted into Israeli military strength, was yielding U.S. leverage at a much higher "rate of exchange" than with any other U.S. military expenditure (while continuing to yield very little diplomatic leverage for Israel itself in those Cold-War days, unlike now).

To be sure, to the extent that Israel-derived U.S. leverage was entirely consumed to solve the Israel-caused conflict, nothing positive was gained by the United States, and that too at some material cost and with some risk. But that accounting is grossly incomplete. For the leverage obtained by the United States over belligerent Arab states was only a by-product of a larger phenomenon, the defeat of Soviet arms and Soviet training by Israel, not once but time after time. And that in turn greatly diminished Soviet influence far beyond the Middle East, precisely at a time when: 1) the Soviet Union was increasingly forced to rely on its military attributes, because of the fading appeal of its ideology and the increasingly evident failure of its model of economic development; 2) the damage to Soviet military prestige was particularly beneficial to the United States because of the damage being concurrently inflicted on its own military prestige by the events of Indochina; and, 3) the North Vietnamese example of successful resistance to the United States with Soviet military support could have found many emulators in the Third World, had it not been offset by the failure of Soviet military support in the Middle East.

Even if all the Israel-derived U.S. leverage in the Middle East itself was consumed to manage the Israel-caused conflict in the Middle East, that still left over the added leverage gained everywhere else. In other words, there had to be a net gain. That regionally specialized U.S. diplomats did not extend their accounting of the costs and benefits of the Israeli connection beyond the loss of congenial postings and assorted convivialities in the Arab world, merely indicates that their contemporary evaluations had little value.

Military Interests and the Military Balance

A similar dissonance obtained between the inherent military interactions between Israel, the Soviet Union and the United States on the one hand, and the protectionist assessments of the military bureaucracies on the other. It should be emphasized, however, that Israel was not at all a victim of discrimination in that regard: U.S. military assessments of *all* Allied capabilities tended to be equally dismissive.

Whenever it was objected in the U.S. Congress that the armed forces did not need some weapon system or force or other, because some ally or other could provide it instead, the military response was always the same: the allied capability in question is qualitatively inadequate; or, the allied capability in question is quantitatively inadequate; or, the allied capability in question will already be fully engaged in combat when it would be needed by the U.S. (the Joint Staff theorem); or, the allied capability in question will be withheld from combat when it would be needed by the U.S. Effective enough in war, in peacetime the U.S. military establishment functions as a sort of factory that embellishes and inflates the raw material of "threats", before converting it into the finished product of budgetary appropriations. It follows that the enemies of the United States are precious threat-providers within that scheme of things, while allies are direct competitors that can deprive the Pentagon of some of its raw material of budget-enhancing threats.

The resulting bureaucratic gamesmanship could not, however, alter the substance of the various military balances. Relevant allied capabilities, including Israeli ones, could be discounted or even ignored by U.S. military planners, but not by Soviet military planners; if anything, their tendency was to overestimate the opposition (it seems that even the Imperial Iranian gendarmerie was part of the troop count in Soviet assessments). Thus, if only by way of Soviet perceptions and reactions, allied military forces, including those of Israel, variously contributed to the global deterrent posture of the United States, sometimes in significant ways, sometimes in ways that were not necessarily obvious. In that regard, the most important nexus between Israeli military capabilities, general Western deterrence and Soviet military power was probably the latent threat of the Israeli air force that weighed on Soviet naval forces in the Mediterranean.

Again, given that the especially well-advertized Soviet fleet operations in the Mediterranean were so much "raw material" for the U.S. Navy's budget process, one may inspect the ocean of U.S. Navy submissions to the U.S. Congress without finding any adequate reckoning of Allied navy capabilities, or even a bare mention of Israeli aerial capabilities. Anyone going by those documents alone would conclude that the U.S. Navy had to cope entirely alone with the Soviet naval presence in the Mediterranean.

THE PRESENT... AND FUTURE

All of the above constitutes a warning for policymakers, and for academic analysts. The former should resist the temptation of demanding explicit recognition of strategic interactions that are situational rather than willed; the latter should resist the temptation of relying on documentary evidence that is not merely biased in predictable ways but systematically misleading in its totality.

The World Setting: The Waning of Great-Power "Geopolitics"

It is gradually being recognized that the end of the Cold War actually marks the end of an even broader and far more protracted phenomenon – the permanent great-power competition for territorial control and influence over the holders of territorial control, a competition that notably accelerated by 1870, that was vented in colonial acquisitions for more than thirty years before the frontal clash of 1914, and that eventually led to the Cold War itself by way of the two fiercely fought world wars. The absence of anything resembling a great-power confrontation in these post-Cold War days of ours is certainly an enormous novelty. That much has been duly recognized, and so has the obvious corollary: the waning of the many local and regional conflicts that had been instigated and materially supported by the Soviet Union, the United States and China during the Cold War years. For Israel of course, the consequences have been especially weighty, and especially beneficial. To confront Syria now, qua Syria whether in war or in peace negotiations, is a wholly different proposition than it was to confront Soviet-client Syria, inherently supported in its military ventures by ample supply and rapid re-supply, inherently dissuaded from seeking a settlement by the very same things.

What has yet to be recognized, however, is that the absence of great-power tensions reflects a yet more momentous absence – of anything that can rightly be called a "great power" among today's leading countries, notably including the United States. It is this absence of functioning great powers that is the cause of today's predicament: the world's inability to cope with the violent disorders that persist even in the absence of great-power instigation or material support. The result is that not only aggressive small powers such as Serbia, not only armed secessionists of all kinds, but even mere armed bands can now impose their will or simply rampage. In today's world, there is neither the danger of great-power wars, nor the relative tranquillity once imposed by each great power within its own sphere of influence.

By the classic definition, great powers were states strong enough to successfully wage war on their own, without allies. But that distinction is now outdated, because the issue today is not whether war can be made with or without allies, but *whether war can be made at all*. For all along there was a tacit pre-condition to great-power status: a readiness to use force whenever it was advantageous to do so, accepting the resulting combat casualties with equanimity – so long as their number was not disproportionate, of course. In the past, that was a precondition too easily satisfied to deserve a mention. While great powers would rely on intimidation rather than actual combat, that was only so because it was taken for granted that they *would* use force when called for – undeterred by the prospect of the ensuing casualties. Nor was there any question for a great power of limiting its use of force to situations in which genuinely "vital" interests – survival interests – were at stake. That was the unhappy predicament of threatened small powers, which might have to fight purely to defend themselves, and could not hope to achieve anything more with their modest military strength. Great powers were different. They could only remain "great" if they were seen to be willing and able to use force even to protect interests far from vital, and indeed to acquire more "non-vital" interests, be they in the form of distant possessions or further additions to their spheres of influence.

To lose a few hundred soldiers in some minor probing operation, to lose some thousands in a small war or expeditionary venture, were routine events for the "great powers" of history. By contrast, it suffices to mention the Somalia debacle was precipitated by the loss of 18 U.S. soldiers, and the Haiti fiasco caused by the fear that some U.S. troops might be killed in defeating that country's military dictatorship, to expose the unreality of the great-power concept in our own day.

Americans might dispute any wider conclusion from those events, reserving for themselves the especial sensitivity that forces policy to change completely because 18 professional soldiers are killed. But the virtue, or malady, are far from exclusively American. Most recently, Britain and France have refused to risk their troops to carry out effective peace-enforcement operations in the former Yugoslavia. To be sure, neither Britain nor France nor any other European power have any "vital" interests at stake in the former Yugoslavia. But that is the very essence of the matter: the conceptual great powers that still confuse our thoughts would have viewed the disintegration of Yugoslavia not as a noxious problem to be avoided but as an opportunity to be exploited. With the need to protect populations under attack as their propaganda excuse, with the restoration of law and order as their ostensible motive, they would have intervened to establish zones of influence for themselves, just as the genuine great powers of history actually did (even distant Russia disputed the Austro-Hungarian annexation of Bosnia-Herzegovina in 1908).

As for why nothing of the kind happened in the former Yugoslavia, the reason is clear: no European government was any more willing than the U.S. government to risk its soldiers in combat. Of Japan, literally nothing need be said on this score. Nor is the refusal to tolerate combat casualties confined to democracies. The Soviet Union was still a totalitarian dictatorship when it engaged in its hyper-classic great-power venture of Afghanistan, only to find that even its tightly regimented society would not tolerate the resulting casualties. At the time, outside observers were distinctly puzzled by the minimalism of Soviet theater strategy in Afghanistan, and by the inordinately prudent tactical conduct of Soviet forces on the ground. Except for a few commando units, they mostly remained confined inside their fortified garrisons. At the time, the explanation most commonly offered was the reluctance of Soviet commanders to rely on their poorly trained conscript troops. We now know better: Soviet headquarters were under constant pressure from Moscow to avoid casualties at all costs, because of the outraged reactions of families and friends.

The same example allows us to eliminate another literally superficial explanation for the refusal to accept even modest numbers of combat casualties: the impact of television coverage. The American experience with full-color, instant-replay television reportage of visibly suffering wounded soldiers, body bags, and grieving relatives from Vietnam to Somalia, looms so large that it might seem downright foolish to dismiss it as fundamentally unimportant. Fresh, living images relayed directly into living rooms, it has been argued again and again, are simply much more compelling than the printed word, or even radio reportage. But of course the Soviet Union never allowed its population to see any U.S.-style television images of war, yet the reaction of Soviet society to the casualties of the Afghan war was essentially identical to the reaction of American society to the casualties of the Vietnam war. In both cases, cumulative totals over the span of many years that did not reach the casualty figures of one day of battle in past wars, were nevertheless deeply traumatic – and politically decisive.

We must therefore look for a more fundamental explanation, and indeed there is one, both obvious and immediately plausible: the family structures of modern, post-industrial societies. In the families of the great powers of history, four, five or six live births were common, with seven, eight or nine less rare than the present one, two or three. On the other hand, infant mortality rates were also high. When it was entirely normal to lose one or more children to disease, the loss of one more youngster in war had a different meaning than it has for today's families, with their two to three children, all of whom are expected to survive, each of whom represents a larger share of the family's emotional economy.

As any number of historical studies have shown, death itself was a much more normal part of human experience when it was not yet confined mostly to the very old. To lose a young family member for any reason was always tragic, yet his death in combat was not the fundamentally unacceptable event that it has now become. Parents and relatives who commonly approve when their children decide to join the armed forces, thereby choosing a career dedicated to combat and its preparation, just as much as the fire-fighting career is dedicated to the fighting of fires, now often react with astonishment and anger when they are actually sent into situations where combat could take place. And they are apt to view their wounding or death as an outrageous scandal, rather than as an occupational hazard. And the Soviet experience of Afghanistan proves that the constraint can become operative even without mass media eager to publicize private grief, with politicians ready to complain at the instance of relatives, or pointed questions being asked in parliament.

What of the Gulf War then, or for that matter of Britain's war to reconquer the Falklands? Do they not suggest a much simpler explanation: that it all depends on the perceived *importance* of the undertaking, on the objective value of what is at stake, or – more realistically – on the sheer ability of political leaders to justify the necessity of combat? It might therefore seem that the new 2.2 child-per-family demography is irrelevant after all, and what counts is only what has always counted, namely the importance of the interests at stake, the political orchestration of the event, and plain leadership.

There is less merit in these contentions than meets the eye. First, if lives can only be risked in situations already dramatic, that in itself rules out the most efficient uses of force – earlier rather later, on a scale smaller rather than larger, to prevent rather than fight wars. More important, to use force only if there is an immediately compelling justification, suits only threatened small powers, such as Israel itself. Usually threatening rather than threatened, a great power must assert claims that far exceed the needs of its own immediate security, notably to protect allies and clients as well as other less-than-vital interests. It must therefore risk combat for purposes that may be fairly recondite, perhaps in distant lands, but certainly in situations in which it is not compelled to fight, but rather deliberately chooses to do so.

Even now, to be sure, exceptional strivings by exceptional leaders can correspondingly widen their freedom of action, overcoming at least in part the effects of the new family demography. That is obviously what happened in the case of both the Gulf intervention and the launching of the Falklands reconquest, impossible undertakings had it not been for the exceptional leadership of President Bush and Prime-Minister Thatcher respectively. And that, clearly, was the decisive factor, not the undoubted significance of keeping Iraq from controlling Saudi as well as Kuwaiti oil, or the equally undoubted insignificance of the Falklands for any practical purpose whatsoever.

The factor of leadership, however, cuts both ways, because the routine functioning of a great power cannot depend on the fortuitous presence of exceptional war-leadership. It will be recalled, moreover, that a very low opinion of Argentine military strength and the resulting belief that casualties would be very low, was crucial to Britain's commitment to war in the Falklands. Likewise, the imperative of minimizing casualties was the leitmotiv of the entire Gulf intervention, from the initial deployment that was originally presented as purely defensive, to the sudden decision to call off the ground war so soon (to be sure there were other considerations as well, notably the fear that Iran would become the next threat if Iraq's army were utterly destroyed). In any case, it seems clear that the freedom of action gained by successful leadership was still rather narrow – it is not hard to guess what would have happened to President Bush and his administration if the casualties of the entire Gulf venture had reached the levels of any one day of serious fighting in either world war.

If the significance of new family demography is accepted, it follows that none of the advanced low birth-rate countries of the world can play the role of a classic great power anymore, not the United States or Russia, not Britain or France, least of all Germany or Japan. They may still possess the physical attributes of military strength or the economic base to develop such strength even on a very great scale, but their societies are so allergic to casualties that they are effectively de-bellicized, or nearly so. Aside from self-defense and exceptional cases, only such combat as can take place without soldiers is likely to be tolerated. Much can be done by airpower, seapower too can be useful, we already have some robotic weapons and we will have more. But Bosnia, Somalia and Haiti remind us that the typical great-power business of "restoring order" is still mainly a ground-force business. In the end, the infantry, albeit mechanized, is still indispensable – and now mostly withheld by the fear of casualties.

There are still many high birth-rate countries of course, but most of them cannot even be small powers, because they cannot wage wars even with allies, owing to ineffectual state bureaucracies and incompetent armed forces. The exceptions are few, and correspondingly important. Those middle wagons in the train of history, such as Egypt, India, Indonesia, Iran, Iraq, Pakistan and Turkey, are neither pre-bellic as are the least advanced countries, nor post-bellic as in the case of the most advanced. With economies at least partly developed, state structures of like quality, and armed forces of at least minimal competence, they are all capable of war, and in fact five out of seven have fought wars in recent years. But even India, Pakistan and Turkey, with their first-rate soldiers and capable administrators lack all the other great-power attributes and certainly any significant strategic reach.

The absence of functioning great powers leaves scholarship with the task of re-thinking the thoroughly outdated traditional conceptions of world politics which feature great powers constantly maneuvering for advantage in the game of alliances and counter-alliances, because they are constantly ready to go to war.

When we survey the central arena of world affairs wherein the advanced countries of the world intersect, only a shadowy ghost of these contentions still remains, as in the controversy over NATO membership for former Warsaw Pact members (under the old *machtpolitik* rules the United States should have been eager to extend its military influence toward the Russian border, instead of being so opposed to NATO's expansion). Within that central arena, only the adversarial industrial policies that I have elsewhere labelled "geo-economic" have a conflictual flavor.[1]

Clearly our textbooks must be rewritten, and our received ideas about the content of statecraft must be cast out.

Israel in Context

Inevitably, there is no comfortable fit for Israel in this new world, internally or externally. Internally, one part of Israeli society is advanced and post-industrial to a fault with birth rates to match, and emphatically resistant to the casualties of war. When Begin tried to obtain support for the 1982 undertaking in Lebanon by stressing that it was Israel's first deliberate, calculated (that is, great power-like) use of force, to gain a security advantage rather than for immediate self-defense, he aroused outrage rather than approval from those who understood him best. Another part of Israeli society is much less advanced and has the demography that allows the uses of force assumed by the norms of classic statecraft – except that in a further complication one part of that part in turn refuses to participate in the armed forces. Still, the knitted-skullcap crowd that opposes withdrawals is certainly consistent, being still focused on territory in the classic manner, and being just as ready to sustain the resulting casualty toll.

Externally, Israel finds itself in the necessity of competing industrially with the advanced, low birth-rate, post-bellic countries that have neither the burdens nor the preoccupations of war, while itself existing in a region of high birth-rate countries societally capable of deliberate war. It does of course have the military skills and technological attributes of its own status, but also the resistance to casualties that comes with that. To the extent that the latter can be made to compensate for the former, by emphasizing remote-attack capabilities of all kinds, a tolerable equilibrium can be maintained in the future, as in the past.

The U.S.-Israeli Strategic Relationship in Context

Threats make alliances, it is said. But that is true only indirectly, and therefore not necessarily. For alliances do not derive their content from consensual threat perceptions, but only from consensual responses to perceived threats. Thus for example, there was a very broad consensus in the rest of Europe that Hitler's Germany was a threat from the moment of its birth. But far from evoking into existence an anti-German alliance, that new threat inspired divergent responses (such as Polish accommodation, British appeasement and Czech resistance etc.), thereby dissolving or at least weakening the pre-existing alliances organized by France from 1919.

Nowadays, Israeli and American policy-makers both tend to perceive Islamic fundamentalism as a threat to Westernizing elites in Islamic countries, their own (and other Western) interests in those countries, and even to their own two countries directly, if only by way of specific terrorist acts in the U.S. case. But that consensual threat perception does not in itself constitute the basis of strategic cooperation, (that is, an alliance) between the two. Only a further consensus on how to respond to Islamic fundamentalism can do that. At present, there is no such consensus.

One view of Islamic fundamentalism is that it is an identity-protecting reaction against the invasion of Western images, sounds and words that erodes the identity-defining culture of Islam. If so, the American response can only be to ignore the problem, inasmuch as a very great proportion of the stimulus that evokes the threat consists of U.S.-made mass culture, whose freedom of expression is itself a fundamental value for Americans, and whose export earnings are more and more significant. Israel by contrast is neither an important exporter of mass-culture products nor wedded to freedom of expression at all costs (as in the censorship of the *Satanic Verses*). There is clearly no basis for a consensual response and thus U.S.–Israeli strategic cooperation in that.

A second view of Islamic fundamentalism is that it amounts to a second-best choice for population groups that are too poor to participate in the Westernizing way of life favored by better-off local elites. If so, the American response can only be to favor the general economic development of the relevant countries, and to encourage a more even income distribution within them. There is not difficulty with any of that as far as the United States or Israel is concerned, but Israel's role as an aid-giver, model and market for Islamic countries could only at best be trivial as compared to that of countries like Japan, Germany and France – even if Israel were identically acceptable to them.

True, Israel has long developed a vocation as a developmental proxy for the United States, notably in Africa; also true, Israeli entrepreneurs and official bodies too have been disproportionately active in the mainly Muslim countries and regions of ex-Soviet Central Asia and the Caucasus. But as far as other Muslim countries are concerned, with very few exceptions, Israel is excluded de jure or deemed an undesirable partner de facto. The old saw of Israel as a technological/developmental conveyor belt and model for the adjacent Muslim/Arab countries reflects a rather pathetic degree of psychological obduracy. To deny a further dimension of (economic) influence to those already viewed as overwhelmingly powerful is only human. There is clearly little basis for a consensual response and thus U.S.–Israeli strategic cooperation in that.

A third view of Islamic fundamentalism sees Iranian propaganda and Iranian funding as its source, or as a very important source among others. There is no difficulty for the United States to oppose the present Iranian regime, anti-American in origin and still anti-American by choice. At the American end there is thus a basis for strategic cooperation, to the extent that Israel has the means to cooperate. Those means are not impressive. Geography rules out a significant Israeli military contribution to the containment of Iran; Israel's intelligence cooperation in that regard is an unknown quantity but still perhaps overshadowed by the Iran-Contra debacle; and Israel's propaganda contribution could only be trivial. That leaves the instrumentalization of Israeli activities in Central Asia in an anti-Iranian role, which might be effective up to a point, but which would also place those activities at risk.

There is, however, a far more basic obstacle to U.S.–Israeli cooperation against Iran: Iran under its present regime is the enemy of the United States, but Iran as a country is Israel's natural and inevitable ally vis-à-vis the intervening Arab states, and certainly Iraq. That strategic pull has occasionally prevailed even over the present regime's extreme ideological hostility to Israel as a Muslim-defeating state to allow explicit acts of cooperation. Far more important, however, is the implicit alignment of the key Iranian and Israeli interest in keeping Iraq as weak as possible. There is clearly little basis for a consensual response and thus U.S.–Israeli strategic cooperation in that.

Hence the attempt to maintain intact the U.S.–Israeli Cold War alliance by simply replacing the Soviet Union with Islamic fundamentalism is entirely unpersuasive.

CONCLUSION

Eppur si muove! There is no Soviet Union anymore and Islamic fundamentalism will not do it, yet the mechanisms of strategic cooperation are not being dismantled. Actually they are still being enhanced, in sundry specialized ways. One factor is bureaucratic momentum. After long resistance, various U.S. bureaucracies have included cooperation with Israel in their repertoire, and now seek to protect it and promote it as with their other activities – and more so, insofar as Congressional support can thereby be earned.

Another much more ephemeral factor is the amity of some key officials in the Clinton administration. But of course by far the most fundamental factor is the organic consensus between U.S. and Israeli elites in the face of an uncertain world.

NOTE

1. See "From Geopolitics to Geo-Economics," *The National Interest*, Summer 1990.

Images of Flawed Paradise:
Israel and the United States

JUDITH N. ELIZUR

THE MEDIA AND IMAGE BUILDING

Before addressing the specific topic of Israel's image in the United States and the United States' image in Israel, a few words of clarification concerning national images and how they are formed.

The conventional wisdom used to be that national images were slow accretions of impressions resulting from the historical events in a nation's past and present which then become part of its political culture. The self-image of any people was held to be the most positive of all images, given the natural tendency to think mainly of one's good side and repress acknowledgement of one's misdeeds.[1] Other nations were viewed more or less favorably, depending on the extent of similarity in values, language and culture. And, of course, the amount of contact between nations, and the resulting historical events, constituted a significant input into this process. Images thus formed were deemed to be stable over generations, making them very difficult to change.[2]

A revisionist approach would query whether images form at such a slow pace today, or whether there is not near-instant image-making as the result of the new medium which has entered our lives since the Second World War. As long as the written medium – books, periodicals, the daily press – had the monopoly on purveying information about the world, one could speak of a process of slow accretion. But television operates at a completely different tempo. We are assaulted daily, whether we are really interested in foreign affairs or not, by pictures from all over the world. Bosnia is in our living rooms, Chechenya, Burundi, South Africa, the West Bank – every trouble spot in the world gets its minute and a half. And the picture plus commentary is superficial (how much can be explained in ninety seconds?), stereotyped (otherwise, how could we comprehend such a

Judith N. Elizur holds a joint appointment in International Relations and in Communications at the Hebrew University of Jerusalem.

quick pass?) and therefore inevitably distorted. Instead of being deeply imbedded in the political culture, such images are often shallow and therefore easy to manipulate.

If the resulting image corresponds to what already exists in the political culture, then the old image will be reinforced. If the image presented on television differs from the pre-existing one, it will either be rejected outright, at least in the short run, or else, if repeated over time, it will begin to modify the original image. For example, the Cold War image of the Soviet Union as a powerful, menacing evil empire was reinforced time and time again by all the media. When the USSR began to disintegrate, at first there was disbelief. But as more and more pictures appeared on our TV screens, as well as words in the press, the extent of its disarray could not be refuted. Now the question is why we did not realize sooner that the emperor had no clothes, that the Soviet economy was near collapse behind that facade of power, and that the ruling elite could not control its disintegration.

Here we must turn to the influence of another element on image formation, that of official policy as reflected in the media. As long as every American administration was determined to view Soviet Russia as a greater or lesser menace to civilization, the old image held sway despite the disintegration taking place behind the Iron Curtain. Too many interest groups – not least the military-industrial complex – had a stake in the maintenance of the old image.

The intellectual effort required to conceive of a world no longer dominated by two Great Powers was almost too great for most policymakers to attempt. And so the old image persisted beyond its demise in reality. Official policy can work to alter images as well: the switch in the Bush administration's policy toward Iraq is but one example. This was an attempt to change the image of Saddam Hussein overnight, from that of the favored party in the Iran–Iraq dispute (despite the fact that he started that war) to that of a menace to the democratic West. Suddenly he became a latter-day Hitler whose human rights violations (the gassing of the Kurds in Halabja, for example) achieved prominence although they had been soft-pedalled for years.

Which image was the greater distortion: that of the dauntless opponent of Iranian fundamentalism or the later analogy to Hitler? Both were the product of the official line, as faithfully portrayed in the media. Which brings us to a brief consideration of the relationship between foreign policy and the media. Again, the conventional wisdom used to be that there is a symbiotic relationship between decisionmakers and journalists. The former need the journalists in order to mobilize public support for policy; the latter need the bureaucrats in order to obtain information – an arrangement more or less between equals.[3] But recently what can be called the "Sarajevo effect" raised the question of who calls the shots. Did the television pictures of the bomb in the Sarajevo marketplace force decisionmakers to act, even though the killing had been going on in smaller doses for months on end?

When this question was put to former Secretary of State Lawrence Eagleburger (in a television interview, it should be noted), he acknowledged that the electronic medium does have an effect on policymakers. First of all, he noted, CNN has on occasion supplied information in real time faster than the regular diplomatic channels are able to do. This had the effect of agenda-setting, because of the impact of the visual message: thus the corpses in the marketplace caused the siege of Sarajevo to be given top priority. However, Eagleburger did not think that when policymakers have a clear idea of their goals, television can change them.[4] He was not asked to compare the influence of television with that of the written press on decisionmakers – but this is a question worthy of some attention as well.

Frequently in the past, and especially in crisis situations, we have seen attempts by governments to manipulate the media in order to insure favorable coverage. Grenada and the Falklands were the most blatant post-Vietnam examples, prior to the Gulf War. The British at least had the grace to consider the notion that their control of the media in the Falklands episode was excessive (they set up a Royal Commission to consider what should be the proper role of government in relation to the media in such situations) but the Pentagon has never indicated that its manipulation of the media in the Gulf War went beyond what a democracy should permit.

A good deal of the blame should be laid at the door of the journalists: the supine acquiescence of the media to the Schwarzkopf snow job was not the finest hour of the free press. And the resulting images could only be distortions: the highly touted technological triumphs that were really failures – such as the Stealth bomber and the Patriot missiles; the pictures of the destruction of Saddam's war machine, when his crack divisions for the most part got away – these are but two examples. The Gulf War illustrated how complete the manipulation of image can be in the absence of the assertion of independence by the media.[5] In this case both the written and the electronic media were guilty of collaboration.

Thus we see that it is not only the nature of the electronic medium that creates distortion but the influence of policy as well. These two elements combine to give us national images that are stereotyped, poor in dimensionality, largely without historical context and almost always biased in the direction that accords with government policy. Newspapers that are imitations of television – those with minimum text, many pictures, big headlines and stress on sensationalism – purvey equally distorted images. Only those papers and periodicals which provide background and analysis can create images that are a more accurate reflection of reality, although they too are subject to the influence of policymakers. Now let us see how these same elements – events, official policy and media treatment – apply in the case before us, that of Israel's image in America and America's image in Israel.

BETWEEN DAVID AND GOLIATH: ISRAEL IN AMERICAN EYES

The basic image of Israel in the United States has always been thought to be a positive one. It stems from underlying sympathy for a fellow democracy having shared values, including respect for human rights and moral state behavior – two cherished American ideals. There is a shared Biblical heritage, evidenced not only in place names and Puritan writings but down to this day, especially in the fundamentalist churches. There are similarities in experience if not in scale – both are nations of immigrants and both had generations of pioneers who pushed back physical frontiers. Israel's Western orientation has never been in doubt and its willingness to fight for its survival has elicited general admiration.

For the most part, American administrations have been sympathetic to Israel. In the Truman era it was viewed primarily as a refuge for the oppressed – the "sanctuary state" image. The struggle to establish a viable democracy in the turbulent Middle East was supported subsequently to a greater or lesser degree. In point of fact, there was not much warmth in the relationship during the 1950s. John Foster Dulles refused to include Israel in his Baghdad Pact of regional actors against the communist menace; the Suez campaign in 1956, in addition to angering Eisenhower, brought the threat of sanctions over the occupation of Sinai and Gaza. Furthermore, opprobrium was heaped on Israel's head from the left, for being party in its eyes to British and French colonialism. However, American public opinion – with the exception of the Jewish community – was not particularly concerned with Israel during its first decades of existence. The ingathering of Jewish refugees in a far-off corner of the world, and the economic hardships that accompanied the process, went largely unnoticed by the general public.

It was a spectacular event, the Six-Day War in 1967, that put Israel on the map of American political awareness. Suddenly what had been viewed as a not very puissant little state acquired the image of a regional power capable of routing its enemies decisively overnight. This was a shocker for those who saw it through the prism of the traditional Jewish image, that of the victim in history, powerless to determine its fate. Some rejoiced that this was no longer the case – in particular, the Jewish community. Others, especially those in churches that held to negative theological notions concerning the role of the Jewish people in history, had difficulty in accepting the image of a self-reliant, assertive nation composed of those who formerly had been viewed as God's rejects.[6] The underdog image which characterized Israel before 1967 was now transferred to the Palestinian refugeees by these critics on the right, joining those on the left who had become disenchanted after Suez.

The dissonance between the new image of a powerful Israel and the old one of an impotent people was so strong, even for Israel's supporters, that this novel aspect of the young State's image began to blot out all its other dimensions. The all-too-frequent confrontations with its Arab neighbors only served to accentuate this tendency. The War of Attrition along the Suez Canal in the late 1960s, the subsequent wars of 1973 and particularly of 1982, and finally, the intifada (Palestinian uprising) from the end of 1987 until 1994 have all but wiped out any picture of Israel other than that of a military machine. Ben-Gurion's vision of Israel as a "light unto the nations" was erased completely by the image of a morally suspect garrison state which lives by the sword.

Reporting from the Middle East concentrates on this aspect of existence almost to the exclusion of any mention of the daily lives of the millions who live there. "Normalcy is not news," say correspondents, who more often than not turn down suggestions that they write about Israeli accomplishments in medicine, agriculture or technology. Their news criteria dictate concentration on the spectacular, the novel and the sensational, especially as coverage more and more comes to be the province of "parachutists" (reporters for both the press and television flown in to cover crisis situations, having little specific knowledge of local conditions). The Middle East as an area of political turbulence (William Scranton first used the term "powder keg" in this regard) and Israel as a stubborn, if not aggressive, player in the power game have become firmly fixed in the political imagery of the United States.

Shifts in official U.S. policy toward Israel are not merely recorded in the media: since they are taken as indications of the national interest, they almost always determine the bias of coverage. Thus, at the time of the Carter administration, which opposed Israel's settlement policy in the territories occupied after 1967, the Likud government came under media fire. The buzzword used to describe it was "intransigent." It did not help matters that the Israeli prime minister, Menachem Begin, seemed to symbolize this trait – especially when compared to that champion media manipulator, Anwar Sadat. The Egyptian leader was responsible for the Arabs reaching a high point in public opinion polls never achieved previously, while Israel's ratings declined.[7]

The efforts of the PLO after the mid-1960s to put the Palestinian case on the international agenda bore fruit. Despite the horrific nature of their terrorist spectaculars, especially in the 1970s, they succeeded in breaking a monopoly on the victim image that formerly had been Israel's. No longer did Israel dominate reporting from the area – the counter-message began to come through loud and clear as reporters began to view every story from two sides. An unprecedented peak of media criticism came at the time of the 1982 Lebanon War. Some of the criticism was overblown: reporters, knowing that their editors at home agreed with the official line, which was critical of Israel, swallowed every atrocity story fed to them by the PLO in Beirut. The mishandling of the press by the Israeli military did little to correct the totally negative image that resulted.

It is interesting to note that, at the outset, TV coverage of the intifada (Palestinian uprising) was tempered somewhat by knowledge of the errors made by both press and TV in the Lebanon War: ignorance of local conditions (attributing the damage at Damour to the Israelis when it was the result of the civil war between Muslims and Christians), lack of historical context (John Chancellor's egregious statement that "Nothing like this has ever happened in the Middle East before"), and uncritical acceptance of claims made by one party to the conflict (for example, the figure of 600,000 refugees spread by PLO sources, which was equivalent to the total population of Southern Lebanon).[8] But as the intifada became a routine story, so did the resulting TV images become stereotyped. The pictures of rock-throwing youths running toward or away from armed Israeli soldiers have not changed from the first months of the uprising until today. Not until the Labor government replaced Shamir's stand-pat policy in 1993 was there any appreciable change in Israel's image in the United States. True, for most of the Reagan years Israel was seen as a "strategic asset" in the fight against the "Evil Empire", and as such was viewed favorably in public opinion polls. But this again put the stress on military might, on the power component in its image. The intifada only reinforced this picture. The Madrid conference (October 1991) was a political breakthrough under American sponsorship, but pictures of diplomats around a conference table did little to blot out the images of constant violence emanating from Gaza and the West Bank.

Only when Rabin and Arafat shook hands at the White House in September 1993 – during the signing ceremony of the Declaration of Principles, reached through the good offices of the Norwegians – did a new image replace the old, enabling rediscovery of the peace-loving aspect in Israel's image. Because Yasser Arafat balked during the signing of the peace agreement in Cairo in May 1994, the opportunity to create an additional positive image was lost. Instead of amity, discord was revealed. All of which demonstrates that even the most carefully pre-planned media event can go awry – can be "hijacked", so to speak – if a participant violates the rules of the game.[9] The subsequent difficulties in implementing the Oslo and Cairo accords have only perpetuated the emphasis on the power element in Israel's image.

It should be noted that there is a special segment of the American public with a somewhat different image of Israel: the Jewish community is part of the general media-consuming public but its minority status makes it much more sensitive to media treatment of Israel and very affected by it. For example, the extremely anti-Israel coverage of the Lebanon War in 1982, as mentioned above, caused widespread protest to be made to newspaper editorial boards and television networks. Moreover, the organized Jewish community has information sources of its own – contacts with Israeli leaders and institutions, reports of visitors, information from relatives – which give it a point of view not always in accord with administration policy or the media presentation of same.[10]

The Jewish community has become concerned lest support for Israel, which while widespread is also probably shallow in many quarters, be diminished by negative media reporting of unremitting violence. Instead of the pre-television era process of slow accretion of impressions which then form the national image, there is worry lest repeated media assaults in the short run have a deleterious cumulative effect on the long-run image, and hence on official policy.

Israel's image since 1967 has veered between that of David and Goliath: when Israel is endangered, as it was in 1973 by the entire Arab World, or in 1991 by Scud missiles from Iraq, it is viewed as David, but when seen only in relation to the Palestinian issue, it becomes Goliath. Both these focuses have to do with the power dimension, which is not necessarily the most attractive one in any national image. For Israel's image to regain its multi-dimensionality, and hence safeguard its positive appeal, a new era of peace with its neighbors is a *sine qua non*. Not the least of image benefits might be a diminution in the Palestinian counter-message, which has reached extremely damaging proportions at times in the past.

An Israel busy with economic and scientific development is undoubtedly more attractive than Fortress Israel, but it may not be of as much interest to the media as Israel in conflict with neighbors near and far. Yet who is to say that Israel has always benefitted from the media's obsession with the latter? What can be said for Israel's image at present is that it resembles that of the little girl in the Mother Goose rhyme: when it is good, it is very very good, but when it is bad, it is horrid.

AMERICA IN ISRAELI EYES

The United States' image in Israeli eyes is a complex matter. Probably Israelis know more about America than Americans know about Israel:

the American image of Israel and the Middle East in general is for the most part stereotyped – camels and desert in a somewhat dangerous faraway place – whereas the Israeli image of the United States is far richer, despite a considerable degree of distortion. This is attributable to a great extent to the existence of additional information channels – unofficial ones such as Hollywood movies and cable TV – which paint a picture of America that reaches the entire world, Israel included.

If we begin with the political image of the United States in Israel, we find that it has many of the same components noted in our analysis of Israel's image in America. In addition to the perceived similarities already mentioned, there is admiration for the world's greatest democracy, for its economic strength and military might. Furthermore, Israelis are well aware of the United States' role as the unique provider of aid, both economic and military. The latter in fact causes great anxiety when an American administration displays what seems in Israeli eyes to be a pro-Arab tilt. The Israeli media echo policymakers' concerns so closely on this score that an observer can almost construct a fever chart on the basis of the media coverage to indicate what official attitudes are.

Here the image of the national leader plays a significant role in determining the degree of cordiality and trust in the U.S.–Israel relationship at any given moment. Just as Golda Meir's grandmotherly image could not be converted into something negative despite her differences with Henry Kissinger, so Richard Nixon's anti-Semitic remarks in private could not alter his image as a staunch friend of Israel after he provided critical assistance at the time of the 1973 Yom Kippur War.[11] Nor did Ronald Reagan appear antagonistic in Israeli eyes at the time of the Lebanon War despite the position of his administration. The situation was very different at the time of the Carter–Begin set-to: in addition to caustic commentary in the press and television, editorial cartoonists on both sides did not spare the opposing national leader. Billy Carter's Libyan connections did not help to create Israeli confidence in his brother's presidential intentions, and Jimmy Carter is viewed to this day in many quarters as pro-Arab, despite his crucial role in the Camp David negotiations.

In fact, there is an almost paranoid tone to speculation in the Israeli media every time there is a change in the American administration: are the new faces friendly or otherwise? Because of Israel's dependence on American aid, military as well as economic, the anxiety is understandable. It is not paralleled in regard to changes in the leadership of any other country. Whereas the generation of American politicians who were veterans of World War II and saw the DP camps in Europe and therefore understood the role of Israel as a haven for the persecuted is vanishing, there is fear lest their successors think of Israel only in terms of its place in America's global strategy. If this strategic role diminishes in importance, what will be the future of U.S.–Israel relations?

Furthermore the Holocaust is apparently so irrelevant to many non-Jews that almost 50 percent of Americans last year said they knew little or nothing about it.[12] Can their leaders then be expected to maintain the special relationship with Israel that has obtained since 1948? Israelis wonder about the depth of American commitment in the future: will it be something transitory, depending on political expedience at any given moment and hence easily manipulated, or is it really deeply rooted and resistant to change?

There is further cause for concern with regard to the role of the president, who is seen as the dominant figure in determining foreign policy. Insofar as political leaders come to symbolize their countries, it must be said that a confused picture often emerges from the American media's current treatment of its national figures. A good case can be made for the contention that the television has destroyed – or nearly destroyed – every president since Lyndon Johnson. Certainly in the wake of Whitewater, it would seem that this has become the media's favorite occupation. The obsession with exposure – whether of sexual peccadillos or political corruption – makes the rest of the world (Israel included) wonder how effective a leader the president of the United States can be. Has the world's greatest democracy become ungovernable? If the media can cripple a president's ability to rule, how should policymakers in other countries relate to him? This is especially crucial to a country like Israel, so dependent on the United States administration for support of every kind.

Thus America, not least because of the megaphone effect created by all the media pulling in the same direction, has come to acquire the image of a land of fads, with its image swinging like a pendulum from one extreme to the other. The debate over political correctness is a case in point. As critics of PC mobilize in the name of First Amendment rights, the rest of the world (again, Israel included) watches somewhat bemusedly, and not always fully comprehending. The Republican triumph in the November 1994 elections makes the picture even more confusing, for to the conservatives now ruling Congress, many of the notions of PC are anathema.

The American image in Israel is not limited to the political or even to the power dimension, as we have seen is the case with the Israeli image in the States. America as a role model in many walks of life is an all-pervasive influence in today's Israel. This goes far beyond the use of English idioms, the presence of Coca-Cola and MacDonald's and an infatuation with MTV. Israeli medical schools and hospitals send graduates and staff to the United States for advanced training; most Israeli academics, especially scientists, take their sabbaticals in the United States. Israeli industry, especially high-tech, looks to

America for development ideas and techniques; many Israeli companies aim for tie-ins with American multinationals despite the fact that their largest market is Europe. Israel was the second country, after Canada and before Mexico, to obtain a free trade area agreement with the United States. Israeli firms are listed on the New York Stock Exchange. Prices for imported goods and in Israeli hotels and restaurants are quoted in dollars. In fact, the American orientation in virtually every field is so pronounced that many Israelis operate as though their country is the 51st state of the Union.

Above all, the American image has long had an extremely powerful dimension, that of its material way of life, especially as projected by Hollywood. So tempting is this element in the image that it has even been the motivation for some Israelis to leave the country in order to improve their economic status. (Needless to say, this is not a symmetrical relationship – Americans who go to Israel know that their standard of living will be lower). Israelis are not unique in seeing America as the land of opportunity, where anyone can attain a standard of living that includes a house, two cars and a swimming pool in the back yard. This image has made the United States a magnet for immigration from all over the world: when Nixon confronted Khrushchev in the model American kitchen at the 1959 Moscow exhibition, even the Russians got the message.

Like the rest of the world, Israel is inundated by Hollywood movies and cable TV. However, these powerful image sources now present a picture of American society that is far more troubled and troubling than it was 50 years ago. America shows itself to the world through these unofficial channels as beset with crime, drugs, violence, urban blight and AIDS. Rich families as portrayed in "Dallas" and other long-running soap operas are beset by sibling rivalry, adultery and alcoholism. News programs are replete with stories of police brutality, serial murders and weird religious cults. Even the geography of the United States has acquired a negative image because only catastrophes are reported – just as in the case of Third World countries. In past years we have seen earthquakes, mudslides and fires in California, floods and tornadoes in the Midwest, hurricanes and blizzards in the East. This last category of images, purveyed in real time, rarely gives a hint of the beauty of the continent, but at least can be labelled an unintentional distortion. Movie makers reinforce this muddled "warts and all" image since they operate on the same assumption as the press and television: for the most part, they also refuse to deal with normalcy. Sadistic killers and sex deviants have dominated Hollywood's output in recent years to the point where one wonders if there is such a thing as a normal family in America. Again, like on television, nature in films is no longer benign or even neutral: people are menaced by dinosaurs in "Jurassic Park", third-generation successors to the sharks in "Jaws" and the birds of Alfred Hitchcock. The pervasive undertones of threat and violence, even where not specifically delineated, create a feeling of unease about American society to the point where one wishes to ask, "Will the real America please stand up?" Certainly the attractiveness of America's high standard of living is diminished by the image of the violent and fear-ridden society that the movies and television portray.

Thus we see the interplay of the same elements – events, government policy and media treatment, here reinforced by Hollywood – operating on the image of the United States in Israel. The world's greatest democracy is seen as Israel's staunchest friend and protector: in this, it has no rival. Indeed the dependence on America is all but total. Yet the image of the United States that obtained 50 years ago has changed, due in no small measure to television. It is still seen as the land of opportunity but the picture now has many dark spots. Its social problems cast a long shadow over the positive aspects in the American image. The impression created in the media of an embattled president does not add to confidence in the country's ability to lead the world in the post-communist era. Yet for Israel the United States remains *the* role model, a shining example of what a democracy should aspire to be, even though at this juncture we know it to be a very flawed Paradise.

N.B. Although this article was written in 1994 – before Rabin's assassination, Peres' brief period at the helm and the return of Likud to power – the foregoing analysis remains valid. *Plus ça change, plus c'est la même chose.*

NOTES

1. Kenneth Boulding, "National Images in the International System", *Journal of Conflict Resolution*, Vol.III, No.2 (1959).
2. Karl Deutsch and Richard Merritt, "The Effect of Events on National and International Images" in Herbert Kelman (ed.), *International Behavior*, (New York: Holt Rinehart & Winston, 1965).
3. Bernard Cohen, *The Press and Foreign Policy* (Princeton: Princeton University Press, 1963).
4. Lawrence Eagleburger, interview on CNN's "Reliable Sources", moderator Bernard Kalb, February 13, 1994.
5. John MacArthur, *Second Front: Censorship and Propaganda in the Gulf War*, 1992.
6. Judith N. Elizur, "The Image of Israel in Protestant Eyes" (unpublished Ph.D. dissertation, Harvard University, 1974).
7. Eytan Gilboa, American Public Opinion towards Israel and the Arab–Israel Conflict (Lexington: D.C.Heath, 1987).
8. Joshua Muravchik, "Misreporting Lebanon", *Policy Review*, Winter 1983.
9. David Dayan and Elihu Katz, *Media Events, the Live Broadcasting of History* (Cambridge, Mass.: Harvard University Press, 1992).
10. Norman Podhoretz, "J'Accuse", *Commentary*, September 1982.
11. Abba Eban, television interview on Israel's Second Channel, program of Rafi Reshef, 25 April 1994; Shlomo Shamir, "Nixon Expressed Himself Against Jews and Blacks", *Ha-aretz*, May 19, 1994.
12. J. Golub and R. Cohen, "What Do Americans Know About the Holocaust?" (New York, American Jewish Committee, 1993).

Bibliography

Ahmad, M. S., "Clinton Supports 'Nuclear Apartheid'," *al-Ahali*, November 17, 1993.

Almond, G. A., *The American People and Foreign Policy* (New York: Praeger, 1950).

Anthony, I., *Arms Export Regulation* (Oxford: Oxford University Press, 1991).

Arbatov, A., in *Disarmament and Security* (Moscow: IMEMO yearbook, 1987).

Ariel, Y. S., *On Behalf of Israel: American Fundamentalism Attitudes toward Jews, Judaism and Zionism, 1865–1945* (Brooklyn, NY: Carlson, 1991).

Ayoob, M., "The Security Problematic of the Third World," *World Politics*, Vol.43, No.2 (January 1991).

Bar-Siman-Tov, Y., *Israel, the Superpowers, and the War in the Middle East* (New York: Praeger, 1987).

Bar-Yosef, A., "Head of American Intelligence: Israel Has Nuclear Capability," *Maariv*, December 1993.

Ben, A., "Arms Control Talks: Discussion of Operating Joint Communication Center in Gulf of Eilat," *Haaretz*, September, 14, 1992.

Ben, A., "Summary of Arms Control Talks: Compromise Between Israel and Egypt," *Haaretz*, September, 20, 1992.

Ben, A., "Cornerstone for Building Trust," *Haaretz*, January 26, 1993.

Ben, A., "Egypt Demanding that Israel Declare Its Willingness to Place Its Nuclear Facilities under International Safeguards," *Haaretz*, February 5, 1993.

Ben, A., "Christopher's Assistant: Israel Must Join the Nuclear Nonproliferation Treaty," *Haaretz*, July 25, 1993.

Ben, A., "U.S. Urging Israel to Join the Biological Weapons Convention," *Haaretz*, August 4, 1993.

Ben, A., "The Understanding with the U.S. Is a Central Pillar of Israel's Nuclear Policy," *Haaretz*, September 29, 1993.

Ben, A., "American Pressure on Israel to Give Up Its Nuclear Weapons May Endanger Its Survival," *Haaretz*, October 17, 1993.

Ben, A., "Jerusalem's Priorities in Demilitarizing the Middle East: Nuclear Weapons – Last," *Haaretz*, November 29, 1993.

Benson, P. L., and D. L.Williams, *Religion on Capitol Hill: Myths and Realities* (San Francisco: Harper & Row, 1982).

Berent, E., and D. Granberg, "Subjective Agreement and the Presidential Candidates of 1976 and 1980," *Journal of Personality and Social Psychology*, Vol.42 (1982).

Berent, M. K., and J.A. Krosnick, "Attitude Importance and Memory for Attitude-Relevant Information," unpublished manuscript, Ohio State University, 1993.

Berent, M. K., and J.A. Krosnick, "Attitude Importance and Selective Exposure to Attitude-Relevant Information," unpublished manuscript, Ohio State University, 1993.

Berry, J. M., "U.S. Plan to Aid Mexico Calms Financial Markets," *Washington Post*, January 14, 1995.

Betts, R., "The Delusion of Imperial Intervention," *Foreign Affairs*, Vol.73 (November/December 1994).

Binder, D., "Anatomy of a Massacre,", *Foreign Policy*, Vol.97 (Winter 1994–95).

Blair, B., *The Logic of Accidental Nuclear War* (Washington: Brookings Institution, 1993).

Bolton, J. R., "Wrong Turn in Somalia," *Foreign Affairs*, Vol.73, No.1 (January/February, 1994).

Boulding, K., "National Images in the International System," *Journal of Conflict Resolution*, Vol.III, No.2, (1959).

Brand, J., "Serbs Take Hostages after Air Strike," *Washington Post*, May 27, 1995.

Breslauer, G., "Soviet Policy in the Middle East, 1967–1972: Unalterable Antagonism or Collaborative Competition," in A.L. George (ed.) *Managing U.S. Soviet Rivalry: Problems of Crisis Prevention* (Boulder, Col.: Westview Press, 1983).

Broder, D., "Hostage to Haiti," *Washington Post*, September 20, 1994.

Brooks, J. E., "The Opinion-Policy Nexus in Germany," *Public Opinion Quarterly*, Vol.54 (1990).

Bulliet, R. W., "The Future of the Islamic Movement," *Foreign Affairs*, Vol.72, No.5 (November/December, 1993).

Bundy, M., W.J. Crowe, and S. Drell, *Reducing Nuclear Danger: The Road Away from the Brink* (New York: Council on Foreign Affairs, 1993).

Ceci, S. J., " How Much Does Schooling Influence General Intelligence and Its Cognitive Components: A Reassessment of the Evidence," *Developmental Psychology*, Vol.27 (1977).

Chandler, C., and M.M. Hamilton, "Loan Guarantees Get Cautious Backing," *Washington Post*, January 14, 1995.

Clark, B., "Old Enemies Make Tricky Friends," *Financial Times*, June 9, 1994.

Clark, W., "A Few Are O.K.: America's Nonproliferation Policy Takes a Turn," *International Herald Tribune*, April 27, 1994.

Clausewitz, K. Von, *On War* (Princeton: Princeton University Press, 1976).

Clymer, A., "Foreign Policy Tug-of-War: Latest in a Long String of Battles," *New York Times*, October 19, 1995.

Cohen, A., "Hawks, Doves, and Ostriches," *Davar*, February 26, 1993.

Cohen, B., *The Press and Foreign Policy*, (Princeton: Princeton University Press, 1963).

Cohen, B. C., *The Public's Impact on Foreign Policy* (Boston: Little, Brown, 1973).

Cohen, R., "CIA Report Finds Serbs Guilty in Majority of Bosnia War Crimes," *New York Times*, March 9, 1995.

Cohen, R., "NATO Jets Bomb Arms Deposit Bosnian Serb Headquarters," *New York Times*, May 20, 1995.

Conable, B. J., and D.M. Lampton, "China: The Coming Power," *Foreign Affairs*, Vol.71, No.5 (Winter 1992–93).

Conover, P. J., V. Gray and S. Coombs, "Single Issue Voting: Elite–Mass Linkages," *Political Behavior*, 4 (1982).

Converse, P. E., "The Nature of Belief Systems in Mass Publics," in D.E. Apter (ed.) *Ideology and Discontent* (New York: Free Press, 1964).

Cooley, J. A., "The War Over Water," *Foreign Policy*, Vol.54 (Spring 1984).

Cooper, K. J., and D. Morgan, "House Votes to Restructure Foreign Affairs," *Washington Post*, June 9, 1995.

Curry, D. C., "Where Have All the Neighbors Gone? Evangelicals and the Marginalization of Religious Influence in American Public Life," *Journal of Church and State*, Vol.36 (1994).

Dahl, R. A., *Preface to Democratic Theory* (Chicago: University of Chicago Press, 1956).

Dahl, R. A., *Democracy and Its Critics* (New Haven: Yale University Press, 1989).

Dallek, R., *The American Style in Foreign Policy* (New York: New American Library, 1993).

David, S. R., *Choosing Sides: Alignment and Realignment in the Third World* (Baltimore: Johns Hopkins University Press, 1991).

Davis, T. R., and S.M. Lynn Jones, "City Upon Hill," *Foreign Policy*, Vol.66 (1992).

Dayan, D., and E. Katz, *Media Events, the Live Broadcasting of History* (Cambridge, Mass.: Harvard University Press, 1992).

De Villiers, J. W., R. Jardine, and M. Reiss, "Why South Africa Gave Up the Bomb," *Foreign Affairs*, Vol.72, No.5 (November/December, 1993).

Dervoy, A., "President Will Ban All Trade with Iran," *Washington Post*, May 1, 1995.

Deutch, K., and R. Merritt, "The Effect of Events on National and International Images," in H. Kellman, (ed.), *International Behavior* (New York: Holt, Rienhart & Winston, 1965).

Devine, D. J., *The Attentive Public* (Chicago: Rand-McNally, 1970).

Devine, P. G., M.J. Monthieth, J.R. Zuwernik, and A.J. Elliott, "Prejudice with and without Compunction," *Journal of Personality and Social Psychology*, Vol.60 (1990).

Devine, P. G., "Stereotypes and Prejudice: Their Automatic and Controlled Components," *Journal of Personality and Social Psychology*, Vol.56 (1989).

Dobbs, M., "NATO Has Initial Talks with Russia," *Washington Post*, June 1, 1995.

Dominguez, J., "Secrets of Castro's Staying Power," *Foreign Affairs*, Vol.72, No.2 (Spring, 1993).

Downs, A., *An Economic Theory of Democracy* (New York: Harper & Row, 1957).

Doyle, M., "Kant, Liberal Legacies, and Foreign Affairs," *Philosophy and Foreign Affairs*, Vol.12, No.3/4 (Summer and Fall 1983).

Drew, E., *On the Edge: The Clinton Presidency* (New York, 1994).

Eberstadt, N., "Can the Two Koreas Be One?" *Foreign Affairs*, Vol.71, No.5 (Winter 1992–93).

Elizur, J. N., "The Image of Israel in Protestant Eyes," (unpublished Ph.D. dissertation, Harvard University, 1974).

Elkins, D. J., *Manipulation and Consent: How Voters and Leaders Manage Complexity* (Vancouver: University of British Columbia Press, 1993).

Epstein, L., *Zion's Call: Christian Contributions to the Origins and Development of Israel* (Lanham, Md.: University Press of America, 1984).

Erlanger, S., "Clinton and Yeltsin Find Way to Ease Strains At Least a Bit," *New York Times*, May 11, 1995.

Erlanger, S., "Russia Says Sale of Atom Reactors to Iran Is Still On," *New York Times*, April 4, 1995.

Erskine, H. G., "The Cold War: Report from the Polls," *Public Opinion Quarterly*, Vol.XXV, No.2 (Summer, 1961).

Ewing, T. N., "A Study of Certain Factors Involved in Changes of Opinion," *Journal of Social Psychology*, Vol.16 (1942).

Fabrigar, L. R., J.A. Krosnick, and J.M. Miller, "What Motivates Issue Public Membership? Distinguishing Between Personal Importance and National Importance," unpublished manuscript, Ohio State University, 1994.

Farah, "To Clinton, Mission Accomplished; to Haitian, Hopes Dashed," *Washington Post*, March 30, 1994.

Feldman, S., "Progress Toward Middle East Arms Control: 1992–1993," in Gazit, S., (ed.) *The Middle East Military Balance: 1993–1994* (Tel Aviv: The Jaffee Center, 1994).

Feldman, S., "Superpower Nonproliferation Policies: The Case of the Middle East," in S.L. Spiegel, *et al.* (eds), *The Soviet–American Competition in the Middle East* (Lexington, Mass.: Lexington Books, 1988).

Feldman, S., *Israeli Nuclear Deterrence: A Strategy for the 1980s* (New York: Columbia University Press, 1982).

Feldman, S., *Israeli Nuclear Deterrence* (New York: Columbia University Press, 1982).

Feuerwerger, M., *Congress and Israel: Foreign Aid Decisionmaking in the House of Representatives* (Westport, Conn.: Greenwood Press, 1979).

Fine, B. J., "Conclusion-Drawing, Communicator Credibility, and Anxiety as Factors in Opinion Change," *Journal of Abnormal and Social Psychology*, Vol.54 (1957).

Fitchett, J., "Western Europe Proposes New Trans-Atlantic Pact," *International Herald Tribune*, February 7, 1995.

Fossedal, G., *The Democratic Imperative* (New York: Basic Books, 1989).

Fowler, R. B., *A New Engagement: Evangelical Political Thought, 1966–1976* (Grand Rapids, Mich.: William B. Eerdman, 1982).

Freedman, G., and M. LeBard, *The Coming War with Japan* (New York: St. Martin's Press, 1991).

Freedman, L., "Why the West Failed," *Foreign Policy*, Vol.97 (Winter 1994/95).

Freedman, R. O., "Israeli Security after the Signing," *Midstream* (June/July 1994).

Friedman, T. L., "Dole Plans Bill to Bar the Use of G.I.s in Haiti," *New York Times*, 18 October, 1993.

Fuller, G., "Islamic Fundamentalism in the Northern Tier Countries: An Integrative View," (Santa Monica, California: Rand Corporation, 1991).

Gaddis, J. L., "International Relations Theory and the End of the Cold War," *International Security*, Vol.17, No.3 (Winter, 1992/1993).

Gates, D., *Non-Offensive Defense: An Alternative Strategy for NATO?* (New York: St. Martin's Press, 1991).

Gazit, M., "Israeli Military Procurement from the United States," in G. Sheffer (ed.), *Dynamics of Dependence*.

Gelman, B., "Assad Agrees to Resume Golan Talks," *Washington Post*, June 11, 1995.

Gibson, J. L., "Political Intolerance and Political Repression During the McCarthy Red Scare," *American Political Science Review*, Vol.82 (1988).

Gilboa, E., "Attitudes of American Jews Toward Israel: Trends Over Time," *American Jewish Year Book*, Vol.86 (1986).

Gilboa, E., "Trends in American Attitudes Toward Israel," in Sheffer, G. (ed.) *Dynamics of Dependence: U.S.–Israeli Relations* (Boulder, Co.: Westview Press, 1987).

Gilboa, E., *American Public Opinion toward Israel and the Arab–Israeli Conflict* (Lexington, MA.: Lexington Books, 1987).

Glock, C. Y., and R. Stark, *Christian Beliefs and Anti-Semitism* (New York: Harper & Row, 1966).

Goldgeier. J., and M. McFaul, "A Tale of Two Worlds: Core and Periphery in the Post-Cold War Era," *International Organization*, Vol.46 (Spring 1992).

Golub, J., and R. Cohen, "What Do Americans Know About the Holocaust?" (New York: American Jewish Committee, 1993)

Gordon, M., "U.S. Warns Russia: Stop Attacking Chechen Civilians," *New York Times*, December 30, 1994.

Gorn, G. J., "The Effects of Personal Involvement, Communication Discrepancy, and Source Prestige on Reaction to Communications on Separatism," *Canadian Journal of Behavioral Science*, Vol.7 (1975).

Greeley, A., "Evidence That Maternal Image of God Correlates with Liberal Politics," *Sociology and Social Research*, 72 (1988).

Green, J. C., " Survey of Americans' Religious Beliefs and Politics," Ray C. Bliss, Institute University of Akron, 1992.

Green, J. C., J.L. Guth, C.E. Smidt, and L.A. Kellstedt, *Religion and the Culture Wars* (Lanham, Md.: Rowman and Littlefield, 1996).

Greenhouse, S., "U.S. Gives Russia Secret Data on Iran to Fight Atom Deal," *New York Times*, April 3, 1995.

Greenhouse, S., "U.S.–Russian Intersection: The Romance is Gone," *New York Times*, March 27, 1995.

Grose, P., *Israel in the Mind of America* (New York: Knopf, 1983).

Guth, J. L., J.C. Green, C.E. Smidt, and M. Poloma, "Pulpits and Politics: The Protestants Clergy in the 1988 Presidential Election," in J. L. Guth and J. C. Green, *The Bible and the Ballot Box: Religion and Politics in the 1988 Election* (Boulder, Col.: Westview 1991).

Guth, J. L., C. E. Smidt, L. A. Kellsted, and J. C. Green, "The Sources of Anti-abortion Attitudes: The Case of Religious Political Activists," *American Politics Quarterly*, Vol.21 (1993).

Haas, R. N. "1,000 Americans on the Golan," *New York Times*, November 21, 1994.

Hadden, J. K., *The Gathering Storm in the Churches* (Garden City, NY: Doubelday, 1969).

Hahn, H., "The Political Impact of Shifting Attitudes," *Social Sciences Quarterly*, Vol.51 (1970).

Halberstam, D., *The Best and the Brightest* (New York: Random House, 1969).

Hammer, A., *Hammer* (New York: Perigee Books, 1987).

Handy, R. T., *A Christian America?*, 2nd ed. (New York: Oxford University Press, 1984).

Hartley, T. and B. Russet, "Public Opinion and the Common Defense: Who Governs Military Spending in the United States?" *American Political Science Review*, 86 (1992).

Hayes, P., "The Realpolitik of the DPRK-IAEA Standoff," *Pacific Research*, Vol.7, No.1 (February, 1994).

Henshaw, S. K., and G. Martire, "Morality and Legality," *Family Planning Perspectives*, Vol.14 (1982).

Herberg, W., *Protestant, Catholic, Jew* (Garden City NY: Doubleday, 1955).

Herring, G. C., "America and Vietnam," *Foreign Affairs*, Vol.70, No.2 (Winter, 1991–1992).

Hersh, S. M., *The Samson Option: Israel's Nuclear Arsenal and American Foreign Policy* (New York: Random House, 1991).

Hertzke, A. D., "An Assessment of Mainline Churches since 1945," in J. E. Wood and D. Davis (eds), *The Role of Religion in the Making of Public Policy* (Waco, Texas.: J. M. Dawson Institute of Church–State Studies, Baylor University, 1992).

Hill, K., "The Domestic Sources of Foreign Policymaking: Congressional Voting and American Mass Attitudes Toward South Africa," *International Studies Quarterly*, Vol.37 (1993).

Hilts, P. J., "Tally of Ex-Soviets' A-Arms Stirs Worry," *New York Times*, March 16, 1992.

Hoagland, J., "End Sanctions on Serbia? Desperate Diplomacy at Work," *International Herald Tribune*, February 20, 1995.

Hoagland, J., "Image Isn't Everything," *Washington Post*, May 31, 1994.

Hockstader, L., "Ex-Allies See Yeltzin Jumping Democracy's Foundering Ship," *Washington Post*, January 1, 1995.

Hoge, D. R., and E. Zuluetta, "Salience as a Condition for Various Social Consequences of Religious Commitments," *Journal for the Scientific Study of Religion*, Vol.24 (1984).

Holbrooke, R., "America: A European Power," *Foreign Affairs,* Vol.74 (March/April 1995).

Homer-Dixon, T. F., J.H. Boutwell, and G.W. Rathgen, "Environmental Change and Violent Conflict," *Scientific American,* Vol.268, No.2 (February 1993).

House, K. E., "Clinton Speaks Loudly and Carries a Twig," *Wall Street Journal,* May 4, 1994.

House, K. E., "The Wrong Mission," *Wall Street Journal,* September 9, 1994.

Hero, A. O., *American Religious Groups View Foreign Policy: Trends in Rank-and-File Opinion, 1937–1969* (Durham, NC: Duke University Press, 1973).

Hughes, B. R., *The Domestic Context of American Foreign Policy* (San Francisco: W. H. Freeman, 1978).

Hunt, M. H., *Ideology and U.S. Foreign Policy* (New Haven: Yale University Press, 1987).

Huntington, S. P., "The Clash of Civilizations?" *Foreign Affairs,* Vol.72, No.3 (Summer 1993).

Isaacson, W., and E. Thomas, *The Wise Men: Six Friends and the World They Made* (New York: Touchstone, 1986).

Iyengar, S., and M. Suleiman, "Trends in Public Support for Egypt and Israel, 1956–1978," *American Politics Quarterly,* Vol.8 (1980).

Jehl, D., "Fearing More Hostility from Iran: U.S. Considers Moves to Isolate It," *New York Times,* May 27, 1993.

Jervis, R., "The Future of World Politics – Will It Resemble the Past?" *International Security,* Vol.16, (Winter 1991/92).

Joffe, J., "Collective Security and the Future of Europe," *Survival,* Vol.34, No.1 (Spring, 1992).

Johnson, C., "Shape Up and Staying Influential in Asia," *International Herald Tribune,* May 26, 1994.

Johnson, J. T., and J. Kelsay, (eds) *Cross Crescent and Sword: The Justification and Limitation of War in Western and Islamic Traditions* (New York: Greenwood Press, 1990).

Kanovsky, E., *Assessing the Mideast Peace Economic Dividend* (Ramat Gan: Besa Center for Strategic Studies, 1994).

Kaplan, R. D., *The Arabists: The Romance of an American Elite* (New York: Free Press, 1993).

Karsh, E. and I. Rautsi, *Saddam Hussein: A Political Biography* (New York: Free Press, 1991).

Kaufman, E., S. Abed, and R. Rothstein, (eds) *Democracy, Peace and the Israeli–Palestinian Conflict* (Boulder, Colorado: Lynne Rienner, 1993).

Kellstedt, L. A. and J.C. Green, "The Falwell Issue Agenda: Sources of Support among White Protestant Evangelicals," in M.L. Lynn and D.O. Moberg (eds), *Research in the Social Scientific Study of Religion,* Vol.1 (Greenwich, Conn.: JAL, 1989).

Kendall, P., *Conflict and Mood: Factors Affecting Stability of Response* (Glencoe, Ill: Free Press, 1954).

Kennedy, E., *Reimagining American Catholicism* (New York: Vintage, 1985).

Kinder, D. R., G.S. Adams, and P. Gronke, "Economics and Politics in the 1984 American Presidential Election," *American Journal of Political Science,* Vol.33 (1989).

Kinder, D. R. and D.R. Kiewiet, "Economic Discontent and Political Behavior: The Role of Personal Grievances and Collective Economic Judgments in Congressional Voting," *American Journal of Political Science,* Vol.23 (1979).

Kinder, D., and Mebane, "Politics and Economics in Everyday Life," in K.R. Monroe (ed.) *The Political Process and Economic Change,* New York: Agathon, 1983.

Kissinger, H., *The White House Years* (Boston: Little, Brown, 1979).

Kissinger, H., *Years of Upheaval* (Boston: Little, Brown, 1982).

Kolko, G., *The Roots of American Foreign Policy* (Boston: Beacon Press, 1969).

Krauthammer, C., "The Unipolar Moment," *Foreign Affairs*, Vol.70, No.1 (1990–91).

Kristof, N. D., "The Rise of China," *Foreign Affairs*, Vol.72, No.5 (November/December, 1993).

Krosnick, J. A., "The Role of Attitude Importance in Social Evaluation: A Study of Policy Preferences, Presidential Candidate Evaluation and Voting Behavior," *Journal of Personality and Social Psychology*, 55 (1988).

Krosnick, J. A, "Attitude Importance and Attitude Change," *Journal of Experimental Social Psychology*, 24 (1988).

Krosnick, J. A., "Government Policy and Citizen Passion: A Study of Issue Publics in Contemporary America," *Political Behavior*, Vol.12 (1990).

Krosnick, J. A. and R.P. Abelson, "The Case for Measuring Attitude Strength in Surveys," in J. Tanur, (ed.) *Questions About Questions: Inquiries into the Cognitive Bases of Surveys* (New York; Russell Sage, 1992).

Krosnick, J. A. and M.A. Milburn, "Psychological Determinants of Political Opinionation," *Social Cognition*, Vol.8 (1990).

Lake, A., "Confronting Backlash States," *Foreign Affairs*, Vol.73 (March/April 1994).

Lancaster, J., "Assad: Threatened by Peace," *Washington Post*, October 25, 1994.

Lancaster, J., and B. Gellman, "National Security Strategy Paper Arouses Pentagon–State Department Debate," *The Washington Post*, March 3, 1994.

Larson, D. (ed.), *The Puritan Ethic in the United States Foreign Policy*, (Princeton, NJ: Van Nostrand, 1966).

Laufer, L. Y., "U.S. Aid to Israel: Problems and Perspectives," in G. Sheffer, *Dynamics of Dependence*.

Lebow, R. N., *Between Peace and War: The Nature of International Crisis* (Baltimore: Johns Hopkins University Press, 1981).

Leege, D. C., "Toward a Mental Measure of Religiosity in Research on Religion and Politics," in T.G. Jelen (ed.) *Religion and Political Behavior in the United States* (New York: Praeger, 1989).

Leege, D. C., J.A. Lieske, and K.D. Wald, "Toward Cultural theories of American Political Behavior: Religion, Ethnicity and Race, and Class Outlook," in W. Crotty (ed.), *Political Science: Looking to the Future* (Evanston, Ill.: Northwestern University Press, 1991).

Leege, D. C., and L.A. Kellstedt, (eds), *Rediscovering the Religious Factor in American Politics* (Armonk, NY: M. A. Sharpe, 1993).

Leffler, M., *A Preponderance of Power: National Security, the Truman Administration and the Cold War* (Stanford: Stanford University Press, 1992).

Levy, J. S., "Domestic Politics and War," in R.I. Rotberg and T.K. Rabb (eds), *The Origin and Prevention of Major Wars* (Cambridge: Cambridge University Press, 1988).

Lilley, J., "Freedom Through Trade," *Foreign Policy*, No.94 (Spring, 1994).

Lindsey, H., *The Late Great Planet Earth* (Grand Rapids, Mi.: Zondervan, 1970).

Lippman, T. W, "White House Sees Iran as Worst 'Outlaw'," *Washington Post* 27, 1994.

Lipson, C., "Why Are Some International Agreements Informal?" *International Organization*, Vol.45 (Autumn 1991).

Little, F. H., *American Protestantism and Anti-Semitism* (Jerusalem: Study Circle on World Jewry, 1985).

Luce, H., *The American Century* (New York: Farrar and Rinehart, 1941).

Lustick, I. S., "Reinventing Jerusalem," *Foreign Policy*, No.93 (Winter, 1993–94).

MacArthur, J., *Second Front: Censorship and Propaganda in the Gulf War*, 1992.

Malcolm, N., "Bosnia and the West: A Study in Failure," *The National Interest*, Vol.39 (Spring 1995).

Marcus, R., and J. Smith, "North Korea Confirms Freeze: U.S. Agrees to Resume Talks," *Washington Post*, June 23, 1994.

Marcus, R., "Clinton Assures Poles of NATO Membership, Eventually," *Washington Post*, July 8, 1994.

Marsden, G. M., *Understanding Fundamentalism and Evangelicalism* (Grand Rapids, Mich.: William B. Eerdaman, 1991).

Martire, G., and R. Clark, *Anti-Semitism in the United States: A Study of Prejudice in the 1980s* (New York: Praeger, 1982).

Marty, M. E., *Righteous Empire: The Protestant Experience in America* (New York: Harper & Row, 1970).

Maynes, C. W., "Containing Ethnic Conflict," *Foreign Policy*, No.90 (Spring, 1993).

McKinnon, R. I., *The Order of Economic Liberalization* (Baltimore: Johns Hopkins University Press, 1993).

Mearshheimer. J., "Back to the Future: Instability in Europe after the Cold War," *International Security*, Vol.15, No.1 (Summer, 1990).

Milbarth, L. W., *Political Participation* (Chicago: Rand-McNally, 1965).

Miller, J. D., *The American People and Policy Science* (New York: Pergamon Press, 1983).

Mishler, W., and R.S. Sheehan, "The Supreme Court as a Countermajoretarian Institution? The Impact of Public Opinion on Supreme Court Decision," *American Political Science Review*, Vol.87 (1993).

Moen, M. C., *The Christian Right and Congress* (Tuscaloosa, Al.: University of Alabama Press, 1989).

Monroe, A. D., "Consistency Between Public Preferences and National Policy Decision," *American Politics Quarterly*, Vol.7 (1979).

Morgenthau, H., *Politics Among Nations* (New York: Alfred Knopf, 1948).

Morse, E., "The Coming Oil Revolution," *Foreign Affairs*, Vol.69, No.5 (Winter 1990/91).

Mueller J., *Retreat from Doomsday: The Obsolesce of Major War* (New York: Basic Books, 1989).

Muravchik, J., "Misreporting Lebanon," *Policy Review*, Winter, 1983.

Murphy, A. R., "The Mainline Churches and Political Activism: The Continuing Impact of the Persian Gulf War," *Soundings*, Vol.76 (1993).

Neuman, R. W., *The Paradox of Mass Politics* (Cambridge: Harvard University Press, 1986).

Nisbett, R. E., and T. Wilson, "Telling More Than We Know: Verbal Reports on Mental Processes," *Psychological Review*, Vol.84 (1977).

Nixon, R., *The Memoirs of Richard Nixon* (New York: Gross and Dunlop, 1978).

O'Flaherty, J. D., "Holding Together South Africa," *Foreign Affairs*, Vol.72, No.4 (September/October, 1993).

Oren, A., "Bamba in the Sense of Bomba," *Davar*, December 3, 1993.

Oren, A., "Sweet Heavy Water," *Davar*, November 17, 1989.

Organsky, A.F.K., *The $36 Billion Bargain: Strategy and Politics in U.S. Assistance to Israel* (New York: Columbia University Press, 1990).

Page, B. I., and R.Y. Shapiro, "Effects of Public Opinion on Policy," *American Political Science Review*, Vol.77 (1983).

Page, B. I., and R.Y. Shapiro, *The Rational Public: Fifty Years of Trends in Americas Policy Preferences* (Chicago: University of Chicago Press, 1992).

Pain, C., and T. Cochran, "So Little Time, So Many Weapons, So Much to Do," *Bulletin of the Atomic Scientists*, Vol.48, No.1 (January/February, 1992).

Pastor, R., "The Latin American Option," *Foreign Policy*, No.88 (Fall, 1992).

Perlmutter, A., "Arafat's Police State," *Foreign Affairs,* Vol.73, No.4 (July/August 1994).

Podhoretz, N., "J'Accuse," *Commentary,* September, 1982.

Pomfert, J., "Carter's Down-Home Style Eased Way for Accord," *Washington Post,* December 22, 1994.

Price, V., and J. Zoller, "Who Gets the News? Alternative Measures of News Reception and their Implications for Research," *Public Opinion Quarterly,* Vol.57 (1993).

Quandt, W. B., "The Urge for Democracy," *Foreign Affairs,* Vol.73, No.4 (July/August 1994).

Quester, G .H., "Some Barriers to Thinking about Conventional Defense," in E. Schmaling (ed.), *Life Beyond the Bomb* (Oxford: Berg, 1990).

Quester, G. H., *Offense and Defense in the International System* (New York: John Wiley, 1977).

Quester, G. H., *American Foreign Policy: The Lost Consensus (New York: Praeger, 1982).*

Quigg, P., *America the Dutiful* (New York: Simon and Schuster, 1971).

Quinely, H., *The Prophetic Clergy* (Berkeley: University of California Press, 1974).

Quinley, H. E. and C.Y. Glock, *Anti-Semitism in America* (New York: Free Press, 1979).

Rausch, D. A., *Fundamentalist Evangelical and Anti-Semitism* (Valley Forge, Pa.: Trinity Press International, 1993).

Redick, J., *Argentina and Brazil: An Evolving Nuclear Relationship* (Southampton: Program for Promoting Nuclear Non-Proliferation Occasional Paper No.7, 1990).

Reid, T. R. and L. Keumhyun, "South Korea Accepts Deal with North on A-Power," *Washington Post,* June 14, 1995.

Reiss, M., *Bridled Ambition: Why Countries Constrain Their Nuclear Capabilities,* (Washington DC, 1995).

Richberg, K., "Back to Vietnam," *Foreign Affairs,* Vol.70, No.4 (Fall, 1991).

Rielly, J. E., "The Public Mood at Mid-Decade," *Foreign Policy,* No.98 (Spring 1995).

Rielly, J. E., (ed.), *American Public Opinion and U.S. Foreign Policy* (Chicago, Il.: Chicago Council on Foreign Relations, 1991).

Robbins, C. A., "Kentucky Senator Handed Keys to Foreign Aid," *Wall Street Journal,* December 13, 1994.

Rokeach, M., "Religious Values and Social Compassion," *Review of Religious Research,* Vol.11 (1969).

Romm, J. J., *Defining National Security: The Nonmilitary Aspects* (New York: Council on Foreign Relations, 1993).

Roof, W. C., and W. McKinney, *American Mainline Religion: Its Changing Shape and Future,* (New Brunswick, NJ: Rutgers University Press, 1987).

Rosenberg, M. J., "Attitude Change and Foreign Policy in the Cold War Era," in J.N. Rosenau (ed.), *Domestic Sources of Foreign Policy* (New York: Free Press, 1967).

Rowen, H., "Administration Ignored Peso Warnings," *Washington Post,* February 5, 1995.

Rubin, U., "How Much Does Missile Proliferation Matter?" *Orbis,* Vol.35, No.1 (Winter 1991).

Russet, B., *Controlling the Sword: The Democratic Governance of National Security* (Cambridge Harvard University Press, 1990).

Sadat, A., *In Search of Identity: An Autobiography* (New York: Harper & Row, 1978).

Safran, N., *The Embattled Ally* (Cambridge Mass.: Belknap Press, 1978).

Safran, N., *Saudi Arabia: The Ceaseless Quest for Security* (Cambridge: Harvard University Press, 1985).

Sagan, S. D., "The Perils of Proliferation: Organization Theory, Deterrence Theory, and the Spread of Nuclear Weapons," *International Security*, Vol.18, No.4 (Spring 1994).

Schattschneider, E. E., *Party Government* (New York: Holt, Rinehart & Winston, 1942).

Schoenbaum, D., *The United States and the State of Israel* (New York: Oxford University Press, 1993).

Schuman, H., and G. Kalton, "Survey Methods," in G. Lindsay and E. Aronson (eds) *Handbook of Social Psychology* (New York: Random House, 1984).

Schuman, H. and S. Presser, *Questions and Answers in Attitude Surveys: Experiments on Question Form, Wording and Content*, New York: Academic Press, 1981).

Schumpter, J. A., *Capitalism, Socialism, and Democracy* (New York: Harper & Row, 1950).

Sciolino, E., "New U.S. Peacekeeping Policy De-emphasizes Role of the U.N.," *New York Times*, May 6, 1994.

Sciolino, E., "Syria and Israel Said to Conduct Talks in Private," *New York Times*, December 31, 1994.

Sciolino, E., "U.S. Pressure Put on Iran and Iraq," *New York Times*, April 5, 1995.

Sciolino, E., "Beijing Rebuffs U.S. on Halting Iran Atom Deal," *New York Times*, April 18, 1995.

Sears, D. O., R.R. Lau, T.R. Tyler, and A.M. Harris, "Self-Interest vs. Symbolic Politics in Policy Attitudes and Presidential Voting," *American Political Science Review*, Vol.74 (1980).

Selznick, G. J. and S. Steinberg, *The Tenacity of Prejudice: Anti-Semitism in Contemporary America* (New York: Harper & Row, 1969).

Shamir, S., "Nixon Expressed Himself against Jews and Blacks," *Haaretz*, May 19, 1994.

Sheffer, G., (ed.) *Modern Diasporas in International Politics*, (New York: St. Martin's Press, 1986).

Sheffer, G., "The End of Dual Loyalty?" manuscript, The Hebrew University, 1994.

Simon, M., *Jerry Falwell and the Jews* (Middle Village, NY: Johnatan David, 1984).

Singer, D., and R. Cohen, *In the Wake of the Palestinian Uprising: Findings of the April 1988 Roper Poll* (New York: American Jewish Committee, 1988).

Smith, H., *The Power Game: How Washington Works* (New York: Ballantine Books, 1988).

Smith, J., "North Korea Broke Nuclear Agreement, Inspectors Conclude," *Washington Post*, May 20, 1994.

Smith, J., "U.S. North Korea Reach Tentative Nuclear Deal," *Washington Post*, June 13, 1995.

Smith, J. and A. Devroy, "U.S. Debates Shift on North Korea," *Washington Post*, June 20, 1994.

Smith, J. R. and D. Williams, "White House to Step Up Plans to Isolate Iran, Iraq," *Washington Post*, May 23, 1993.

Snetsinger, J., *Truman, the Jewish Vote and the Creation of Israel* (Stanford, CA.: Hoover Institution Press, 1974).

Spector, L., *Nuclear Ambitions* (Boulder: Westview Press, 1990).

Spolar, C., "Freed U.N. Soldiers 'In Good Spirit'," *Washington Post*, June 4, 1995.

Stansilaw, J., and D. Yergin, "Oil: Reopening the Door," *Foreign Affairs*, Vol.72, No.4 (September/October 1993).

Stark, R., B. D. Foster, C. Y. Glock, and H. E. Quinely, *Wayword Shepherds: Prejudice and the Protestant Clergy* (New York: Harper & Row, 1971).

Steinberg, G., "Israeli Responses to the Threat of Chemical Warfare," *Armed Forces and Society*, Vol.20, No.1 (Fall 1993).

Stockton, R. L., "The Falwell Core: A Public Opinion Analysis," paper presented to the annual meeting of the Society for the Scientific Study of Religion, Chicago, 1984.

Stockton, R. R., "Christian Zionism: Prophecy and Public Opinion," *Middle East Journal*, Vol.41 (1987).

Telhami, S., "How to Lose Friends in the Persian Gulf," *Los Angeles Times*, June 4, 1995.

Tesser, A., "Self-Generated Attitude Change," in L. Berkowitz (ed.), *Advances in Experimental Social Psychology*, Vol.11 (San Diego, Cal.: Academic Press, 1978).

Tilly, C., "Reflections on European State-Making," in C. Tilly (ed.) *The Formation of National States in Western Europe* (Princeton: Princeton University Press, 1975).

Tumin, M. M., *Social Stratification* (Englewood Cliffs, NJ: Prentice-Hall, 1967).

Vallone, R. P., L. Ross, and M.R. Lepper, "The Hostile Media Phenomenon: Biased Perception and Perceptions of the Media Bias in Coverage of the Beirut Massacre," *Journal of Personality and Social Psychology*, Vol.49 (1985).

Van Evra, S., "Primed for Peace: Europe after the Cold War," *International Security*, Vol.15, No.3 (Winter 1990/91).

Van Evra, S., "The United States and the Third World: When to Intervene?" in K. Oye, R. Lieber, and D. Rothchild (eds) *Eagle in a New World: American Grand Strategy in the Post-Cold War World* (New York: Harper Collins, 1992).

Vaux, K. L., *Ethics and the Gulf War: Religion, Rhetoric, and Righteousness* (Boulder, Col. Westview, 1992).

Vogel, S., "U.S. Proposes NATO 'Partnerships' for Former Warsaw Pact Nations," *Washington Post*, October 26, 1993.

Wakberg, J., "Sample Methods for Random Digit Dialing," *Journal of the American Statistical Association*, Vol.50 (1978).

Waltz, K., "The Spread of Nuclear Weapons: More May Be Better," *Adelphi Papers*, No.171 (London: IISS, 1981).

Wald, K. D., "Religious Elites and Public Opinion: The Impact of the Bishops' Peace Pastoral," *Review of Politics*, Vol.54 (1992).

Wald, K., D., *Religion and Politics in the United States*, 2nd. Ed. (Washington, DC: CQ Press, 1992).

Wald, K. D., "The Religious Dimension of American Anti-Communism," *Journal of Church and State*, forthcoming.

Walvoord, J. F., *Armageddon, Oil and the Middle East Crisis*, Rev. Ed. (Grand Rapids, Mi.: Zonervan, 1990).

Weber, T. P., *Living in the Shadow of the Second Coming: American Premillennialism 1875–1982* (Chicago: University of Chicago Press, 1987).

Wertheimer, J., *A People Divided: Judaism in Contemporary America* (New York: Basic Books, 1993).

Wilkenfeld. J., "Domestic and Foreign Conflict Behavior of Nations," *Journal of Peace Research*, No.5 (1968).

Williams, D., "Carter Provides Cover for Another U.S. Shift," *Washington Post*, December 21, 1994.

Williams, D., "Russia Joins NATO Plan," *Washington Post*, June 23, 1994.

Young, J., E. Borgida, J. Sullivan, and J. Aldrich, "Personal Agendas and the Relationship between Self-Interest and Voting Behavior," *Social Psychology Quarterly*, 50 (1987).

Zimmermann, W., "The Last Ambassador: A Memoir of the Collapse of Yugoslavia," *Foreign Affairs*, Vol.74 (March/April 1995).

Index